DISCOURSE, INTERACTION AND COMMUNICATION

PHILOSOPHICAL STUDIES SERIES

VOLUME 72

Founded by Wilfrid S. Sellars and Keith Lehrer

The titles published in this series are listed at the end of this volume.

DISCOURSE, INTERACTION AND COMMUNICATION

Proceedings of the Fourth International Colloquium on
Cognitive Science (ICCS-95)

Edited by

XABIER ARRAZOLA
ILCLI,
San Sebastián, Spain

KEPA KORTA
ILCLI,
San Sebastián, Spain

and

FRANCIS JEFFRY PELLETIER
University of Alberta,
Edmonton, Alberta, Canada

KLUWER ACADEMIC PUBLISHERS
DORDRECHT / BOSTON / LONDON

A C.I.P. Catalogue record for this book is available from the Library of Congress.

ISBN 0-7923-4952-0

Published by Kluwer Academic Publishers,
P.O. Box 17, 3300 AA Dordrecht, The Netherlands.

Sold and distributed in North, Central and South America
by Kluwer Academic Publishers,
101 Philip Drive, Norwell, MA 02061, U.S.A.

In all other countries, sold and distributed
by Kluwer Academic Publishers,
P.O. Box 322, 3300 AH Dordrecht, The Netherlands.

Printed on acid-free paper

Printed in the Netherlands

To Víctor Sánchez de Zavala
(1926-1996)

TABLE OF CONTENTS

A LOGICAL APPROACH TO REASONING ABOUT UNCERTAINTY: A TUTORIAL
Joseph Y. HALPERN

HOW COMMITMENT LEADS TO COORDINATION: THE EFFECT OF INDIVIDUAL REASONING STRATEGIES ON MULTI-AGENT INTERACTION
Martha E. POLLACK

BUILDING A COLLABORATIVE INTERFACE AGENT
Candace L. SIDNER

INTRODUCTION

DISCOURSE, INTERACTION, AND COMMUNICATION

Co-organized by the Department of Logic and Philosophy of Science and the Institute for Logic, Cognition, Language, and Information (ILCLI) both from the University of the Basque Country, the Fourth International Colloquium on Cognitive Science (ICCS-95) gathered at Donostia - San Sebastián from May 3 to 6, 1995, with the following as its main topics:

1. Social Action and Cooperation.
2. Cognitive Approaches in Discourse Processing: Grammatical and Semantical Aspects.
3. Models of Information in Communication Systems.
4. Cognitive Simulation: Scope and Limits.

More than one hundred researchers from all over the world exchanged their most recent contributions to Cognitive Science in an exceptionally fruitful atmosphere. In this volume we include a small though representative sample of the main papers. They all were invited papers except the one by Peter Juel Henrichsen, a contributed paper that merited the IBERDROLA - Gipuzkoako Foru Aldundia Best Paper Award, set up in ICCS-95 for the first time.

Concerning the contents of the volume, the papers go from the extremely abstract to the extremely specific, reflecting not only what happened at ICCS-95 but also the current state of Cognitive Science. The collection can be seen as either a broad overview of the field or as a repository of many excellent particular studies and three general ones. The title "Discourse, Interaction, and Communication" tries to capture the main issues addressed in the book and gives an intuitive idea of its contents. We can classify the papers under three main subjects: Language, Social Action, and Foundations of Cognitive Science. Language has been a central theme in all editions of ICCS. This is also the case in this fourth edition, and the title shows it. Henrichsen, Pelletier, and Recanati's papers are directly concerned with natural language. Fenstad's and Lakoff's are too; but they can also be grouped as works on the foundations of Cognitive Science, along with Silvers' paper. Tuomela's, Halpern's, Pollack's, and Sidner's papers are all focused on social action.

1. Language

The provocative title of Peter Juel Henrichsen's paper, "Does the sentence exist? Do we need it?", gives a clear idea on its aim. The answers to the questions are, of course, negative. He proposes to abandon the concept of 'sentence', since this seems to be the reason for formal linguistic theory to neglect two crucial properties of natural language, namely, that "(i) language perception is an incremental process, which (ii) does not hinge on the identification of sentence boundaries." He proposes an alternative grammar, called *Semicolon Grammar* (;**G**), which takes into account these two properties, and does not assume such a thing as a 'final' syntactic constituent, i. e., a sentence. ;**G** consists essentially in a recursive technique for adding new information to old, based on the Lambek calculus, modified by an insight from dynamic predicate logic. He develops a detailed technical apparatus for a natural explanation of categories usually described as inter-sentential like interjections and connectives, and syntactic-semantic borderline cases such as cross-sentential binding and ellipsis. In sum, we have a very suggestive (and iconoclastic) proposal of a promising programme in grammar. It merited, as we said before, the IBERDROLA - G. F. A. Best Paper Award at ICCS-95.

François Recanati's paper, "Contextual Domains" addresses the issue of how to specify the variable domains of discourse for quantifiers, incomplete description and some other linguistic elements. The phenomenon is best illustrated by examples like 'The burglar took everything', where 'everything' ranges over the domain of valuable objects in the house and not everything in existence. Instead of an ellipsis theory, according to which these sentences would be elliptical for longer sentences such as 'The burglar took everything valuable in the house', Recanati proposes a theory of contextually restricted domains, based on an attempt of reconciliation of the Austinian semantics of situation theorists and the cognitive semantics of Gilles Fauconnier. It should be noted that Recanati the notion of contextual domain defended by Recanati encompasses both 'genuine' domains involving real situations and intensional domains which involve worlds other than the actual world. He assumes that we only *pretend* to refer to non-actual, intensional domains, but that, linguistically, real and pretended domains are on a par.

Jeff Pelletier's "Thinking of 'Not'" questions the way cognitive scientists characterize the mental items that a person has which are supposed to represent the meaning or interpretation for that person of public language utterances. Whatever these internal items are—images, combinations of concepts, patterns of neural firings, etc.—they are *objects* and therefore they cannot directly be the type of thing to which a truth-function like 'not' applies. Pelletier considers two directions open to those cognitive scientists who wish to give a coherent account of negation. One direction is to embrace the fact that the mental items are objects, and therefore that the notions of identity and non-identity can coherently hold amongst them. Pelletier presents various ways to use these notions as a method to indirectly give appropriate meanings for natural language negations. The other direction is to accept that these mental items have semantic properties—such as "falling into the same applicability range"—and to try to use the resulting notions (e.g., incompatibility) to give an appropriate notion of natural language negation.

2. Foundations of Cognitive Science

Lakoff, in his paper entitled "The Metaphorical Conception of Events and Causes: Some Implications of Cognitive Science for Philosophy", presents a large sampling of his results on conceptual metaphor, which can be understood as located in the transition between two generations of Cognitive Science. Lakoff characterizes the First Generation as "Cognitive Science and the Disembodied and Unimaginative Mind." This view coalesced in the mid-seventies from ideas in classical artificial intelligence, information processing psychology and generative linguistics. However, he continues, research into color categories, basic-level concepts, image schemas, prototypes, and conceptual metaphors have called into question certain First Generation views, in particular the view that Reason is Logic. According to Lakoff, this research has lead to the Second Generation of Cognitive Science, characterized as "Cognitive Science of the Embodied and Imaginative Mind". The importance of this Second Generation for Philosophy is that it rejects the principle that human concepts and human reason provide access to an objectively existing world, independent of human psychology.

Jens Erik Fenstad's paper, "Formal Semantics, Geometric, and Mind" is also focused also on the foundations of Cognitive Science. He begins with a critical review of standard logical semantics and its ontology, characterizing the standard logical approach to reasoning and understanding as a search for ever more sophisticated proof procedures. But he claims that the sophistication that has been achieved by this methodology is illusory. The illusion lies in the ontology of first order logic: it is an ontology of lists; there are no structurally defined hierarchies, so the model is "flat". Fenstad claims that this is not enough. Some notion of geometry needs to be introduced into model theory. After reviewing the historical disengagement of logic and geometry, Fenstad cites a few cases where geometry is crucial to linguistic meaning and reviews Gärdenfors' work on conceptual space in some detail, as an example of how model theory can be enhanced though geometry. Fenstad then looks to neurology for justification of the geometrical view of model theory used in conceptual space, making strong claims about the relationship between neurological structure and cognitive processes. Fenstad's overall goal, started in this paper, is to triangulate natural language, cognition, and neurobiology in a rigorous mathematical framework.

Stuart Silvers, in his paper "Informational Semantics and Epistemic Arrogance", addresses the philosophical discussion on naturalized epistemology. He considers critically Fodor's proposals in *The Elm and the Expert* for how informational semantics is supposed to elucidate his version of naturalized epistemology of human knowledge while retaining our self-proclaimed human rationality. He argues in particular that Fodor's constraints on semantic content requires him to adopt the same sort of explanatory apparatus that he decries in his archenemy, namely, meaning holism. In addition, Silvers claims that Fodor's syntax-driven computational model of mind is too idealized and abstract for a naturalized theory of human rationality.

3. Interaction

The word "Interaction" in the title of the volume represents the other main topic of the book. Within Cognitive Science an increasing concern on social aspects of cognition has arisen during the last several years. Many disciplines are turning their focus from the individual to society. Four papers in this volume form a good selection of this new direction in Cognitive Science. From different perspectives Tuomela, Halpern, Pollack, and Sidner are all concerned not with an isolated individual facing the world but with individuals in groups and societies that faces the world together.

Raimo Tuomela's paper "Collective Goals and Cooperation" uses his previous research on cooperation and social action to provide a philosophical explanation of the notion of an intended collective goal in its full-blown sense. A state or action is an intended collective goal in a group, according to Tuomela's analysis, when the members intend to contribute—together with the others—to the satisfaction of that goal, and they mutually believe or know that the others similarly have that goal and intend to contribute together with the others to its achievement. The resulting notion of a collective goal is stronger than what game-theory delivers or indeed is capable of delivering, and Tuomela argues for its centrality in understanding human cooperation.

Joseph Halpern, in his paper entitled "A Logical Approach to Reasoning about Uncertainty: A Tutorial", considers a logical framework for modeling uncertainty, based on the use of possible worlds, that incorporates knowledge, probability, and time. After defining what is knowledge for a single agent in this sort of framework, he considers that single agents exist in *multi-agent systems* and posses information about the environment of these systems. He presents a concrete framework for modeling knowledge and time in multi-agent systems, applying it to the solution of various well-known puzzles of reasoning about uncertainty.

Martha Pollack's paper, "How Commitment Leads to Coordination: The Effect of Individual Reasoning Strategies on Multi-Agent Interaction", is a concise summary of her work on reasoning strategies for single agents in dynamic environments, together with an extension to multiple agents. The central assumptions are that agents are situated in dynamic environments in which the agent is not the only source of change, and that agents have computational resource limits. The outcome is that the environment may change during the time the agent is reasoning; moreover, it may change in ways that undermine the agent's active assumptions that are being used in this reasoning. More generally, an agent who ignores the interplay between its computational resources and environmental change is apt to make poor decisions. Pollack's approach is to develop strategies for deciding what to reason about when, and for how long. She also explores the possibility of generalizing the single-agent case to the multi-agent case, where coordination and cooperation can arise among the agents.

The final paper in the volume is Candace Sidner's "Building a Collaborative Agent Interface," which outlines the construction of an intelligent software agent for collaboration with a human in plannning an air-travel itinerary by means of a standard graphical user interface. The agent, named TT, is presented anthropomorphically and interacts with the user as well as with the software environment. The agent is both communicative (it behaves in accordance with Sidner's work on human discourse structure), and collaborative (it understands the user's goals well enough to collaborate in their achievement).

The papers in this volume represent leading edge work by well-known scholars on the three topics mentioned in the volume's title: discourse, interaction, and communication. They report work done from widely divergent points on the theoretical spectrum of Cognitive Science, and from different disciplinary starting points (Philosophy, Psychology, Logic, Linguistics, Artificial Intelligence). Not only do these works faithfully represent the main topics and the wide range of differing positions presented at ICCS-95, but despite their differences (or perhaps because of these differences) they also display many clear directions for future research in these three central areas of Cognitive Science.

Acknowledgements: Thanks for their economic support to the sponsors of this Fourth Colloquium: the Secretary of State of Education and Science (Ministerio de Educación y Ciencia) of the Spanish Government, the Secretary of Education of the Basque Government, the Secretary of Culture of the County Council of Gipuzkoa (Gipuzkoako Foru Aldundia), the Kutxa Foundation, and Iberdrola Electric Company. Thanks also to the members of the Organizing and Program Committees of the Colloqiuum. An anonymous referee and the responsibles from Kluwer, especially Keith Lehrer and Maja de Keijzer, deserve a special mention here, for their help and patience during the process of producing this volume. María Frías (ILCLI) did an invaluable work in typing and formatting.

The Editors.

DOES THE SENTENCE EXIST?
DO WE NEED IT?

P. J. HENRICHSEN
Institute of General and Applied Linguistics (IAAS)
University of Copenhagen
pjuel@cphling.dk

1. Introduction

> "In defining syntax, a dictionary will usually refer to the *sentence*. But of all linguistic units this is the most problematic, and the one whose nature has been most debated."
> P. H. Matthews, *Syntax*, Cambridge (1981).

> "Sometimes every speaker of English will agree that a particular sentence is unacceptable. But many sentences are liable to provoke disagreement, sometimes quite angry disagreement."
> N. Fabb, *Sentence Structure*, Routledge (1994).

In this paper I'll demonstrate how a formal grammar can be set up without explicit reference to problematic entities like 'sentences' and 'syntax trees'; instead, the basic unit is taken to be the never-ending discourse itself. The project is nicknamed *Semicolon Grammar* (;G).

Formal syntax of today is mostly preoccupied with short, well-demarcated strings of words in null-context, with the time factor abstracted away. Every linguist is confronted with an artificial choice: Will he study sentences? Or will he study discourse? I propose that something along the lines of ;G could do as the missing link between free discourse and formal grammar.

In order to keep both feet on the ground, I'll prepare and define a small lexicon, demonstrating that ;G is well suited to analyse the following kinds of phenomena:

- categories usually described as inter-sentential (interjections, connectives)
- syntactic-semantic borderline cases (cross-sentential binding, ellipses)

By the end of the paper, the general issue is resumed, and the results are summed up.

The reader not interested in Lambek Calculus should feel free to skip over the technical sections.

1

X. Arrazola et al. (eds.), Discourse, Interaction and Communication, 1–24.
© 1998 *Kluwer Academic Publishers. Printed in the Netherlands.*

1.1. A BUILT-IN PROBLEM IN PSG

When a human language user is taking part in a conversation he is engaged in high level semantic reasoning *every moment*. Long before the hearer has identified a sentence boundary (if he does so at all) he is deeply involved in guessing and anticipating the intentions of the speaker. If the speaker halts—even in the middle of a constituent—it is perfectly normal for the hearer to continue his flight of words.

In the early seventies, Marslen-Wilson showed that the hearer does not depend on a completed syntactic analysis of a constituent in order to begin understanding it—i.e. to start reflecting on its consequences. On the contrary, he can utilize his knowledge on all linguistic levels at any one time. He is able to discover irregularities with as little delay as one or two syllables—and this is true for not only local morphological errors but also for syntactic, logical-semantic, and even the highest levels of pragmatic anomalies (Marslen-Wilson (1975), Tyler & al (1977)).

We can illustrate Marslen-Wilson's results on language perception with a left-branching tree:

(1)
```
                                                    aha!
                                          _____
                                     aha!
                            _____
                   aha!
          _____
    aha!
  _____
  token₁     token₂        token₃        token₄        token₅       etc.
```

In the tradition of formal semantics, compositionality is almost always taken to be a desideratum—"I would not know of a competing principle," says Theo Janssen [(1986), p.2]. Following the principle of compositionality, the meaning of any constituent can be deduced from the meaning of its subparts.

It is puzzling, then, that many languages seem to prefer *right*-associative syntactic structures. In the PSG-literature, including G&B, the right-branching tree occurs far more often than its mirror image.

(2)   [Nina [doesn't [see [a [green [bottle]]]]]]

This oddity is also pointed out in Steedman (1987) and Haddock (1988), which are in some ways similar to the present approach (not questioning the Sentence, though); see also Kempen (1987) and de Smedt (1990). Why is it that the evolution of language hasn't favoured the inverse kind of structures? That would seemingly give a much simpler access to the meaning of constituents.

That is, if PSG-description is at all appropriate for models of language perception.

1.2. CATEGORIAL GRAMMAR

The same peculiarity appears in a Categorial Grammar (CG) analysis of the example above.

In simple CG, the syntactic category A/B (resp. $B\backslash A$) means: Find a category matching B on your right (resp. left), in order to make an A. The intransitive verb, for example, is categorized as NP\S, defining it as a token able to combine with a subject (NP) on its left, thereby becoming a full sentence (S). The semantics of that sentence is computed as the semantics of the NP applied to the semantics of the verb by functional application[1].

(3)
Nina	.. NP	.. **N**
doesn't	.. $(NP\backslash S)/VP_{inf}$	.. $\lambda P\lambda y.\neg P(y)$
see	.. VP_{inf}/NP	.. $\lambda x.\textbf{see}(x)$
a	.. NP/CN	.. $\lambda c.\textbf{exist}(c)$
green	.. CN/CN	.. $\lambda c.\textbf{green}(c)$
bottle	.. CN	.. **bottle**

Here, too, it is not at all obvious how to map the first two tokens 'Nina doesn't' onto a meaning representation. Actually, the parser must process the sequence perfectly right-to-left, even though humans demonstrably do it the other way round.

1.2.1. *Lambek Calculus*
The /- and \-rules above constitute the simplest workable (directional) CG, sometimes called AB-calculus after its earliest advocates, Ajdukiewicz (1935) and Bar-Hillel (1964). AB is strongly equivalent to the context-free grammars; it is therefore not surprising that AB-analysis has the same shortcomings in the case above.

But the problem can be overcome by a more flexible interpretation of the two slashes.

(4)

Lambek Calculus (sequent presentation)

$$\frac{\Sigma \Rightarrow B..Y \quad \Delta\ A..X(Y)\ \Gamma \Rightarrow C..Z}{\Delta\ \Sigma\ B\backslash A..X\ \Gamma \Rightarrow C..Z}\backslash_L \qquad \frac{\Sigma \Rightarrow B..Y \quad \Delta\ A..X(Y)\ \Gamma \Rightarrow C..Z}{\Delta\ A/B..X\ \Sigma\ \Gamma \Rightarrow C..Z}/_L$$

$$\frac{B..Y\ \Sigma \Rightarrow A..X}{\Sigma \Rightarrow B\backslash A..\lambda Y.X}\backslash_R \qquad \frac{\Sigma\ B..Y \Rightarrow A..X}{\Sigma \Rightarrow A/B..\lambda Y.X}/_R \qquad \frac{true}{A..X \Rightarrow A..X}\text{axiom}$$

A, B, C are syn. categories; X, Y, Z are sem. formulae; Γ, Δ, Σ are strings of signs
underlined = non-empty

These five rules together are called the Lambek Calculus (L) after its inventor (Lambek (1958)).

A characteristic of L is that it offers structural completeness, in the sense that a certain sequence of tokens can be analysed in any order one may suggest. If two adjacent categories do not fit together the left rules won't work, but nevertheless the right rules can combine them by way of (lambda-) abstraction.

Turning to L, 'Nina doesn't' becomes analysable by means of /R.

(5)

	Nina	doesn't		Nina^doesn't
	.. NP	.. $(NP\backslash S)/VP_{inf}$	$\Rightarrow_L$	.. S/VP_{inf}
	.. N	.. $\lambda P.\lambda x.\emptyset P(x)$		.. $\lambda S.[\lambda P.\lambda x.\neg P(x)](S)(N)$

For perspicuity, the syntactic and the semantic part of the proof are presented separately; the active divisor in every sequent is underlined. From here on, $\Rightarrow$ and $\Rightarrow_L$ are used interchangeably. Note that L-proof trees read most easily bottom-up.

(6)

$$
\frac{
\frac{true}{VP_{inf} \Rightarrow VP_{inf}}\ ^{ax}
\quad
\frac{
\frac{true}{NP \Rightarrow NP}\ ^{ax}
\quad
\frac{true}{S \Rightarrow S}\ ^{ax}
}{
NP \quad NP\backslash S \Rightarrow S
}\ ^{\backslash L}
}{
\dfrac{NP \quad (NP\backslash S)\underline{/}VP_{inf} \quad VP_{inf} \Rightarrow S}{NP \quad (NP\backslash S)/VP_{inf} \Rightarrow S\underline{/}VP_{inf}}\ ^{/R}
}\ ^{/L}
$$

(7)

$$
\frac{
\frac{[S \leftarrow Q]}{Q \Rightarrow S}\ ^{ax}
\quad
\dfrac{
\dfrac{[y \leftarrow N]}{N \Rightarrow y}\ ^{ax}
\quad
\dfrac{[R \leftarrow (\lambda P\lambda x.\neg P(x))(S)(y)]}{(\lambda P\lambda x.\neg P(x))(S)(y) \Rightarrow R}\ ^{ax}
}{N \quad (\lambda P\lambda x.\neg P(x))(S) \Rightarrow R}\ ^{\backslash L}
}{
\dfrac{N \quad \lambda P\lambda x.\neg P(x) \quad Q \Rightarrow R}{N \quad \lambda P\lambda x.\neg P(x) \Rightarrow Formula}\ ^{/R[\ Formula\,\leftarrow\,\lambda Q.R\,]}
}\ ^{/L}
$$

After beta-reduction[2] of *Formula*, the result is: $\lambda S.\neg S(N)$, a function from properties (namely the following VP) to propositions (the eventual sentence). The formula—just as the utterance of the two words—stands for the assertion that whatever follows, Nina doesn't do it[3].

(8)

$$
\frac{
\dfrac{
\dfrac{
\dfrac{\neg\mathbf{see(exist(green(bottle)))(N)}}{\lambda c.\ \neg\mathbf{see(exist(green}(c)\mathbf{)))(N)}}
}{\lambda c.\ \neg\mathbf{see(exist(}c\mathbf{))(N)}}
}{\lambda x.\ \neg\mathbf{see(}x\mathbf{)(N)}}
}{\lambda Q.\ \neg Q(\mathbf{N})}
$$

Nina	doesn't	see	a	green	bottle

Now every sentence can be processed strictly left-to-right. The same does not hold for the discourse as a whole, though; we will come back to this point later.

1.2.2. *L-Sequents With Uninstantiated Consequents*

When combining the two signs NP and $(NP\backslash S)/VP_{inf}$, we simply took it for granted that the consequent was to be S/VP_{inf}. This is the simplest possibility, but by no means the only one. In all cases where the consequent is unknown—and that is the typical situation when parsing incrementally—the number of valid instantiations is infinite. Usually, only a few of them are useful:

(9)	(i)	NP	NP\S	$\Rightarrow$	S
	(ii)	NP	NP\S	$\Rightarrow$	$S/(S\backslash S)$
	(iii)	NP	NP\S	$\Rightarrow$	$S/((NP\backslash S)\backslash(NP\backslash S))$
	(iv)	NP	NP\S	$\Rightarrow$	$(((VP_{inf}/CN)/NP)\backslash VP_{inf})/((NP\backslash S)\backslash CN)$

Here, we have a subject and an intransitive verb resulting in (i) a concluded sentence, (ii) a sentence waiting for a sentential adverb, and (iii) a sentence waiting for a VP-modifier. It is rather more difficult to see the use of (iv). We need a system to effectively prune the search space.

One such system is the calculus M of Moortgat (1988). M consists of a small number of lemmas—uninstantiated L-proofs created by partial deduction. Every one of the lemmas covers a finite area of the infinite search space, and by adding to the lemma-base one can gain new territory in a controlled way.

Another way of restricting the calculus is to accept only consequents which are combinable with existing lexemes; this strategy which could be called 'lexical guidance', would allow for (i) always, and for (ii) and (iii) insofar as the lexicon contains lexemes of category S\S and $(NP\backslash S)\backslash(NP\backslash S)$. This 'lexical guidance' can be refined in many ways, and together with M it effectively zooms in on the relevant consequents.

See Milward (1995) for a different tackling of indeterminacy in incremental CGs.

1.3. DYNAMIC SEMANTICS

In the Montague-tradition, the meaning of a sentence is, of course, determined by its truth conditions. If the two sentences, (i) 'The Earth is smaller than the Sun', and (ii) 'Spain is large' are both true, then they mean exactly the same (in the actual world). It is different with a sentence containing a pronoun: (iii) 'It's bigger than the Moon'. The meaning of (iii) is relative to the context—a fact that is easily appreciated when comparing (iii)'s truth value in the two discourses (i)(iii) and (ii)(iii). So, in some cases a sentence can be described by its truth conditions, in other cases it cannot. This inconsistency is an old tripwire of formal semantics.

In dynamic semantics, on the other hand, the meaning of a sentence is not linked to its truth value, but rather to its context change potential—(i) and (ii) needn't be taken as being synonymous, as the logic can capture the fact that (i) introduces two discourse referents ('Earth' and 'Sun'), and (ii) only one ('Spain'). So in the two cases (i)(iii) and (ii)(iii), (iii) is evaluated on two different backgrounds. Hence, it is no longer paradoxical that one and the same sentence has two different evaluations.

In Dynamic Predicate Logic (Groenendijk & al (1991)), a sentence is interpreted as a relation between an information state (called the input state) and a set of information states (the output states). An information state is simply a variable assignment function, i.e. a function from variable names to entities.

(10) $i = [\,x{\leftarrow}\textbf{Earth},\ y{\leftarrow}\textbf{Sun},\ \text{(all others undefined)}\,]$

Consider the assignment function i. On evaluating the discourse (i)(iii), the information state just before (iii) could very well be i, in which case the following pronoun 'it' must tie to either x or y. Both unifications will render (iii) a true statement. Conversely, in discourse (ii)(iii) where the only available binder for 'it' is 'Spain' (iii) is false.

2. Decomposition of the Sentence

Now putting together L and DPL, we have an *almost* left associative model of the discourse.

(11)

But there is still an unmotivated discontinuity, seen from a processing point of view. The alleged phase transitions around the S-nodes do not correspond to perceptible mental gear shifts. In real dialogue, it is often very hard indeed to identify the supposed sentence boundaries, as anyone will know who has ever tried to write down a lively discussion. Language users are engaged in meaning retrieval on-line, and no one is really concerned with the full stops. In many writing codes (runic letters, early Latin, classical Chinese), the full stop is even non-existent. It would probably be very hard to make writers of these codes acknowledge that 'The sun is shining, I'm hungry' are two sentences, while 'The sun is shining and I'm hungry' is only one. Indeed, I find it counterintuitive myself.

(12)   Nina   runs   'n   she   is   hungry
            NP   NP\S   (S\S)/S   NP   (NP\S)/(CN/CN)   CN/CN   ⇒   S

In traditional grammar, this string is analysed as a sentence—but if we left out the barely perceptible *'n*, the analysis would be fundamentally different, the evaluation now hinging on a discourse theory detached from the grammar itself. So what good are the S-boundaries? What would it take to get rid of them?

   If this derivation were valid: S S ⇒ S, then the phase transition would dissolve. The derivation above would be equally valid with and without the connective, and in general we could have a strictly left-branching analysis tree. This would mean an uncompromised compositionality, even on the discourse level. It would also mean that we no longer had the usual evaluation platforms based on the sentence boundaries, where the discourse machinery is normally engaged. There wouldn't be two distinct levels of description, only one single grammar. Hence, all discourse decisions would have to be made on-line, by the sentence parser alone (or, if you prefer: the discourse parser).

2.1. THE CATEGORY OF THE TRADITIONAL SENTENCE

Among the infinitely many instantiations of A that validate $A\ A \Rightarrow_L A$, one is particularly interesting, viz. $A = D\backslash D$, D being a basic category[4]. All other As are much more complex (with the obvious exception of D/D), since the number of basic categories in A must be even (Henrichsen (1995)).

Changing a syntactic category affects the corresponding semantic formula, since the λ-formulae must match the functor-argument structure of the categories. This parallelism between syntactic form and semantic content, which is one of the distinctive features of Montague Grammar, is often called the rule-to-rule-paradigm.

So if we reinterpret the primitive S as a complex category D\D, this is bound to have semantic consequences. Category D\D cannot be matched by a simple truth value, and it cannot be a DPL-style one-to-many relation either. Rather, it is a *function* (with identical domain and range).

2.2. SENTENCES AS DISCOURSE MODIFIERS

The sentence is now interpreted as a semantic function—from what to what, then?

The simplest choice is of course $\langle t,t \rangle$, functions from truth values to truth values. This is the traditional type of sentence adverbials like 'yesterday', 'luckily', and perhaps the tag 'y'know'. A characteristic of adverbs is their ability to join a constituent without changing its syntactic properties, exactly the role we want the sentence to play at the discourse level.

(13)	Nina	runs,	she	is		hungry		
	NP	NP\(D\D)	NP	(NP\(D\D))/ADJ		ADJ	$\Rightarrow$	D\D

runs	..	$\lambda\lambda a_i.\ a\ \&\ \mathbf{run}(x)$
is	..	$\lambda P\lambda x\lambda a_i.\ a\ \&\ P(x)$
hungry	..	$\lambda x.\ \mathbf{hungry}(x)$

The formula produced: $\lambda a_i.\ a\ \&\ \mathbf{run}(\mathbf{N})\ \&\ \mathbf{hungry}(she)$. One may rightly ask what the strange abstraction a over truth values is good for—it seems to be an artifact of the system. Also, it is not possible to attribute a proper semantics to 'she', the only available choice being an unbound variable. Obviously, the sentence type $\langle t,t \rangle$ is too banal.

Inspired by DPL, the next suggestion is $\langle \tau,\tau \rangle$, where type τ designates the set of variable assignment functions. This option seems more promising.

3. Dynamic λ-calculus

It's now time to introduce a slightly altered notation for λ-formulae. All formulae are written as usual, except those of type τ, which now may have the form: $o_\tau\{PROG(x,y,z...)\}$. Informally speaking, *PROG* is a program having $x,y,z...$ as input and o as output.

If we, for a start, regard proper names (PNs) as members of the basic category NP, and verbs as functions from multiple NPs to discourse modifiers—i.e. take the most conservative view—the analysis of 'Nina knows John' doesn't reveal much new.

(14)   Nina .. NP.. **N**   knows .. (NP\Đ)/NP   John .. NP.. **J** $\Rightarrow$

$\qquad\qquad\qquad\qquad\qquad\qquad\qquad\qquad$ Đ .. $\lambda i.\ i\{$ EVAL(**know(J)(N)**) $\}$

runs	.. NP\Đ	.. $\lambda x\lambda i.\ i\{$ EVAL(**run**(x)) $\}$
knows	.. (NP\Đ)/NP	.. $\lambda x\lambda y\lambda i.\ i\{$ EVAL(**know**$(x)(y)$) $\}$
gives	.. ((NP\Đ)/NP)/NP	.. $\lambda x\lambda y\lambda z\lambda i.\ i\{$ EVAL(**give**$(x)(y)(z)$) $\}$

Đ is short for D\D, and EVAL is the interpretation function. The evaluation of **know(J)(N)** amounts to a simple check whether Nina actually knows John or not, in the model representing the actual world. The input i is returned unchanged, so for the moment, the utterance of a name does not change the information state.

4. The ;G lexicon

4.1. PRONOUNS

In CG, the pronouns are often taken to be *type-raised* noun phrases, i.e. to be functions over properties. The same approach is taken here, for reasons to be explained.

(15)   she .. Đ/(NP\Đ)   .. $\lambda P\lambda i.\ P(z)(j)\{$ DREF$_e\,(z, i, j)$ $\}$

$\qquad\quad$ her .. (Đ/NP)\Đ   .. $\lambda P\lambda i.\ P(z)(j)\{$ DREF$_e\,(z, i, j)$ $\}$

$\qquad\qquad\qquad\qquad\qquad\qquad\qquad$ (P is of type $\langle e,\langle \tau,\tau\rangle\rangle$, 'dynamic properties')

DREF$_e$ is the locus of 'discourse referent administration'. In a call like DREF$_e\,(Item,i,j)$, *Item* is of type e (entity), and i and j of type τ (assignment functions). Procedurally speaking, i is input and j is output. *Item* is either: If *Item* is a variable, DREF$_e$ instantiates it with a suitable binder in i; if *Item* is a constant, i is updated with *Item* (or left unchanged if *Item* was present already). In both cases, *Item* is then fronted in i, and the result exported as j.

The pronouns have now gained access to the information state. Consider an information state [**N.J**], a situation where (only) Nina and John have been mentioned in the preceding discourse[5]. Now someone utters 'she runs'.

(16)   she runs $\Rightarrow$ Đ .. $(\lambda P\lambda i.\ P(z)(j)\{$ DREF$_e\,(z, i, j)$ $\})(\lambda x\lambda i'.\ i'\{$EVAL(**run**$(x)$) $\})$

This unfriendly-looking consequent reduces to $\lambda i.j\{\text{DREF}_e\,(z,i,j),\mathbf{run}(z)\}$ in a few steps. Notice that $(k\{PROG_2\})\{PROG_1\}$ is equivalent to $k\{PROG_1,PROG_2\}$, where $(PROG_1,PROG_2)$ is a program sequence consisting of $PROG_1$ and $PROG_2$ in that order.

She^runs has now been translated into a function from an information state i to an information state j. Instantiating i with [N,J] makes z become N—the only suitable binder—and $\mathbf{run}(\mathbf{N})$ is evaluated with respect to the model. Since no new binders have been introduced, the outcome is $j\leftarrow[\mathbf{N},\mathbf{J}]$.

4.2. PROPER NAMES

But how did Nina and John enter the information state in the first place? The utterance of 'Nina' doesn't suffice, since names do not have context change potential (cf. section 3.). In my view, this is a drawback of DPL: Predicates are considered *tests*; the evaluation of, say, $\mathbf{run}(\mathbf{N})$ cannot add anything—such as a new discourse referent—to the information state. In other words, if a PN binder is needed, it must be introduced in the information state by a daemon.

In the present setting, it is quite easy to equip names with binding potential. All that is needed is type-raising over Đ, as with the pronouns.

(17)　　Nina$_{\text{subj}}$　.. Đ/(NP\Đ)　.. $\lambda P\lambda i.\,P(\mathbf{N})(j)\{\,\text{DREF}_e\,(\mathbf{N},\,i,\,j)\,\}$

　　　　Nina$_{\text{obj}}$　.. (Đ/NP)\Đ　.. $\lambda P\lambda i.\,P(\mathbf{N})(j)\{\,\text{DREF}_e\,(\mathbf{N},\,i,\,j)\,\}$

Now the semantics contains a subformula of type τ, where an updating of the information state can take place. The type of PNs has changed from e to $\langle\langle e,\langle\tau,\tau\rangle\rangle$, $\langle\tau,\tau\rangle\rangle$, functions from dynamic properties $\langle e,\langle\tau,\tau\rangle\rangle$ to discourse modifiers $\langle\tau,\tau\rangle$.

This is on a par with Montague's treatment; in PTQ[6], all NPs, quantified or not, are given the same type: $\langle\langle e,t\rangle,t\rangle$ (ignoring the s-indices for now). In PTQ, the PNs do not actually make use of the added semantic power, as they reduce back to the minimal type e during analysis; the convention just smartens up the logic.

However, in logic good looks are often a sign of a good interior. There are actually a few independent arguments for choosing the PTQ-style PN, an important one being appositional constructions. NPs like 'old Tom', 'Billy the Kid', and 'Mary, who had a little lamb' are not easily analysed with PNs of type e, but unproblematic with the type raised version (NP$_\uparrow$).

(18)　old　　　　　　　　Tom　　　　　　　　old^Tom

　　.. NP$_\uparrow$/NP$_\uparrow$　　　　.. NP$_\uparrow$　　$\Rightarrow$　　.. NP$_\uparrow$

　　.. $\lambda G\lambda P.G(\mathbf{old})\ \&\ G(P)$　.. $\lambda Q.Q(\mathbf{T})$　　　.. $\lambda P.\mathbf{old}(\mathbf{T})\ \&\ P(\mathbf{T})$

The consequent denotes a *set* which either is empty (if Tom is not old) or contains all of Tom's properties (including **old**), in which case 'Tom' is synonymous with 'old Tom'.

However, the main reason for type-raising is that it offers a more realistic description of PNs when processing incrementally. Imagine a situation where someone has just uttered: 'Father Christmas ...'

(19)   (i)   Father_Christmas   .. NP   .. **F C**
            (ii)   Father_Christmas   .. NP↑   .. $\lambda P.P(\mathbf{FC})$.

Whereas (i) does not allow for any kind of syntactic or semantic predictions (unless we design an external device for exactly that purpose), (ii) makes the parser expect a VP. This does not force the speaker to actually produce one, he could also continue 'with all his reindeer', or even to halt or correct himself. In any case, the parser has access to the properties of the PN immediately, making the analysis of certain ellipses much more elucidating: 'Dracula! [accessible information: *'is a bloodthirsty beast'*, accessible inference: *'is coming'*]'.

 We conclude for now that the projection of names onto collections of properties (generalized quantifiers) instead of individuals is not only harmless, it is indeed desirable.

4.2.1. *Notational variants*
A generalized quantifier can be lexicalized in one of two versions.

(20)   (i)   Nina$_{subj}$ .. Đ/(NP\Đ)   .. $\lambda P \lambda i.\ P(\mathbf{N})(j)\{\ \mathrm{DREF}_e(\mathbf{N},i,j)\ \}$
           (ii)   Nina$_{subj}$ ... D\(D/(NP\Đ))   .. $\lambda i \lambda P.\ P(\mathbf{N})(j)\{\ \mathrm{DREF}_e(\mathbf{N},i,j)\ \}$

(i) and (ii) are L-equivalent by theorem *(21)*, called *associativity* (cf. Moortgat (88)).

(21) $(B\backslash A)/C .. X$ $\Rightarrow$ $B\backslash(A/C) .. \lambda Y \lambda Z.X(Z)(Y)$

So the choice between (i) and (ii) is a purely cosmetic one. Whereas (i) makes the kinship between classical CG and ;G clear (the traditional category being S/NP\S), (ii) exposes the special ability of PNs to interact with the context.

 In this paper, all syntactic categories will appear in their 'classical' form.

4.3. CONJUNCTION — ?

In the PSG-tradition, as well as in CG, the sentential 'and' is usually taken to be a function over two arguments: the preceding sentence, and the following one.

(22)   S   → S CONJ S   S   S\S/S S $\Rightarrow$ S
           CONJ   → and

This definition leads to multiple analyses of constituents like [S$_1$ and S$_2$ and S$_3$ and S$_4$], but as long as the strings under consideration are short and have a well-defined end, the structural ambiguity is tolerable.

 Real discourse is not short. Still, language users don't seem to be burdened by an exponentially growing process-time-per-sentence. In ;G there is room for a description of the sentential 'and', not as a *conjunction*, but as a semantically empty *modifier*—a stand-by particle.

(23)   and .. D\D .. $\lambda i.i\{\}$

Rather than a heavy-duty function over *two* sentences, the 'and' is now a modifier over a single information state; as a result, the structural ambiguity is gone.

Logicians will point out that we do find ambiguous cases like ((apples and pears) or oranges) *vs.* (apples and (pears or oranges)). However, if ambiguities like these occur at all on the discourse level, the speaker will presumably put a heavy stress on 'and', making it distinguishable from the every-day use which is covered by the present description.

The new lexicalization of 'and' makes discourses like 'Fido barks, and, and, and, Nina yawns' analysable—before rejecting these as downright ill-formed, try to read them aloud![7]

4.4. INTERJECTION — ?

In formal grammar, the interjections are often left out in the cold. This is hardly surprising, since words like 'yes' and 'hello' are not easily incorporated in syntax trees. The very term *interjection* seems to indicate that this is an old sin of omission.

Intuitively speaking, interjections are not a marginal category—they are used very frequently in conversation, not just as sentence glue but as important carriers of meaning. Moreover, they do not really form a demarcated collection, since expressions like 'excuse me', 'thank you' and 'how are you' seem to have a least *some* sentence-nature left. Indeed, most interjections are interchangeable with traditional sentences.

(24) α_1:   No, but I'll ...

           α_2:   I won't do so, but I'll ...

           β_1:   Thank you, and goodbye.

           β_2:   I appreciate that; have a good day.

Otto Jespersen took an extreme position: "'Yes' and 'No,' and interjections like 'Alas!' or 'Oh!' or the tongue-clicks inadequately spelt 'Tut' and 'Tck' are to all intents and purposes sentences just as much as the most delicately balanced sentences ever uttered by Demosthenes or penned by Samuel Johnson" (Jespersen (1925), p.307). This very liberal sentence definition has often since been criticized—the present approach offers the luxury of *not taking sides*, and doing so on principled grounds.

When taken as standard discourse modifiers, Đ, iteration and coordination of interjections come for free (cf. section 4.3.). Now, these particles aren't really *inter*jections any longer, since they are not in between anything.

(25)

(*context*)	Thanks,	but	I'll	walk;	goodbye	(*new context*)	
D	Đ	Đ/Đ	Đ/VP$_{inf}$	VP$_{inf}$	Đ	$\Rightarrow$	D

As for their semantics, many interjections seem to require a more detailed picture of the information state than is given here, even for a minimal description; since they are typically speech acts ('thanks', 'hello') or immediate reactions ('gosh!', 'tut!'), the respective information states should at least include a representation of the speaker's idea about the hearer's point of view.

4.5. VERBS

Even if the prototypical binder is the proper name (it can introduce new discourse referents, no matter how subordinate their occurrence), binding potential is by no means restricted to names, nor to nominals in general.

(26) α_1.   Nina$_i$ yawns$_j$; her$_i$ dog does so$_j$ too
         α_2.   [Nina yawns]$_j$; it$_j$ irritates Fido

         β_1.   Nina [kicks Fido]$_j$; John does so$_j$ too
         β_2.   [Nina kicks Fido]$_j$; it$_j$ provokes John
         β_3.   ? [Nina kicks]$_j$ Fido; it$_j$/so$_j$/this$_j$ ...
         β_4.   Nina [kicks]$_j$ the dog; John, $_{(j)}$ the cat

         γ.   Nina runs ten miles every day; last year it was only six

         δ_1.   Nina$_i$ yawns$_j$ — and her$_i$ dog $_{(j)}$
         δ_2.   Nina has no dog$_k$; Mary has two $_{(k)}$
         δ_3.   Nina's dog$_k$ yawns; Mary's $_{(k)}$ does too
         δ_4.   John$_i$ washes$_k$ Nina$_j$'s [dirty trousers]$_l$, and she$_j$ $_{(k)}$ his$_i$ $_{(l)}$
         δ_5.   John$_i$ washes$_k$ Nina$_j$'s [trousers whenever Fido has lain on them
                          and wetted them]$_l$, and she$_j$ $_{(k)}$ his$_i$ $_{(l?)}$

To keep things simple, we'll take 'so' as referring exclusively to properties, and 'it' to discourse modifiers. It is important to realize that 'it' *could not* be described as standing for one traditional sentence (whatever that is); in the present framework, there is no qualitative syntactic difference between a single and a whole sequence of discourse modifiers: 'Nina drinks; she smokes pot; she never does the dishes$_j$; it$_j$ doesn't seem to bother her boyfriend, though'. Of course, in practice there must be some restrictions, but they are not likely to be syntactic in nature.

Considering discourses like α_{1-2} and β_{1-4}, the evaluation of verbs must include an updating of the information state with pointers to at least three objects: the lexical form itself (**ywn**, **kick**, **give**), the VP-predication (**kick**(obj), **give**(obj_2)(obj_1)), and the saturated proposition (**ywn**($subj$), **kick**(obj)($subj$), **give**(obj_2)(obj_1)($subj$)).

This is not the end of the story, though—compare γ.

Adding binding potential to the verbs forces higher-order items into the information states, and therefore from now on the e-index of DREF$_e$ is skipped. This marks the definitive farewell to DPL.

4.5.1. *Nina yawns; her dog does so too*
In this section, we'll trace the processing of the discourse α_1, 'Nina yawns, her dog does so too'.

The first operation needed is to combine the current information state (called *init*) with 'Nina': D Đ/(NP\Đ) $\Rightarrow$ D/(NP\Đ). The consequent is what could be called a 'situated' (or 'extensionalized') subject. All stages from this point and up to 'too' are shown in the table below.

(27)

Nina	..	$\Theta/(NP\backslash\Theta)$	.. $\lambda P\lambda i.\,P(\mathbf{N})(j)\{\ \mathrm{DREF}(\mathbf{N},i,j)\ \}$
yawns	..	$NP\backslash\Theta$	.. $\lambda x\lambda i.\,j\{\ \mathrm{DREF}(\mathbf{ywn},i,i'),$
			$\mathrm{DREF}(\mathbf{ywn}(x),i',j),$
			$\mathrm{EVAL}(\mathbf{ywn}(x))\ \}$
her$_{gen}$	..	$(\Theta/(NP\backslash\Theta))/CN$	.. $\lambda P\lambda Q\lambda i.Q(y)(P(y)(j))\{\mathrm{DREF}(x,i,j),\mathrm{EVAL}(\mathbf{has}(y)(x))\}$
dog	..	CN	.. $\lambda x\lambda i.\,j\{\mathrm{DREF}(\mathbf{dog},i,i'),\mathrm{EVAL}(\mathbf{dog}(x)),\mathrm{DREF}(x,i',j)\}$
does	..	$(NP\backslash\Theta)/VP_{inf}$	.. $\lambda P\lambda x\lambda i.\,P(x)(i)\{\}$
so	..	VP_{inf}	.. $\lambda x\lambda i.\,j\{\mathrm{DREF}(P,i,i'),\mathrm{DREF}(P(x),i',j),\mathrm{EVAL}(P(x))\}$

The adverb 'too' is not considered here, as it calls for a refinement of the lexicon not relevant for the present discussion. As for the various lexicalized DREF-calls, their raison d'etre are suggested by the examples only, in order to keep the text reasonably short.

(28)

New word	New actions	New instantiations	New expectations
Nina	$\mathrm{DREF}(\mathbf{N},\,init,j)$	$j\leftarrow[\mathbf{N}|init]$	$D/(NP\backslash\Theta)$ .. $\lambda P.P(\mathbf{N})(j)$
yawns;	$\mathrm{DREF}(\mathbf{ywn},j,i)$ $\mathrm{DREF}(\mathbf{ywn}(\mathbf{N}),i,j')$ $\mathrm{EVAL}(\mathbf{ywn}(\mathbf{N}))$	$j'\leftarrow[\mathbf{ywn}(\mathbf{N}),\mathbf{ywn},\mathbf{N}|init]$	D .. j'
her	$\mathrm{DREF}(x,j',j'')$ $\mathrm{EVAL}(\mathbf{has}(y)(\mathbf{N}))$	$x\leftarrow\mathbf{N}$ $j''\leftarrow[\mathbf{N},\mathbf{ywn}(\mathbf{N}),\mathbf{ywn}|init]$ $(y\in\{\mathbf{\$},\mathbf{Fido},\mathbf{£}\})$	$(D/(NP\backslash\Theta))/CN$ .. $\lambda P\lambda Q.Q(y)(P(y)(j''))$
dog	$\mathrm{DREF}(\mathbf{dog},j'',i')$ $\mathrm{EVAL}(\mathbf{dog}(y))$ $\mathrm{DREF}(y,i',j''')$	$y\leftarrow\mathbf{Fido}$ $j'''\leftarrow[\mathbf{Fido},\mathbf{dog}|j'']$	$D/(NP\backslash\Theta)$ .. $\lambda Q.Q(\mathbf{Fido})(j''')$
does	*(none)*	*(none)*	D/VP_{inf} .. $\lambda Q.Q(\mathbf{Fido})(j''')$
so^(too)	$\mathrm{DREF}(P,j''',i'')$ $\mathrm{DREF}(P(\mathbf{Fido}),\,i'',k)$ $\mathrm{EVAL}(\mathbf{ywn}(\mathbf{Fido}))$	$P\leftarrow\mathbf{ywn}$ $k\leftarrow[\mathbf{ywn}(\mathbf{Fido}),\mathbf{ywn}|j''']$	D .. k

$\{\mathbf{\$},\mathbf{Fido},\mathbf{£}\}$ are things belonging to Nina. Processing α_1 has made the information state change from *init* to state $k = [\mathbf{ywn}(\mathbf{Fido}),\mathbf{ywn},\mathbf{Fido},\mathbf{dog},\mathbf{N},\mathbf{ywn}(\mathbf{N})\,|\,init]$.

According to this description, the collection of discourse referents is monotonically increasing[8], and this is definitely the preferable linguistic point of departure. Of course, taking part in a real conversation involves a lot of 'unlearning'; but the same is true for all kinds of mental data processing, so allocating the long-term 'down dating' of information states to the grammar itself would be too narrow-minded—it would block off some important generalizations on the cognitive level.

4.5.2. *Nina yawns; it irritates Fido*

As for α_2, the lexicalization of the pronoun 'it' is somewhat tricky, when 'it' is taken as a variable over discourse modifiers. We can obviously not ascribe it to category Đ/(NP\Đ), as this would corrupt the semantics. On the other hand, the logically natural choice Đ/(Đ\Đ) leads to overgeneration[9]. Sooner or later, however, the calculus has to be enhanced with morphological features etc. anyway, and hopefully this will solve the problem.

For now, we simply lexicalize 'it' as Đ/(P\Đ), P being an ill-defined quasi-proposition, and p a semantic variable of the corresponding type. As long as the only duty of P is to mediate between subject and verb, the deception seems harmless.

(29)

it	.. Đ/(P\Đ)	.. $\lambda U\lambda i.U(p)(j)\{\text{DREF}(p, i, j)\}$
she	.. Đ/(NP\Đ)	.. $\lambda Q\lambda i.\ Q(z)(j)\{\text{DREF}(z, i, j)\}$
so	.. VP$_{\text{inf}}$	.. $\lambda x\lambda i.\ j\{\text{DREF}(P, i, i'),\ \text{DREF}(P(x), i', j),\ \text{EVAL}(P(x))\}$
continues	.. P\Đ	.. $\lambda p\lambda i.\ j\{$ DREF(con, i, i'),
		EVAL(con(p)),
		DREF(con$(p), i', j$) $\}$
irritates	.. (P\Đ)/NP	.. $\lambda x\lambda p\lambda i.\ j\{$ DREF(irr, i, i'),
		EVAL(irr$(x)(p)$),
		DREF(irr$(x), i', i''$),
		DREF(irr$(x)(p), i'', j$) $\}$
Fido$_{\text{obj}}$	.. (D/NP)\D	.. $\lambda T.\ j\{\text{DREF}(\text{Fido}, T(\text{Fido}), j)\}$

The signs 'she' and 'so' are repeated here for comparison with 'it'. Note that only 'so' inserts new material into the information state (namely $P(x)$, the tacitly introduced proposition). The intransitive verb 'continues' is added for comparison with 'irritates'.

(30)

New wd.	New actions	New instantiations	New expect.
Nina^ yawns;	*(cf. fig.28)*	$k \leftarrow [\mathbf{ywn(N)}, \mathbf{ywn}, \mathbf{N}\|init]$	D .. k
it	$\text{DREF}(p, k, k')$	$p \leftarrow \mathbf{ywn(N)}$ $k' \leftarrow [\mathbf{ywn(N)}, \mathbf{ywn}, \mathbf{N}\|init]$	$D/(P\backslash\!D)$ .. $\lambda U.U(p)(k')$
irritates	$\text{DREF}(\mathbf{irr}, k', i)$ $\text{EVAL}(\mathbf{irr}(x)(\mathbf{ywn(N)}))$ $\text{DREF}(\mathbf{irr}(x), i, i')$ $\text{DREF}(\mathbf{irr}(x)(\mathbf{ywn(N)}), i', k'')$	 $(x \in \{\mathbf{J}, \mathbf{Fido}\})$ $k'' \leftarrow [\mathbf{irr}(x)(\mathbf{ywn(N)}), \mathbf{irr}(x), \mathbf{irr}\|k']$	 D/NP .. $\lambda x.\, k''$
Fido	$\text{DREF}(\mathbf{Fido}, k''', l)$	$k''' \leftarrow (\lambda x.\, k'')(\mathbf{Fido})$ $x \leftarrow \mathbf{Fido}$ $l \leftarrow [\mathbf{Fido}, \mathbf{irr(Fido)(ywn(N))},$ $\mathbf{irr(Fido)}, \mathbf{irr},$ $\mathbf{ywn(N)}, \mathbf{ywn}, \mathbf{N} \| init\,]$ D .. l	

The resulting information state l is [**Fido, irr(Fido)(ywn(N)), irr(Fido), irr, ywn(N), ywn, N** | *init*], and as l now contains *two* propositions, a following utterance as 'it makes no sense' should be ambiguous. This seems to be correct, even though 'it' is predicted to prefer **irr(Fido)(ywn(N))** to **ywn(N)**, the former being the freshest. This is perhaps less obvious, since a repeated pronoun tends to stick to the same referent. As it stands, the grammar has no feeling for rhetorical effects such as *epanaphora*.

In the examples, we take programs to be run as soon as they are constructed. This is not necessitated by the logic itself, and it is easy to imagine a parser always estimating the costs before running a program; such a parser would postpone evaluation when confronted with, say, a lot of abstraction (such as right after a determiner 'the'). See Johnson-Laird (1977) and van der Linden (1992) for two different angles on this topic.

4.6. A NOTE ON GRAMMATICAL OBJECTS

Observe that Fido_{obj} is given the category $(D/NP)\backslash D$, rather than the expected $(D\!\!/NP)\backslash D\!\!/$. The lowered object type is easier to work with, since (i) doesn't involve as much abstraction as (ii) (cf. 1.2.2.):

(31)   (i)   *(situated subject)* .. $D/(NP\backslash\!D\!\!/)$ *(verb)* .. $(NP\backslash\!D\!\!/)/NP$ $\Rightarrow$ D/NP

       (ii)   *(situated subject)* .. $D/(NP\backslash\!D\!\!/)$ *(verb)* .. $(NP\backslash\!D\!\!/)/NP$ $\Rightarrow$ $D/((D\!\!/NP)\backslash\!D\!\!/)$

The semantic consequence of lowering the object type is that objects are not linked directly to the current information state (the underlined D in $(D/NP)\backslash(\underline{D}\backslash D)$), but rather depend on the subject-verb-complex for their input. This makes no difference, as long as a subject or a verb has appeared by the onset of the object.

Of course, English (and presumably all languages) has object-initial forms too, and they demand the full object-category for an incremental analysis; otherwise, parsing a sequence like: *(context)^him^I^would^like^to...* cannot relate 'him' to *context* before the mediating 'I' has arrived.

(32) Fido_{obj} .. $(D/NP)\backslash D$ .. $\lambda P\lambda i. \; P(\textbf{Fido})(j)\{\text{DREF}(\textbf{Fido}, i, j)\}$ (normal object-type)

  Fido_{obj} .. $(D/NP)\backslash D$ .. $\lambda T. \; j\{\text{DREF}(\textbf{Fido}, T(\textbf{Fido}), j)\}$ (lowered object-type)

5. Ellipsis as Syntactic Disturbance

Consider the mildly irregular forms, repeated here:

(33) δ_1. Nina_i yawns_j — and her_i $\text{dog}_{(j)}$

  δ_2.   Nina has no dog_k ; John has two $_{(k)}$

  δ_3.   Nina's dog_k yawns; John's $_{(k)}$ does so too

  δ_4. John_i washes_k Nina_j's [dirty $\text{trousers}]_l$, and $\text{she}_{j\,(k)}$ $\text{his}_{i\,(l)}$

  δ_5. John_i washes_k Nina_j's [trousers whenever Fido has lain on them

  and wetted $\text{them}]_l$, and $\text{she}_{j\,(k)}$ $\text{his}_{i\,(l?)}$

Are they ill-formed? Are they perfectly well-formed? Would we like a grammar of English to generate them or not? If one believes in an independent syntactic level of description, these questions must all have clear answers yes or no.

Another perhaps more perspicuous strategy is the following: Whenever the parser is not able to incorporate a newly encountered sign, the syntactic grip is loosened—the semantic fastened.

To be more precise, the 'incorporation' of new categories is defined in terms of *complexity*:

- The complexity COM of a category A is equal to the number of basic categories in A; COM($(NP\backslash D)/NP$) is thus 4 (cf. Buszkowski (1988) p.72)
- Consider a sequent consisting of a current category, a new category, and a consequent: *Current New* $\Rightarrow$ *Conseq*. If there is an instantiation of *Conseq* making the sequent valid, such that COM(*Conseq*) < COM(*New*) + COM(*Current*), then *New* is said to be *incorporated* in *Current*.
- The syntactic *gain* is computed as COM(*New*) + COM(*Current*) − COM(*Conseq*), *Conseq* being a valid consequent of the lowest complexity possible.

The examples α_1 and α_2 were parsed without syntactic conflicts, i.e. all words could be incorporated on arrival. In the tables below, $n<n'+n''$ signifies that the *gain* factor is positive, n, n' and n'' being COM(*Conseq*), COM(*New*) and COM(*Current*).

(34)

α_1	Nina 4<1+5	yawns; 1<4+3	her 5<1+6	dog 4<5+1	does 2<4+4	so (too) 1<2+1
α_2	Nina 4<1+5	yawns; 1<4+3	it 4<1+5	irritates 2<4+4	Fido 1<2+3	

The gain factor should be taken with a grain of salt: We have not been very specific in defining VP_{inf} and P, and consequently the gain of an incorporation like $D/VP_{inf}\ VP_{inf} \Rightarrow D$ can only be specified as *at least* 2. Similarly, if we install the full object type (cf. section 4.6.), the gain figures of α_2 change from 2;6;2;6;4 to 2;6;2;2;10.

Nevertheless, the *sign* of the gain factor is significant, as exemplified in the following table where the indigestible words make the gain factor drop to zero.

(35)

δ_1	Nina 4<1+5	yawns, 1<4+3	and 1<1+2	her 5<1+6	dog; 4<5+1	(but) **8=4+4**		
δ_3	Nina 4<1+5	's 5<4+11	dog 4<5+1	yawns; 1<4+3	John 4<1+5	's 5<4+11	does **9=5+4**	(so too)

Now the parser has a well-defined way of detecting incorporation conflicts—but how to solve them?

5.1. JOHN WASHES NINA'S DIRTY TROUSERS, AND SHE HIS

The following analysis is rather tentative—the present grammar is in its early childhood, and seen from there everything seems possible. But even if the framework presented here really is too slight for a thorough analysis of ellipses, I believe the intuitions behind it to be basically correct.

(36)

John$_{subj}$ .. D/(NP\D) .. $\lambda P\lambda i.\ P(\mathbf{J})(j)\{DREF(\mathbf{J},i,j)\}$

washes .. (NP\D)/NP .. $\lambda x\lambda y\lambda i.\ j\{\ DREF(\mathbf{wsh},\ i,\ i'\ ),$
$EVAL(\mathbf{wsh}(x)(y)),$
$DREF(\mathbf{wsh}(x),\ i',\ i''),$
$DREF(\mathbf{wsh}(x)(y),\ i'',j)\ \}$

Nina's$_{obj}$ .. ((D/NP)\D)/CN .. $\lambda P\lambda T.\ P(y)(j)\{EVAL(\mathbf{has}(y)(\mathbf{N})),$
$DREF(\mathbf{N},T(y),j)\}$

dirty .. CN/CN .. $\lambda P\lambda x\lambda i.P(x)(j)\{EVAL(\mathbf{dty}(x)),$
$DREF(\mathbf{dty},\ i,\ i'),$
$DREF(\mathbf{dty}\cap P,\ i',j)\ \}$

trousers .. CN .. $\lambda x\lambda i.\ j\{DREF(\mathbf{trs},i,i'\ ),$

$$\text{Eval}(\text{trs}(x)),$$
$$\text{Dref}(x,i',j) \}$$

and	.. Đ	.. $\lambda i.i\{\}$
she	.. Đ/(NP\Đ)	.. $\lambda Q\lambda i.\ Q(z)(j)\{\text{Dref}(z,i,j)\}$
his$_{obj}$	.. ((D/NP)\D)/CN	.. $\lambda P\lambda T.\ P(z)(j)\{\text{Dref}(x,T(z),j),$
		$\text{Eval}(\text{has}(z)(x))\}$

(37)

New wd.	New actions	New instantiations	New expectations
John	$\text{Dref}(\mathbf{J}, init, j)$	$j\leftarrow[\mathbf{J}\|init]$	D/(NP\Đ) .. $\lambda P.P(\mathbf{J})(j)$
washes	$\text{Dref}(\mathbf{wsh}, j,i),$		
	$\text{Eval}(\mathbf{wsh}(y)(\mathbf{J}))$	$(y \in \{\mathbf{Nds},\mathbf{Jds},\mathbf{Ndt},\mathbf{Jdt},\mathbf{Nct},\mathbf{Jct}\})$	
	$\text{Dref}(\mathbf{wsh}(y),i,i')$		
	$\text{Dref}(\mathbf{wsh}(y)(\mathbf{J}),i',j')$	$j'\leftarrow[\mathbf{wsh}(y)(\mathbf{J}),\mathbf{wsh}(y),\mathbf{wsh}\|j]$	D/NP .. $\lambda y.\ j'$
Nina's	$\text{Eval}(\mathbf{has}(y)(\mathbf{N}))$	$(y \in \{\mathbf{Nds},\mathbf{Ndt},\mathbf{Nct}\})$	
	$\text{Dref}(\mathbf{N},j',j'')$	$j''\leftarrow[\mathbf{N}.\mathbf{wsh}(y)(\mathbf{J}),\mathbf{wsh}(y),\mathbf{wsh}\|j]$	D/CN .. $\lambda P.P(y)(j'')$
dirty	$\text{Eval}(\mathbf{dty}(y)),$	$(y \in \{\mathbf{Nds},\mathbf{Ndt}\})$	
	$\text{Dref}(\mathbf{dty},j'',i'')$		
	$\text{Dref}(\mathbf{dty}\cap P,i'',j'')$	$j'''\leftarrow[\mathbf{dty}\cap P,\mathbf{dty},\mathbf{N}\|j'']$	D/CN .. $\lambda P.P(y)(j''')$
trousers	$\text{Dref}(\mathbf{trs},j''',i''')$	$P\leftarrow\mathbf{trs}$	
	$\text{Eval}(\mathbf{trs}(y))$	$y\leftarrow\mathbf{Ndt}$	
	$\text{Dref}(\mathbf{Ndt},i''',k)$	$k\leftarrow[\mathbf{Ndt},\mathbf{trs},\mathbf{dty}\cap\mathbf{trs},\mathbf{dty},\mathbf{N}\|j''']$	D .. k
and	*(none)*	*(none)*	D .. k
she	$\text{Dref}(z,k,k')$	$z\leftarrow\mathbf{N}$	D/(NP\Đ)
		$k'\leftarrow[\mathbf{N},\mathbf{Ndt},\mathbf{trs},\mathbf{dty}\cap\mathbf{trs},\mathbf{dty}\|j'']$	.. $\lambda Q.Q(\mathbf{N})(k')$
his	*(conflict)*	?	?

The current information state is: $k'\leftarrow[\mathbf{N}, \mathbf{Ndt}, \mathbf{trs}, \mathbf{dty}\cap\mathbf{trs}, \mathbf{dty}, \mathbf{wsh}(\mathbf{Ndt})(\mathbf{J}),$ $\mathbf{wsh}(\mathbf{Ndt}), \mathbf{wsh}, \mathbf{J} \mid init]$. $\mathbf{Ndt}$ is supposed to be some dirty trousers of Nina's, $\mathbf{Jct}$ some clean ones of John's, et cetera. The $\cap$-operator computes the meet of two properties: $P\cap Q \equiv_{def} \lambda x\lambda i.\ Q(x)(P(x)(i))$.

How to bridge the gap? It goes without saying that the hypothetical intercalated category *InterC* should be incorporatable in the sequent *Current InterC* $\Rightarrow$ *Current'*, and the following category *New* too, in *Current' New* $\Rightarrow$ *Conseq*; but this is not enough to guarantee *InterC* to be of finite complexity, even if *Current'* and *Conseq* are known (which we wouldn't want to presuppose anyway).

The solution proposed here is to assume that the speaker, in producing a syntactic conflict, exploits his knowledge of the hearer's information state: By deliberately turning down his syntactic lantern, he signifies that the semantic goal is not far.

(38)

Intercalation algorithm

If a syntactic conflict is detected and *Current = A/B..λX.Y,* then
(i)   find and apply a fresh, suitable binder X' of type $f(B)$ in the information state; check that *New* can be incorporated in A, preferably by application. Resume parsing: $A..(\lambda X.Y)(X')$ *New* ...
(ii)   if (i) fails, find a fresh, suitable binder $\lambda Z.X'$ of type $f(B/C)$ in the information state, such that *New* can be incorporated in A/C, preferably by application. Resume parsing: $A/C..\lambda Z.(\lambda X.Y)X'$ *New* ...

Of course, this constitutes only one corner of an algorithm, but it's enough for the examples at hand, as well as quite a few commonly heard ellipses[10].

(39)

New wd.	New actions	New instantiations	New expectations
John^...^she	*(cf. fig.37)*	*(see k' below)*	$D/(NP\backslash D) .. \lambda Q.Q(N)(k')$
(washes)	DREF(**wsh**, $k'.i$).		
	EVAL(**wsh**$(y)(N)$)	$(y \in \{$**Nds, Jds, Ndt,**	
	DREF(**wsh**$(y), i, i'$)	**Jdt, Nct, Jct**$\}$)	
	DREF(**wsh**$(y)(N), i', k''$)		$D/NP.. \lambda y. k''$
his	DREF($x,(\lambda y.k'')(z), k'''$)	$x \leftarrow$ **J**	
	EVAL(**has**$(z)(J)$)	$(z \in \{$**Jds, Jdt, Jct**$\}$)	$D/CN .. \lambda P. P(z)(k''')$
(dirty^	EVAL(**dty**(z))	$(z \in \{$**Jds, Jdt**$\}$)	
trousers)	DREF(**dty**, k''', j)		
	DREF(**dty**$\cap$**trs**, j, j')		
	DREF(**trs**, j', j'')		
	EVAL(**trs**(z))	$z \leftarrow$ **Jdt**	
	DREF(**Jdt**, j'', out)		$D..out$

$k' \leftarrow$[**N, Ndt, trs,** **dty**$\cap$**trs, dty, wsh(Ndt)(J), wsh(Ndt), wsh, J** | *init*]
$k'' \leftarrow$[**wsh**$(y)(N)$, **wsh**(y), **wsh, N, Ndt, trs, dty**$\cap$**trs, dty, wsh(Ndt)(J), wsh(Ndt), J** | *init*]
$k''' \leftarrow$[**J, wsh**$(z)(N)$, **wsh**(z), **wsh, N, Ndt, trs, dty**$\cap$**trs, dty, wsh(Ndt)(J), wsh(Ndt)** | *init*]
$out \leftarrow$[**Jdt,trs,dty**$\cap$**trs,dty,J,wsh(Jdt)(N),wsh(Jdt),wsh,N,Ndt,wsh(Ndt)(J),wsh(Ndt)**|*init*]

Had the next sign after 'she' been, say, 'but' ('John washes Nina's dirty trousers, and she; but...'), then option (i) of the intercalation algorithm would have applied, since NP\Ð can be incorporated in D/(NP\Ð) , and D\(D/Ð) in D, both by application.

(40)   ˆshe..D/(NP\Ð)   (intercal)..NP\Ð   but..D\(D/Ð)   ⇒   Conseq

The relatively low salience of this utterance is not unexpected, the many intervening non-suitable binders of the correct type taken into consideration: **trs, dty∩trs, dty**. The only (fairly) plausible binder is **wsh(Ndt)**, and if the utterance *has* to mean something, this seems to be the best bid. Compare δ_1 and δ_2, which are processed using option (i) with the intended result:

(41)   ˆdog .. D/(NP\Ð)   (intercal)..NP\Ð..**y w n**   but..D\(D/Ð)   ⇒   Conseq
        ˆtwo .. D/CN   (intercal)..CN..**dog**   but..D\(D/Ð)   ⇒   Conseq

Now back to John's laundry, 'John washes Nina's dirty trousers, and she his':

(42)   ˆshe..D/(NP\Ð)   InterC   his.. (D/NP)\(D/CN)   ⇒   Conseq

InterC = NP\Ð fails, since (D/NP)\(D/CN) cannot be incorporated in D. By option (ii), *InterC* is instantiated with (NP\Ð)/NP..$\lambda x \lambda y \lambda i.j$, for which we have a first class candidate in **wsh**.[11]

Immediately, yet another conflict is detected—and easily resolved by option (i).

(43)   ˆhis..D/CN   (intercal)..CN.. **dty∩trs**   (reset)..D\D   ⇒   Conseq

dty∩trs is preferred to **trs** presumably because it narrows down the set of object-entities more efficiently, making it the more salient of the two (see Steedman (1990) for purely syntactic CG-treatments of similar ellipses).

Rather than using a dummy 'but', we now have the interrupt count as D\D itself. Whenever we want the parser to begin intercalating *before* a non-incorporatable sign has arrived, we must do so by explicitly cancelling its syntactic expectations. This seems very similar to what goes on prosodically at the end of discourses like δ_1, δ_2 and δ_4: If pronouncing the last word unstressed and with neutral intonation, the speaker keeps the hearer waiting for more[12].

6. Does the Sentence Exist?

"Nonbeing must in some sense be, otherwise what is it that there is not? This tangled doctrine might be nicknamed Plato's beard; historically it has proved tough, frequently dulling the edge of Occam's razor."
W. Quine, *From a Logical Point of View*.

Over these pages, I've used words like 'sentence', 'interjection', 'conjunction' and 'ellipsis' time and again, claiming them either to be unfit names or to refer to questionable categories. Apparently, the terms are needed in order to be rejected ...

There *are* sentences, just as there are heroes, fools, and timeservers. Anyone can point out good examples of fools, and educated people can point out good examples of sentences (but that is almost as far as it goes).

We need the sentence in order to establish a lexicon, especially in Categorial Grammar; otherwise, not even the verb can be defined. On the other hand, no category of English grammar needs more than a handful of words for a minimal example: 'Mary yawns', 'John kicks Fido', 'The shirt smells', 'It is very dirty', and so on. This is the way it's done in any reasonable dictionary. Accepting these examples doesn't commit us to acknowledge each and every systematic expansion of their constituents as a qualified piece of discourse. This is not to say that long or semantically anomalous periods are *non*-sentences; rather, they are not very well characterized by an abstract feature [± *well-formed*], that is, if the sentence is taken to be a 'natural kind'. A more sensible criterion is to what degree they are incrementally understandable. 'Colorless green ideas sleep furiously' is simply not a very good example of a sentence—just as Chomsky is not a very good example of a timeserver.

The peculiar fact is that this is a perfectly uncontroversial standpoint in *discourse* theory, where judgments are typically based on coherence, salience, felicity—while in *syntax* theory it is almost heresy.

Now, if the Sentence is really not reliable as the basic unit of a combined syntax- and discourse-grammar, what is? Information states, and words. Words are much more real than sentences—we *know* they exist, we know they have a sound and a meaning. Of course, the demarcation of 'word' has been disputed as well; still, we can hardly imagine a natural language without a word for 'word', whereas sentence-hood belongs to the realm of educated, written language. A pop song called 'Sentences Don't Come Easy To Me' would never become a hit.

6.1. SEMICOLON GRAMMAR — STATE OF THE ART

The present approach is different from most formal syntactic theories in a number of ways.

Firstly, time has a direction. Every word contributes immediately, syntactically as well as semantically, to the informational background on which the following words are interpreted. That is why anaphors are preferred to 'cataphors', topic-comment to comment-topic, filler-gap to gap-filler, etc. Most theories of the CG- and PSG-tradition do not have any principled preferences in these cases—they are just as well suited to describe the non-language Hsilgne as the language English, the former being identical to the latter with all sentences worded backwards[13].

Secondly, right-associative structures are preferred to left-associative (cf. 1.1.). Thanks to L, any sequent can be analysed left-to-right, the right-branching (i) as well as the left-branching (ii).

(44)	(i)	A/B	B/C	C/D	D	$\Rightarrow$	A
	(ii)	D	D\C	C\B	B\A	$\Rightarrow$	A

In (ii), the incorporation of every new sign closes off a constituent; in (i), by contrast, the constituents are kept open, favouring *prediction* (cf. fig. 37). Being able to predict the syntactic and semantic developments of the discourse is a powerful means of robustness, making communication more efficient.

Thirdly, we don't need to lament the throngs of existing sentence definitions, since the question of sentence-hood is not taken as a fundamental one.

(45) δ_4.   John washes Nina's dirty trousers, and she his

   δ_5.   John washes Nina's dirty trousers whenever Fido has lain on them and
            wetted them, and she $\downarrow$ his

Discourse δ_5 is just 'not as understandable' as δ_4 because of the intervening material between the V_t-binder and the gap. δ_5 would hardly be generated, since at point $\downarrow$, **wsh** wouldn't be a very suitable binder any more, making the speaker prefer another mode of expression in order not to confuse the hearer; but there is no need for labelling δ_5 as 'ill-formed'. And we can forget about questions like: Is δ_4 really *one* or *two* sentences?

Now for the buts. Even if the sketched programme seems promising, its implementation is still imperfect, to put it mildly. The lexicon presented here is small and arbitrary[14], and the intercalation algorithm is far too liberal, accepting almost any irregularity as a likely ellipsis.

Another more principled objection is that the underlying logic is not very strong, L being only context-free. Does this mean that the proficiency badges of traditional grammar are out of reach—discontinuous dependencies, passivisation, raising, stranding?

I am not quite sure what to think about this yet. In general, I'm not happy with a too detailed comparison; what is considered to be important areas of research seen from one point of view, might appear as fata morgana from the other. Who says that there is *stranding*? Or *fronting*? These metaphors really only make sense with reference to delimited written strings of words. As for *raising* and *government*, they don't mean anything in a theory without syntax trees.

A more promising approach is to take human dialogue as the prime manifestation of language. This means trading the long lists of well-formed sentences for a picture of the speaker working every moment on levelling out the differences between his own intentions and his idea of the hearer's information state. Meaningful questions to a language model like that would then be of the following kind: What is *at this point* the purpose of saying 'herself' rather than 'her'? Of putting a grammatical object where something else was expected, even if it creates syntactic disturbance? Of postponing the preposition, instead of saying: 'Take off it'?

For this strategy to have a fair chance, a logic is needed which is guaranteed to get something out of *Current New* $\Rightarrow$ *Conseq*, irrespective of the instantiation of the antecedent. We wouldn't want a logical breakdown, just because an unforeseen word turned up—this would be as absurd as giving up a journey, just because the car couldn't get past a gate.

That is why L was chosen. L is a calculus with fine, well described, consistent qualities, inspiring confidence. L is defined by a very small number of rules; it offers structural completeness, cut-freeness, and efficient parsing. Adding just one extra structural rule, such as permutation or expansion, turns L into a far stronger and more intractable logic which doesn't have the least similarity with a NL-parser. This would call for a lot of ad hoc restrictions.

L is context-free only (Pentus (1993)), but this needn't count for the language model as a whole. We have shown that some forms usually considered elliptic (and obviously non-context-free) can be treated in ;G without fiddling with the logic itself, by considering *why* anyone would say like that—building heuristics on the firm grounds of L.

We conclude for now that the choice of L suggests a maxim: *Be context-free* (if you're not, you must have your reasons). Whether this strategy is feasible, or whether we have to install another logic, the future will show.

Later, much later, we would expect to end up—by abstracting over communication situations—where traditional syntax begins.

Acknowledgements

Thanks to Peter Rossen Skadhauge for checking the logical deep structure of this paper and to Britt Keson for checking the English surface.

Notes

[1] A lexical sign consists of three fields: *Phon* .. *Syn* .. *Sem*. In this paper, *Phon* is simply an orthographical form, while *Syn* is a syntactic category, and *Sem* the related semantics as represented by a (slightly non-standard) λ-formula. Where irrelevant, one or two of the fields are left implicit. Logical predicates of arity ≥ 2 are written Curry-style, i.e. as embeddings of one-place predicates; $A(B,C,D)$ is thus written $((A(D))(C))(B)$, or just $A(D)(C)(B)$.

[2] For thorough introductions to λ-calculus, L, and CG in general, see van Benthem (91) and Morrill (94).

[3] From a semantic point of view, we could as well take it as an assertion about what *precedes* or *surrounds* the utterance; observe that this is paralleled by the everyday-use of ellipses like 'Nina doesn't'. More on this later.

[4] $D\backslash D$ $D\backslash D$ $\Rightarrow$ $D\backslash D$ is a special case of the L-theorem called *(functional) composition*: $A\backslash B..Y$ $B\backslash C..X \Rightarrow A\backslash C..\lambda Z.X(Y(Z))$ (see Moortgat (1988)).

[5] [N,J] is short for [$x\leftarrow$N, $y\leftarrow$J, (all others undefined)].

[6] 'The Proper Treatment of Quantification in Ordinary English', ref. Montague (1970).

[7] All the other sentential connectives ('but', 'while', 'then again', stressed-'and' etc.) are much less redundant, and much less frequent. They do leave their stamp on the interpretation of the following discourse, and their type must reflect this, suggesting the category $D\backslash(D/(D\backslash D))$, or equivalently: D/D. This, of course, reintroduces the structural ambiguity.

[8] Not order preserving, though, since the order of referents change when old ones are touched up.

[9] The produced semi-acceptable forms are not devoid of interest. A typical example is: 'Nina smokes, it, John yawns', or in categories: D $D/(NP\backslash D)$ $NP\backslash D$ $D/(D\backslash D)$ $D/(NP\backslash D)$ $NP\backslash D$. This sequence, which is not very far from spoken language, is parsable using e.g.: $D/(D\backslash D)..Q$ $D..M \Rightarrow D..Q(\lambda N\lambda i.M(N(i)))$ (combining *init*^Nina^smokes^it + John^yawns). The resulting information state is [ywn(J), ywn, J, smoke(N), smoke, N, *init*]; interestingly, items 4, 5 and 6 has been actualized (moved in front) during the processing of 'it'.

[10] Taking ellipses as identical to syntactic conflicts is of course an over-simplification. Resumptions like 'If he comes—I said if—then he...' are out of reach; as for now, conflicts always lead to destruction of syntactic information.

[11] Compare δ_3, which uses option (i), but needs functional *composition* rather than application in incorporating 'does'.

[12] Analysing an interrupt as a *sign* $D\backslash D$ is just to keep the algorithm simple. A more correct analysis is: *Current InterC* $\Rightarrow$ D.

[13] The existence of Hsilgne of course stands or falls by the existence of the Sentence—but as the Sentence is above suspicion in formal syntax, there is really no paradox here.

[14] A few ;G toy lexicons developed in different directions are described in Henrichsen (1995); a time-aspect-extension building upon Muskens (1992), a quantifier-version a la Dinsmore (1993) allowing for incremental parochial reasoning, and a Prolog-version.

References

Ajdukiewicz, K. (1935) 'Die Syntaktische Konnexität'. Eng. transl. 'Syntactic Connexion', in McCall, S. (1967) *'Polish Logic 1920-1939'*, Oxford.

Bar-Hillel, J. (1964) *'Language and Information'*, Addison-Wesley.

van Benthem (1991) *'Language in Action: Categories, Lambdas and Dynamic Logic'*, North-Holland.

Buszkowski, W. (1988) 'Generative Power of Categorial Grammars', *in* Oehrle & al (1988).

Dinsmore, J. (1991) *'Partitioned Representations'*, Kluwer.

Garfield, J.L. (1987) *'Modularity in Knowledge Representation and NL Understanding'*, MIT Press.

Groenendijk, J.A.G.; M.B.J.Stokhof (1991) 'Dynamic Predicate Logic', *Linguistics and Philosophy* 14 p.39-100.

Haddock, N.J. (1988) 'Incremental Semantics and Interactive Syntactic Processing', PhD thesis, Univ. of Edinburgh.

Henrichsen, P.J. (1995) 'Det Inkrementelle Leksikon', Tietgen prize diss. (in Danish), Copenhagen Business School.

Janssen, T.M.V. (1986) *'Foundations and Applications of Montague Grammar 1'*, CWI, A'dam.

Jespersen, O. (1925) *'The Philosophy of Grammar'*, edition London: Allen & Unwin (1975).

Johnson-Laird, P.N. (1977) 'Procedural Semantics', *Cognition* 5 p.189-214.

Kempen, G.; Hoenkamp, E. (1987) 'An Incremental Procedural Grammar for Sentence Formulation', *Cognitive Science* 11 p.201-258

Lambek, J. (1958) 'The Mathematics of Sentence Structure', in Buszkowski, W. & al (1988) *'Categorial Grammar'*, John Benjamins, A'dam.

van der Linden, E.-J. (1992) 'Incremental Processing and the Hierarchical Lexicon', *Comp. Ling.* 18/2 p.219-238.

Marslen-Wilson, W.D. (1975) 'Sentence Perception as an Interactive Parallel Process', *Science* 189 p.226-228.

Milward, D. (1995) 'Incremental Interpretation of Categorial Grammar', Proceedings of the 7th EACL.

Montague, R. (1970) 'The Proper Treatment of Quantification in Ordinary English', in Thomason (1974).

Moortgat, M. (1988) *'Categorial Investigations: Logical and Linguistic Aspects of the Lambek Calculus'*, Foris.

Morrill, G.V. (1994) *'Type Logical Grammar: Categorial Logic of Signs'*, Kluwer.

Muskens, R. (1992) 'Tense and the Logic of Change', ITK Research Report No. 35, Univ. of Tilburg.

Oehrle, R.T. & al (1988) *'Categorial Grammars and NL Structures'*, Reidel.

Pentus, M. (1993) 'Lambek Grammars are Context Free', Proceedings of the 8th IEEE Symposium on Logic in Computer Science, p.429-433.

de Smedt, K.J.M.J. (1990) 'Incremental Sentence Generation', PhD thesis, Univ. of Nijmegen.

Steedman, M. (1987) 'Combinatory Grammars and Human Language Processing', in Garfield (1987).

Steedman, M. (1990) 'Gapping as Constituent Coordination', *Linguistics and Philosophy* 13, p.207-263.

Thomason, R.H. (1974) *'Formal Philosophy: Selected Papers of Richard Montague'*, Yale Univ.

Tyler, L.K.; W.D.Marslen-Wilson (1977) 'The On-Line Effects of Semantic Context on Syntactic Processing', *Journal of Verbal Learning and Verbal Behavior* 16 p.683-692.

CONTEXTUAL DOMAINS

F. RECANATI
CREA (Ecole Polytechnique/CNRS)
1 rue Descartes, 75005 Paris
France

1. Contextually restricted quantifiers

Natural language quantifiers often seem implicitly restricted. Thus when we say 'The burglar took everything', we have the feeling that 'everything' ranges over the domain of valuable objects in the house—not everything in the world. (In this case, it can be argued that there *has to be* some contextual restriction or other, for a totally unrestricted notion of 'everything in the world' hardly makes sense.) In the same way, someone who says 'Most students came to the party' is likely to have a particular group of students in mind, such that most students in that group came to the party.

Similar phenomena can be found which do not involve overt quantifiers. If, when asked whether I have eaten, I reply 'I've had breakfast', I clearly mean that I've had breakfast on the day of utterance. In contrast, an utterance like 'I've been to China' is likely to mean that the speaker has been to China once—not (or not necessarily) that he has been to China on the day of utterance (Sperber and Wilson 1986: 189-90). This difference can be accounted for in terms of a contextually variable domain of discourse (Recanati 1989b: 305-6). If we accept Davidson's analysis of action sentences, we can treat 'I've had breakfast' as meaning approximately: 'there is a past event which is my having breakfast'. Contextually the domain of quantification is restricted; the utterance 'concerns' only what happened so far on a certain day.

Among the phenomena which seem amenable to a treatment in terms of contextually restricted quantification we find incomplete descriptions. Often we use a description 'the F' even though Russell's uniqueness condition is not satisfied. Thus I say 'Close the door', knowing full well that there is more than one door in the universe. Does this object to Russell's analysis of descriptions? Not if we accept the notion of a contextually restricted domain of quantification. If we do, we can say that the uniqueness condition *is* satisfied—not in the world, but in a relevant portion of the world. The latter is the domain of discourse for incomplete descriptions. Such an analysis has been offered many times, e.g. in Kuroda (1982), Barwise & Perry (1983), Fauconnier (1985), Recanati (1987), Barwise & Etchemendy (1987).

An alternative analysis has it that sentences such as 'Everybody went to Paris' are elliptical for longer sentences such as 'Every philosopher in the department went to Paris'. On this view, the sentence is not interpreted with respect to a contextually restricted domain; rather, its interpretation proceeds in two steps: the sentence is first completed, then interpreted with respect to the total world. This analysis is widespread, and many philosophers like it better than the analysis in terms of contextual domains; yet I think it can be objected to on several grounds. Be that as it may, I will not discuss

X. Arrazola et al. (eds.), Discourse, Interaction and Communication, 25-36.

the ellipsis theory here. What I want to do is elaborate the domain theory and respond to some of the objections it faces.

2. Austinian semantics

The notion of a contextually variable domain of discourse can be generalized in two directions. First, it can be argued that a contextually determined domain of discourse is involved whether or not the utterance includes a quantifier. Following Barwise, Perry and their colleagues, we can view the domain of discourse as a 'situation' tacitly referred to in the discourse. Whenever there is quantification, it is relative to the situation tacitly referred to, but the generalized notion of domain of discourse as 'parameter situation' applies whether or not the utterance involves some form of quantification. Barwise and Etchemendy give the following example (Barwise and Etchemendy 1987:121-2). Looking at a poker game, I say 'Claire has a good hand'. I describe the situation I am witnessing as a situation in which Claire has a good hand. If I am mistaken and Claire is not a constituent of the situation (if she is not among the players of the game I am watching, contrary to what I believe), my utterance is not true—even if Claire is playing poker in some other part of the city and has a good hand there; the utterance is not true because the situation referred to is not of the type described. If we did not have partial situations as domains of evaluation for our statements, but only the total world, we would have to say that the utterance is true, provided Claire is playing poker in some other part of the city and has a good hand there. So we see that utterances, like quantifier phrases, are interpreted relative to some partial, contextually determined domain of discourse rather than relative to a fixed, total world.

John Austin's semantic theory, presented in 'Truth', 'How to Talk' and a few other papers (Austin 1970), explicitly relies on the notion of a parameter situation relative to which utterances are to be interpreted. An utterance is true, Austin says, if the 'historic' situation it refers to is of the type with which the sentence is associated by the descriptive conventions of the language. Thus 'Claire has a good hand' is true iff the situation it refers to (viz. the poker game the speaker is watching) is a situation in which Claire has a good hand.[1] Contemporary 'situation theorists' follow Austin in describing the complete content of an utterance as a pair consisting of a parameter situation and a type of situation. The type of situation is very much like a 'proposition' in the traditional sense, but in Austin's semantics the utterance's semantic content (the 'Austinian proposition', as Barwise & Etchemendy say) is richer: it also involves the situation tacitly referred to by the utterance. If we abstract from the Austinian situation contextually provided, the content of the utterance is a proposition classically understood (I call it the 'propositional nucleus'). The 'Austinian proposition' results from adding to that propositional nucleus a situation implicitly referred to by the speaker. Austinian semantics therefore adds a further contextual parameter to those associated with standard indexicals: the situation talked about. The absolute and the restricted interpretations of a quantified sentence such as 'Everybody went to Paris' (everybody in the world vs. everybody in a certain group) result from different ways of filling out the situational slot in semantic structure. On this theory (in contrast to the 'ellipsis theory') the linguistic meaning of the sentence is the same on both interpretations; what varies is the value of a contextual parameter. This is easy to express in a Kaplanian framework: the 'character' of the sentence is a function from a rich 'context' including not only a speaker, a time, etc. but also a situation of reference, to a 'content' which is an Austinian proposition, i.e. a pair consisting of a situation and a proposition in the standard sense (the 'propositional nucleus'). Different Austinian propositions are expressed depending on the situation contextually referred to.

I said that the notion of a contextual domain of discourse could be generalized in two directions. Austinian semantics represents the first type of generalization: every utterance refers to a situation with respect to which it is presented as true. (A special case, perhaps, is that in which the situation in question is the total world.) The second generalization results from extending the notion of domain to counterfactual situations, belief worlds, fictional worlds, and the like. While the first, Austinian generalization has been advocated by some philosophers (namely situation theorists), the second generalization has been advocated by some linguists (namely cognitive semanticists such as Fauconnier). Before discussing the second generalization, however, we must consider an objection to the minimal notion of a contextual domain of discourse. This objection, originally due to Lewis and McCawley, suggests that the notion of a contextual domain cannot do the work we expect it to do—that of accounting for the interpretation of incomplete quantifiers.

3. Domain shift

The objection goes as follows:

> It is not true that a definite description "the F" denotes x if and only if x is the only F in existence. *Neither is it true that "the F" denotes x if and only if x is the one and only one F in some contextually determined domain of discourse.* For consider this sentence: "The pig is grunting, but the pig with floppy ears is not grunting" (Lewis). And this: "The dog got in a fight with another dog" (McCawley). They could be true. But for them to be true, "the pig" or "the dog" must denote one of two pigs or dogs, both of which belong to the domain of discourse. (Lewis 1979: 240-1; emphasis mine)

According to Soames (1986), Lewis's example (L), insofar as it is an example of a sentence which can be true, constitutes a decisive counterexample to Austinian semantics:

(L)   The dog got in a fight with another dog

In order to deal with a true instance of (L), the Austinian semanticist would have to posit a situation in which (i) there is one and only one dog (in order to satisfy the uniqueness requirement conveyed by the description 'the dog') and (ii) there are two dogs (in order to make the sentence true). Austinian semantics is taken to be refuted by those cases where certain constituents of the sentence 'place demands on situations that conflict with those arising from other constituents in the sentence' (Soames 1986: 357).

But is Austinian semantics really refuted by (L)? I do not think so. The attempted refutation relies on the crucial assumption that there is at most one situation referred to by a given utterance. According to Austinian semanticists, however, the situation talked about may change within the limits of a single utterance. This means that there can be more than one domain corresponding to a given utterance. As Barwise and Perry say, 'there is no reason to suppose that there is at most one resource situation per utterance any more than there should be only one thing around referred to by IT in a given utterance' (Barwise and Perry 1983:153). Now, if there are more than one domain, more than one situation, then an utterance like 'The dog got in a fight with another dog' no longer raises an insuperable problem: it can be accounted for by positing *two* situations, one in which there is one and only one dog, and another one in which there are two dogs.

The situation talked about is a feature of the 'context'. Now it is well-known that the context changes as the utterance takes place, to a large extent as a result of the utterance itself. Thus the earlier part of an utterance often affects the context in which the later part is interpreted. This phenomenon of intra-sentential variability has been noted many times in the literature on context-change, in connection with conjunctions, conditionals, and the defeasibility of presuppositions (see e.g. Stalnaker 1974, 1978). It is therefore not surprising that the domain of discourse itself can change in mid-utterance. The 'shifty' nature of the contextual domain of discourse is particularly obvious in Kuroda's framework. In Kuroda's 'indexed predicate calculus', sentential constituents are indexed and the indices refer to the domains (or 'mini-worlds') with respect to which the constituents are to be interpreted. The constituents within a single sentence can but need not be co-indexed. Thus Kuroda gives the following example (among many others):

(1)
    Since it was so stuffy in the house, Mary went up to the attic and opened the window

An utterance of (1) talks about a situation involving Mary and a particular house (whose identifiability is presupposed by the description 'the house'). Let us call this situation 'i'. 'The house' is interpreted with respect to i: the house is the house of the situation. 'The attic' is interpreted with respect to a different domain j, namely the house that is a constituent of situation i: the attic is the attic of the house. Here we have a case of *domain focalization:* the domain is restricted to a given portion of the initial domain. This sub-domain is easy to focus on, for it is made salient by the description 'the house'. A further, and more significant, shift of domain occurs when the third description, 'the window', is tokened. Under pragmatic pressure, a new domain k is selected: the introduction of the attic as a new topic makes it possible to interpret 'the window' as the window of the attic, rather than (implausibly) as the window of the house (Kuroda 1982:46). This is a standard instance of domain shift. It is driven by the process of 'accommodation' described by Lewis in the same paper in which the dog counterexample is presented (Lewis 1979). Using indices to represent domains of discourse (though not quite in Kuroda's manner), (1) can be represented as follows:

(1*)
    (Since it was so stuffy in (the house)$_i$, Mary went up to (the attic)$_j$ and opened (the window)$_k$)$_i$

i = the situation the global utterance talks about
j = the house
k = the attic

    This example shows that the 'domains of discourse' posited by the Austinian semanticist *can* be associated with expressions at all levels, from constituents of sentences to extended pieces of discourse. (All the authors I mentioned earlier as having appealed to contextually restricted domains of discourse make this point explicitly.). The Austinian semanticist is therefore happy to grant that 'contextual supplementation [i.e. the provision of a contextual domain] works at the level of constituents of sentences or utterances' (Soames 1986: 357). It is true that Austinian semantics locates the tacit reference to a situation at the global, utterance level. But, contrary to what Soames suggests,[2] nothing prevents the pragmatic process of domain provision from working both at the level of constituents and at the level of global utterances. Thus in (1*), there is a 'main' domain, namely i, corresponding to the global utterance. The main domain is the situation the utterance as a whole talks about (the 'historic' situation referred to, in Austin's terminology). Local domains, such as j and k in (1*), are not alternatives but additions to that main domain.

To illustrate the dialectic between local domains and main domains, consider the following variant of Barwise's example: 'Claire has a better hand than the bearded man'. Let us assume that the global utterance is interpreted with respect to a particular situation, namely the poker game, as in the original example. Now the description 'the bearded man' must be interpreted with respect to a partial situation in which there is only one bearded man. This opens up two possibilities: either the two situations are the same, or they are not. The case is simpler if the bearded man is the bearded man of the poker game (i.e. the one and only male participant in the poker game to have a beard), but this need not be the case. It is easy to imagine a context such that the bearded man referred to in the utterance 'Claire has a better hand than the bearded man' is no longer bearded in the poker situation referred to, but was bearded in a prior situation of which both the speaker and the listener are aware and which serves as 'resource situation' for the interpretation of the description. In such a case the description is interpreted with respect to a local domain distinct from the main domain (the poker situation):

(2*)   (Claire has a better hand than (the bearded man)$_i$)$_j$

i = *local domain (the previous encounter with the 'bearded man')*
j = *main domain (the poker situation)*

Ruth Kempson gives another example in which the shift of domain is of a temporal nature. Think of the contrast between (3) and (4):

(3)   The hostages were systematically ill-treated
(4)   The hostages were welcomed home by the President

In the domain framework, the contrast can be represented as follows:

(3*)   ((the hostages)$_i$ were systematically ill-treated)$_i$
(4*)   ((the hostages)$_i$ were welcomed home by the President)$_j$

i = *the 'hostage' situation*
j = *the 'welcome' situation*

As Kempson says,

> The interpretation of (3) implies that throughout the time described as one in the past with respect to the time of the utterance, a set of people who were being held hostages were systematically ill-treated. In (4), however, at the point in time in the past at which a set of people is welcomed home by their president, they are transparently no longer hostages. But the assertion made by (4) may yet be true. The

resource situation, s_0, against which a definite NP is evaluated demonstrably need not be the same as the described situation (Kempson forthcoming, p.15).

In other words, (4) involves a temporal shift of domain. Such shifts are pervasive in everyday discourse.

Now we see how the dog counterexample can be disposed of. It is easy to imagine true instances of (L) analysable as involving a shift of domain, for example a temporal shift.[3] Suppose we hear a dog barking at some distance. 'It's a dog', I say. But after some time, still concentrating on what I hear, I say 'The dog got in a fight with another dog'. Here again, time is the dimension along which the domain of discourse shifts. The situation we start with has one and only one dog, barking; then the situation changes. Even if the situation attended to does not really change (there were two dogs from the start, but we paid attention to only one of them) at least we re-analyse it and our representation changes. (The change occurs in 'processing time', in Langacker's terminology.) Be that as it may, the initial situation, with only one dog, gives way to a different situation with two dogs. The latter situation is what the global utterance talks about, but the description 'the dog' is still interpreted with respect to the earlier situation (described by the previous utterance, 'It's a dog'). (L) can therefore be analysed as follows:

(L*)   ((The dog)$_i$ got in a fight with another dog)$_j$

i = *the earlier situation (described by 'It's a dog')*
j = *the new situation (described by (L))*

Such an utterance would be true, if the dog which is a constituent of the initial situation i had got in a fight with another dog in the main situation j.

4. Mental spaces

So far the situations we have talked about are portions of the actual world. But the notion of a contextual domain of discourse can be (and has been) extended to situations which are not actual.

Sometimes it seems that an utterance does not talk about the actual world, nor a portion thereof, but about e.g. a fictional world. Thus an utterance such as 'Sherlock Holmes lives at 221B Baker Street' does not describe (a portion of) the actual world but, rather, the world of Conan Doyle's novels. There are also utterances which describe hypothetical situations. Thus I can say: 'Suppose that P', and then state that Q: what this means is that Q holds in the hypothetical world(s) or situation(s) introduced by the supposition that P. There are also utterances that describe belief worlds (i.e. the world as it is according to a certain person) rather than the actual world. So-called 'free indirect speech' can be analysed along those lines (Recanati 1987: 62). Suppose someone says:

(5)
        John is completely paranoid. Everybody wants to kill him, including his own
        mother!

Here, arguably, the sentence 'Everybody wants to kill him' is to be evaluated with respect to John's belief-world. The speaker somehow projects herself into John's mind. She does not really assert that everybody wants to kill John; it is his thought, not her own, that she expresses. The utterance is presented as 'true with respect to John's belief-world'—not as true with respect to the actual world:

(5*)   (John is completely paranoid.)$_i$ (Everybody wants to kill him.)$_j$

i = *the actual world*
j = *John's belief world*

Counterfactual situations, belief worlds, fictional worlds and the like can play the role of the contextual domain of discourse and affect the interpretation of quantifiers. Consider the following example. Suppose Peter wrongly believes that Ann is your sister; Ann is coming over and I say to you, ironically:

(6)   Hey, 'your sister' is coming over.

Although the utterance as a whole is about the actual world, the description 'your sister' is to be interpreted with respect to Peter's belief-world. In this context, the description refers to Ann, whereas in another context it would refer to Nicole, your actual sister. Here the domain of discourse shifts within the utterance, as in the examples above.

(6*)   ((Your sister)$_j$ is coming over)$_i$

i = *the actual world;*
j = *Peter's belief world*

There are examples of the same phenomenon occurring outside ironical speech (Recanati 1994:158-9). Imagine the following situation: John wrongly believes that Bush is the President of the USA. Knowing that Bush is in the next room, I say:

(7)
       If he goes in the next room, John will be surprised to meet the President of the USA.

Here the description 'The President of the USA' refers to Bush rather than to the actual President (Clinton) because it is intended to be interpreted with respect to a world, namely John's belief-world, in which Bush is the President of the USA. Thus the consequent of (7) can be analysed as follows:

(7*)
       (John will be surprised to meet (the President of the USA)$_k$)$_j$.

       j = *the hypothetical situation in which John goes in the next room*
       k = *John's belief world*

The consequent of (7) is presented as true in the hypothetical situation in which John goes in the next room; but the description 'the President of the USA' is evaluated in John's belief world rather than in the hypothetical situation. It is Bush (the person whom John thinks is President) whom John is surprised to meet, in the hypothetical situation in which John goes in the next room.

A fuller analysis of (7) would have to take into account the fact that, by describing a hypothetical situation j, a hypothetical statement like (7) describes the actual world i as a world in which that situation is possible. The analysis therefore becomes:

(7**)
> (If he goes in the next room, (John will be surprised to meet (the President of the USA)$_k$)$_j$)$_i$.

> i = *the actual world*
> j = *the hypothetical situation in which John goes in the next room*
> k = *John's belief world*

A further complication stems from the fact that (7) involves an attitude verb: 'to be surprised that...' Now attitude reports in general can be analysed as involving a mandatory domain shift. It is part of the semantics of 'believe' and other attitude verbs that their complement (e.g. the embedded sentence) is to be interpreted with respect to the attitude-world of the ascribee. An utterance like 'John believes that grass is green' therefore involves two domains, one (the 'parent space', in Fauconnier's terminology) for the interpretation of the global utterance, and another one (the ascribee's belief world) for the interpretation of the complement clause:

> (John believes that (grass is green)$_j$)$_i$
> i= *parent space (e.g. the actual world)*
> j= *John's belief world*

Applied to (7), this yields:

(7***)
> (If he goes in the next room, (John will be surprised that (John meets the President of the USA)$_k$)$_j$)$_i$.
> i = *the actual world*
> j = *the hypothetical situation in which John goes in the next room*
> k = *John's belief world*

This is not an alternative to (7**); for the description itself must be indexed, as it can be interpreted either with respect to k ('opaque' reading, with the description denoting Bush) or with respect to j ('transparent' reading, with the description denoting Clinton). The two readings can be represented as follows:

> (If he goes in the next room, (John will be surprised that (John meets (the President of the USA)$_k$)$_k$)$_j$)$_i$.

> (If he goes in the next room, (John will be surprised that (John meets (the President of the USA)$_j$)$_k$)$_j$)$_i$.

> i = *the actual world*
> j = *the hypothetical situation in which John goes in the next room*
> k = *John's belief world*

As Fauconnier (1985) has shown, it is one of the main advantages of the domain framework that it permits to handle intensional ambiguities (such as transparent/opaque or specific/nonspecific) easily and straightforwardly. This is particularly clear when we consider phenomena which raise difficulties for classical analyses in terms of scope. To this issue I now turn.

5. Domains vs. scope

Consider (8):

(8)   Teri believes that a spy is following her

This example exhibits the specific/non-specific 'ambiguity'. According to the traditional scope analysis, (8) can be analyzed either as:

(8') $(\exists x: \text{spy } x)$ (Teri believes (x is following Teri))

or as:

(8")   Teri believes $((\exists x: \text{spy } x)$ (x is following Teri)).

In the domain framework another analysis of the ambiguity is available—one that does not appeal to scope. In 'Teri believes that a spy is following her', there are two worlds at stake, the actual world (where we find Teri and her beliefs) and the world of her beliefs (which the complement clause describes). The embedded sentence is evaluated with respect to the belief world: in Teri's belief world j, a spy is following her.

(8*)   (Teri believes that (a spy is following her)$_j$)$_i$.

The ambiguity of the indefinite description 'a spy' stems from the fact that it can be interpreted with respect to either of the two domains at stake, the belief world j and the parent space i. The two readings are:

(8**)   (Teri believes that ((a spy)$_i$ is following her)$_j$)$_i$.

(8***)   (Teri believes that ((a spy)$_j$ is following her)$_j$)$_i$.

In (8***) there is a double 'domain shift'. A first domain shift is linguistically encoded; as I said earlier, it is part of the meaning of 'believe' that the embedded sentence must be interpreted with respect to a domain (the belief world) distinct from the domain with respect to which the global utterance is evaluated (e.g. the actual world). But the description, in the sentence, can be evaluated with respect to i, despite the fact that the sentence where it occurs is evaluated with respect to j. This is another instance of domain shift. On this analysis, the 'ambiguity' of the description comes from the fact that two domains are contextually available for its evaluation. It's not really an ambiguity, in the technical sense, but rather a particular form of semantic indeterminacy. While it is semantically mandatory for the embedded sentence to be evaluated with respect to the ascribee's belief world, the description's domain of evaluation is not semantically constrained in this manner.

F. RECANATI

So we have two ways of analysing the specific/nonspecific ambiguity: the scope analysis and the domain analysis. At this stage they need not be considered as alternative analyses; perhaps it is the scope of the description which determines which domain is relevant. However, the scope analysis is much more restricted in its application than the domain analysis. For the specific/non-specific ambiguity can be found also in sentences *without* sentential complement, like:

(9)   Teri painted a mountain.

On one reading, there is a particular mountain (say, Mount Everest) which Teri represented in her painting; on the other reading there is no particular mountain—Teri's painting merely happens to be a 'mountain-representation' (as Goodman would say). Now the scope analysis does not apply to examples like (9). We can represent the specific reading as

(9') $(\exists x: \text{mountain } x)$ (Teri painted x)

but how shall we represent the non-specific reading? We can do so only by doing 'some violence to both logic and grammar', as Quine admits (Quine 1956: 186). Thus we have to equate the painting of an object (the mountain) with the painting of a state of affairs (viz. the fact that there is a mountain):

(9")   Teri painted $(\exists x: \text{mountain } x)$

The same problem arises for Quine's example, 'I want a sloop' (Quine 1956). In spite of Quine's best efforts, the scope analysis is clumsy and implausible when applied to such examples (see Kaplan 1986: 266-8).

This problem does not exist for the analysis in terms of contextual domains. In 'Teri painted a mountain', 'a mountain' can be interpreted with respect to the actual world (there is a real mountain, which Teri represented in her painting) or with respect to the world of the painting (in the painting, there is a mountain):

(9*)   (Teri painted (a mountain)$_i$)$_i$
(9**)   (Teri painted (a mountain)$_j$)$_i$

The second phenomenon which the domain framework permits to handle is that of 'intermediate' readings. Consider (10):

(10)   Tom is looking for a fish.

On the standard 'specific' reading (10) means: there is a fish Tom is looking for. On the 'non-specific' reading, Tom is looking for some fish or other. But there is an intermediate reading: Tom is looking for the fish Max claimed he saw (but which does not exist in reality). Even if the first two readings could be handled in terms of scope, à la Quine, the third reading would still raise a problem—a problem which vanishes in the domain framework (Fauconnier 1985). What characterizes the intermediate reading in this case is the fact that the indefinite description is interpreted with respect to Max's belief-world.

(10*)   (Tom is looking for (a fish)$_i$)$_i$.

(10**)   (Tom is looking for (a fish)$_j$)$_i$.
(10***)   (Tom is looking for (a fish)$_k$)$_i$.

i = *the actual world*
j = *Tom's target situation*
(= *the situation he is trying to bring about: a situation where he finds a fish*)
k = *Max's belief world*

6. Intensional domains and pretended reference

The suggested extension of the notion of domain of discourse to cases involving worlds other than the actual world (intensional domains, as I call them) raises an obvious problem. Domains of discourse consist of situations we *refer to I*. This is the gist of Austinian semantics. Like other philosophers, I believe that, in order to be referred to, something must be real—it must exist in the actual world. (This follows from the theory of Direct Reference—see Recanati 1993.) Extending the framework to cases in which the domains are intensional and concern fictional or other non-actual worlds raises the problem of reference to the non-existent. It seems that we face a dilemma here. Like Barwise and his colleagues we can refrain from extending the framework to fictional worlds, belief-worlds, hypothetical worlds, etc.; this is unattractive for this extension yields significant dividends—difficult issues become easy to deal with in the extended framework. Or, like Fauconnier and others, we can decide to extend the framework, at the cost of giving up the standard theory of reference. (Thus Bencivenga 1983 advocates an 'epistemic theory of reference'). This is also unattractive, to most philosophers at least. This dilemma explains why there are two opposite camps among those who appeal to contextual domains of discourse. With some exceptions, philosophers insist on the centrality of the relation between words and the actual world; as a result, they do not appeal to intensional domains. Cognitive semanticists, on the other hand, insist on descriptive adequacy and emphasize the centrality of the relation between words and mental constructs—representations of the world, or 'represented worlds'. Cognitive semantics posits mental worlds populated with mental referents; it scorns Russell's 'robust sense of reality' as a philosophical prejudice.

The dilemma is not genuine, however. I think Fauconnier and others following him are right to extend the notion of domain of discourse to fictional words, belief-worlds, and the like. The advantages of doing so are, I think, overwhelming. But in order to do so we need *not* undermine the entire framework by giving up the only clear notion of reference we have.

The notion of *pretended reference* provides a way out of the dilemma. When we 'refer' to something non-actual—something fictional, say—we *pretend* to refer. As the 'referent' does not exist, it cannot be really referred to; but it can be fictively referred to (Lewis 1978, Walton 1990, Currie 1990). What is true of individuals is true of situations: in the same way as we can pretend to refer to Sherlock Holmes, as if he existed, we can pretend to refer to the situation described by the Sherlock Holmes story, as if it was real.

When an utterance (or an utterance part) is interpreted with respect to a counterfactual situation, the reference to that situation is merely pretended. Pretended or fictive reference is not genuine reference; it is only 'quasi'-reference (Geach 1972: 161sq). Yet, as cognitive semanticists keep stressing, the difference does not matter from a strictly linguistic point of view. For we use the same linguistic material, with the same linguistic meaning, whether we genuinely refer or only pretend to refer. This follows from the very notion of 'pretense'. Hence, linguistically, there is no difference between 'Holmes lives at 221B, Baker Street' and 'Recanati lives in Paris'. Nor is there any significant difference, from a linguistic point of view, between intensional domains and 'genuine' domains involving real situations. It is therefore legitimate, for linguistic purposes, to use a notion of 'domain of discourse' which encompasses both.

Notes

[1] This is not quite what Austin would say; for Austin would be reluctant to include the reference of 'Claire' (i.e., Claire) in the type of situation conventionally associated with the sentence. Referents, for Austin, belong to the 'historic' situation referred to by the utterance, insofar as they are determined by 'demonstrative conventions'. The problem for Austin is that Claire is not part of the situation referred to (the poker game) in the Barwise-Etchemendy example. Be that as it may, I cannot go into the details of Austin's theory here, nor discuss the difference between that theory and the interpretation offered by Barwise and Etchemendy.

[2] 'Contextual supplementation works at the level of constituents of sentences or utterances, *rather than* the level of the sentences or utterances themselves' (Soames 1986: 357).

[3] True instances of (L) are perhaps easier to imagine when the description 'the dog' is understood as attributive, but this difficulty is exogenous; it relates to another aspect of the semantics of descriptions and should not, or not necessarily, interfere with issues concerning domains of discourse.

References

Austin, J. L. (1970) *Philosophical Papers*. Second edition, Clarendon Press, Oxford.
Barwise, J. and Etchemendy, J. (1987) *The Liar*. Oxford University Press, New York.
Barwise, J. and Perry, J. (1983) *Situations and Attitudes*, MIT Press, Cambridge, Mass.
Bencivenga, E. (1983) An Epistemic Theory of Reference. *Journal of Philosophy* 80, 785-805.
Currie, G. (1990) *The Nature of Fiction*. Cambridge University Press, Cambridge.
Fauconnier, G. (1985) *Mental Spaces: Aspects of Meaning Construction in Natural Language*. MIT Press/Bradford Books, Cambridge, Mass.
Geach, P. (1972) *Logic Matters*, Basil Blackwell, Oxford.
Kaplan, D. (1986) Opacity, in L. Hahn and P. A. Schilpp (eds.), *The Philosophy of W. V. Quine*, Open Court, La Salle, Illinois, pp. 229-89.
Kempson, R. (forthcoming) *Language and Cognition: A Licensing Grammar*.
Kuroda, S.Y. (1982) Indexed Predicate Calculus. *Journal of Semantics* 1, 43-59.
Langacker, R. (1987) *Foundations of Cognitive Grammar*. vol. 1. Stanford University Press, Stanford.
Lewis, D. (1978) Truth in Fiction. *American Philosophical Quarterly* 15, 37-46.
Lewis, D. (1979) Scorekeeping in a Language Game, in D. Lewis, *Philosophical Papers*, vol. 1, Oxford University Press, 1983, New York, pp. 233-49.
McCawley, J. (1981) *Everything that Linguists have Always Wanted to Know about Logic*. Basil Blackwell, Oxford.
Quine, W. v. O. (1956) Quantifiers and Propositional Attitudes, in W. v. O. Quine, *The Ways of Paradox and Other Essays*, revised edition. Harvard University Press, 1976, Cambridge, Mass. pp. 185-196.
Recanati, F. (1987) Contextual Dependence and Definite Descriptions. *Proceedings of the Aristotelian Society* 87, 57-73.
Recanati, F. (1989a) Referential/Attributive: A Contextualist Proposal. *Philosophical Studies* 56, 217-49.
Recanati, F. (1989b) The Pragmatics of What is Said. *Mind and Language* 4, 295-329.
Recanati, F. (1993) *Direct Reference: From Language to Thought*. Basil Blackwell, Oxford.
Recanati, F. (1994) Contextualism and Anti-Contextualism in the Philosophy of Language, in S. Tsohatzidis (ed.), *Foundations of Speech Act Theory*, Routledge, London, pp. 156-66.
Soames, S. (1986) Incomplete Definite Descriptions. *Notre Dame Journal of Formal Logic* 27, 349-75.
Sperber, D. and Wilson, D. (1986) *Relevance: Communication and Cognition*, Basil Blackwell, Oxford.
Stalnaker, R. (1974) Pragmatic Presuppositions, reprinted in S. Davis (ed.), *Pragmatics: A Reader*, Oxford University Press, New York, 1991, pp. 471-82.
Stalnaker, R. (1978) Assertion, in P. Cole (ed.), *Syntax and Semantics 9: Pragmatics*, Academic Press, 1978, New York, pp. 315-22.
Walton, K. (1990) *Mimesis as Make-Believe*. Harvard University Press, Cambridge. Mass.

THINKING OF 'NOT'

F. J. PELLETIER
Department of Philosophy
University of Alberta
Edmonton, Alberta
Canada T6G 2E5
jeffp@cs.ualberta.ca

> Another faculty we may take notice of in our minds, is
> that of discerning and distinguishing between the several
> ideas it has.... Unless the mind has a distinct perception
> of different objects and their qualities, it would be
> capable of very little knowledge... On this faculty of
> distinguishing one thing from another, depends the
> evidence and certainty of several, even very general
> propositions, which have passed for innate truths;
> because men, overlooking the true cause why those
> propositions find universal assent, impute it wholly to
> native uniform impressions: Whereas it in truth depends
> upon this clear discerning faculty of the mind, whereby it
> perceives two ideas to be the same, or different.
> (Locke, *Essay Concerning Human Understanding* II.xi.1)

1. Introduction

A certain direction in cognitive science has been to try to "ground" public language statements in some species of mental representation. A central tenet of this trend is that communication—that is, public language—succeeds (when it does) because the elements of this public language are in some way correlated with mental items of both the speaker and the audience so that the mental state evoked in the audience by the use of that piece of public language is the one that the speaker wanted to evoke. The "meaning", therefore, of an utterance—and of the parts of an utterance, such as individual sentences and their parts, such as the individual words, etc.—is, in this view, some mental item. Successful communication requires that there be widespread agreement amongst speakers of the same public language as to the mental entities that are correlated with any particular public words.

Such a view of meaning is variously called "cognitive" or "internalist" or "subjectivist" or "solipsistic" or (sometimes) "representationalist" (these terms having, however, further connotations which set them apart from one another in other ways), and

X. Arrazola et al. (eds.), Discourse, Interaction and Communication, 37–47.

can be found in a wide variety of writers who do not agree on many other things. It is opposed to views that take the meaning of an utterance to be an item of "reality," however defined. In different writers this latter view is called "externalist" or "objectivist" or "realist" or (sometimes) "representationalist," always with the idea that there is something other (or at least, more) than the mental state of speakers and hearers that determines meaning. The literature is rife with arguments between internalists vs. externalists, subjectivists vs. objectivists, cognitivists vs. realists, on such topics as "truth" and "synonymy" and "twin earth" and "arthritis" (to mention only a few). I do not plan to engage this literature here. Instead I wish to point to a different problem: a problem concerning the *type* of internal, mental entities that are invoked as meanings for the public language, a problem that seems to infect a wide range of, perhaps all, internalist theories.

There are different types of cognitivist theories of meaning, of course, and when trying to describe the underlying problem I will attempt to remain neutral as to what the mental items are that imbue public terms with meaning. If I sometimes slip into a "mental language of thought" idiom, or into a "mental images" idiom, or into a "mental models" idiom, etc., I ask the reader to attempt to read the point being made in the broadest way possible. Although I think that none of the cognitivist theories of meaning have in fact adequately addressed the problem to be introduced, I do think that some of the theories could mount more reasonable answers to this issue than others can. So at the end I will try to show the sorts of cognitivist theories I find able to provide an answer to the problem, and indicate what theories will have (what I take to be) insurmountable difficulties.

2. How Cognitivism Deals with Problems in Naïve Semantics

Naïve semantics is the view that expressions of natural language get their meaning from the aspect of reality that they name or describe. A sentence, for example, might describe an event, or an action, or a state of affairs. The described entity is what counts as the meaning of this sentence, and the sentence is true if and only if the event, action, state of affairs actually obtains. An immediate problem with naïve semantics concerns names that do not denote anything, such as 'The Easter Bunny' and 'Vulcan.' Since there is no rabbit that doles out colored eggs, nor any planet orbiting between Mercury and the sun, there are no events or actions or states of affairs involving The Easter Bunny or Vulcan; from which it follows that any sentence using such names is meaningless—a conclusion that seems to fly in the face of common sense concerning the meaning of these kinds of sentences.

Naïve semantics is, of course, a kind of realist semantic theory. The problem presented, therefore, is really only a problem for certain realist semantic theories; for, it is only they who might view meaning as some class of items in "reality." But it can be seen that the central presupposition of naïve semantics—that *something* is correlated with each sentence to give it meaning—is a principle that holds more widely than just for realist theories. In fact this principle is presupposed by all "non-holistic" cognitive semantic theories. And it is these non-holistic cognitivist theories in which I am interested here. It is interesting to see what cognitivist theories of meaning have to say about problems that naïve semantics brings up, and to see whether it's really true, as some cognitivist theorists believe, that these problems do not apply to their theories.

What gives a public sentence meaning, these non-holistic cognitivist theories say, is a mental image or other representation (such as a statement in a "mental language") of the event or state of affairs envisaged by the sentence. And this holds regardless of whether the various items mentioned in the sentence exist in "reality," because what counts according to these theories is that they exist "in the mind." So long as the speaker and audience have mental correlates of the item, then the public sentence has an appropriate grounding for its meaning.[1] So a sentence about The Easter Bunny has meaning for a speaker if s/he has a mental item correlated with this term, and communication with an audience succeeds only if they both have a representation which is occasioned in the correct manner.

There is a second, related problem brought out by naïve semantics which perhaps does not find so convenient an account in cognitivist views on meaning, and that is the issue of "negative existentials." A sentence like 'Vulcan does not exist' is self-refuting in a naïve semantics, for if there is something in reality that answers to the name 'Vulcan' then the sentence is false, while if there is not anything answering to the name then there is nothing about which we can say that it does not exist. So on naïve semantics negative existentials are either false or meaningless. And any semantic theory that admits there to be sentences whose truth presupposes their own meaninglessness is surely a self-refuting semantic theory. Cognitive theories of meaning need to provide some explanation of how negative existentials can be meaningful.

What can a cognitivist view say about this problem? The expedient of simply deferring the meaning to some mental structure in the same way as done with the first problem does not work without some modification; for, although such a theorist might want to say that they have a mental image or other item that means/represents 'Vulcan,' we need in addition to have some sort of distinction drawn between terms that represent non-existing items and terms that represent existing items. Otherwise we will be unable to distinguish the meanings of 'Vulcan exists' and 'Vulcan does not exist.' (Of course, in an internalist semantics, this is a matter of whether the speaker *thinks* it exists or doesn't exist, not whether "in reality" it does or does not exist). So, the mental model of the world that the speaker grounds his/her meaning in must contain a distinction between items that (are believed to) exist and those that do not. In effect a negative existential says that the subject-term of the sentence is correlated with an object in the "doesn't exist" portion of the mental theory, while a positive existential says that an object in the "existence" portion of the mental story is being indicated. In at least this feature the cognitivist account resembles the account of Meinong, who wanted to make a similar distinction within "reality"; and one might wonder whether the criticisms commonly brought to bear against Meinongian metaphysics don't also apply to our cognitivist.

I shall not raise that issue here but instead ask whether and how this general account can be extended. First, can it be extended to hold of negative existential *general* statements, such as 'Unicorns do not exist'? Presumably the cognitivist theory takes the mental item corresponding to 'unicorn' and somehow places it into the "doesn't exist" area. We return later to what this might mean, but it is not at all clear how the same move can be made with sentences like 'Round squares do not exist,' for under some versions of what these mental correlates are there cannot be one for items that cannot *possibly* exist. Some of the cognitive theories might, for example, assign some mental picture of a unicorn, or a combination of prototypical unicorn-properties, as the meaning of 'unicorn.' But such theories would have a very difficult time in giving this type of meaning to 'round square'; at least, some other type of restatement will be needed for these types of phrases.

Whatever the particular solution to general negative existentials is chosen, we see a certain strategy being pursued. The cognitivist theory attempts to restate certain troublesome sentences of public language by a paraphrase that does not involve this new restatement in the same difficulty that the naïve semantic theory posed for the original public statement. The idea in a (non-holistic) cognitive semantic theory is to show systematically which mental items are correlated with each public sentence, and to do it in such a way that the resulting system of mental representation of public language does not fall afoul of the semantic puzzles raised by naïve semantics. The method to be employed when one of these puzzles seems to come into play is to *paraphrase the offending portion of the public language* by some inoffensive portion of the mental correlate.

In the next section I will explain one of these puzzles and look at whether there is a way to effect an appropriate paraphrase. In my explanation I will often use the term "mentalese" or "mental language" for what might more neutrally (but awkwardly) be called "the system of mental representation of public language which gives meaning to the public language." And I will often talk as if it is a matter of "translation" of the public language into this mentalese. Much of this is in accordance with common usage in the cognitive science literature, but I do not wish for anyone to think that the resulting mental system has to be language-like in the way envisaged by certain believers in The Language of Thought. For, exactly the same points hold (I contend) for those who take the mental system to be a system of imagistic items, or categories of prototypes plus rules, or combinations of any of the well-known candidates. What is relevant to the issue is merely that the cognitive theory hold there to be *some* mental structure which gives meaning to any particular public sentence. And whatever the theory claims is the relation that directly holds between the public and the mental is what I call "translation"; and what I call "paraphrase" occurs when the straightforward application of the translation method does not yield an appropriate mental meaning, but instead one needs to employ some more complicated rewording in these cases rather than merely applying the translation method. This more complicated method might be most easily understood as saying that the original public sentence should be viewed differently from its apparent form (by paraphrasing it as another sentence of the public language, and then applying the standard method of translation into mentalese to this paraphrase).

3. Predicative Negation

We have mentioned negation in conjunction with existence, generating naïve semantic puzzles for negative existentials of various types. But although negative existentials have been the traditional source for semantic puzzles of this kind, similar puzzles can also be generated for naïve semantics by negating predicative expressions, and they do not seem to have similar solutions. The sentences 'Kim is not plump', 'Dogs are not fish', 'The

Axiom of Choice does not follow from the other axioms of Zermelo-Fraenkel set theory'
all have a predicate negation...which intuitively has the effect of saying that the predicate
in question does not apply to the referent of the subject of the sentence. The reason for
its lack of application is different in the different examples: it may be a matter of fact
about the world, it may be an issue in the taxonomy of concepts, or it may be a matter
of mathematical necessity. And doubtless there are other reasons a predicate might fail to
hold. Note that, on the surface, there is no item or group of items which are said not to
exist here, unlike the case with negative existentials.

Recall that naïve semantics holds that the meaning of a linguistic item, including a
sentence, is the item being described by that item. Within a realist framework, a sentence
would describe an event or state of affairs or some such thing. Yet this seems self-
refuting in the case of predicate negation, as it did in the case of negative existentials,
because the very sentence asserts that the relevant event or state of affairs is *not*
occurring...and so the relevant meaning couldn't be there if the sentence were true.

When a cognitivist attempts to give the same response to this problem as was given
to the problem of negative existentials, it is soon discovered that new factors come into
play with predicative negation. The main difference comes with the category of item that
is to give meaning to these two different constructions. In the case of negative
existentials where the subject term is a singular term, such as 'The Easter Bunny', the
corresponding mental item is a "singular item"....just what a singular item amounts to
depends on the mental theory, but it might be an idea or image of an individual, or a
name in a Language of Thought. In either case it seems reasonably straightforward
simply to put this mental item onto the "doesn't exist" section of one's mental theory.
When the negative existential is about a general term, such as 'unicorn', the
corresponding mental item is a "general"....just what a general item amounts to depends,
once again, on the mental theory, but it might be an idea or concept of a class of things,
or a general term in a Language of Thought. In either case the placement of this type of
mental item into the "doesn't exist" section of one's mental theory amounts to saying
there are no instances (in my mental theory) corresponding to this concept. (Of course a
concept's being in the "doesn't exist" portion of the mental theory does *not* amount to
saying that the concept itself does not exist!) So, in the cases concerning negative
existentials, the type of mental item that is supposed to give such sentences meaning is
an idea or image or concept or term which is appropriately located in one's mental
economy.

But sentences are different. To them corresponds some *combination* of concepts,
ideas, images or terms. In cognitivist theories that invoke a language-like mental
representation, this combination is some syntactic-like nexus of the representations of
the items that correspond to the parts of this combination. In such theories, the mental
language contains some "mentalese glue" to make these parts form a whole in much the
same way that the syntactic combining of words/phrases employs a "syntactic glue" to
form a sentence of the public language out of a mere list of words. Imagistic cognitivist
theories likewise envision a meaning assigned to a public sentence by a combination,
but this time it is by combining the various "images" that correspond somehow to the
parts of the public sentence to form them into an image which represents the entire
sentence.

When this picture of meaning of sentences encounters negative predications there will be a problem. The meaning of the negation, recall, is made up somehow from the meaning of its parts, which includes the positive of the sentence. And by hypothesis the positive has no meaning; for although the mental items corresponding to the concepts, ideas, images, and terms mentioned in the sentence are presupposed to exist, they happen not to be combined in the way the (positive of the) sentence mandates. Yet the *combination* is not the kind of item that can be placed in the "doesn't exist" section of the mental model, for it is neither an individual nor a general concept.

4. Two Inadequate Answers to Problem of Predicate Negation

Consider our sentence 'Kim is not plump.' What could a cognitivist theory assign as a meaning of this sentence? It seems clear that it should in some way be constructed from the meaning of 'Kim is plump,' but how? Naïve semantics says that the meaning of a negation amounts to saying the positive does not occur—there is no state of affairs of Kim's being plump; it then points out that this is precisely to say that the negative sentence has no meaning. (And since the same point could hold for any negative sentence, the overall conclusion is that negative predications are self-refuting: if their preconditions for truth are met, then they cannot have any meaning).[2]   Negative predications are thus self-refuting. So how can a cognitivist theory accommodate negation, and the idea that negative sentences are a function of the meanings of the components of the underlying positive sentence, without running afoul of this naïve semantics puzzle?

One way might be to posit the existence of items exactly corresponding to these negations. So not only does there exist a combination of the Kim-concept and the Intelligent-concept to give a meaning to the public sentence 'Kim is intelligent', but also there exists a combination of the Kim-concept and the Plump-concept and the Not-concept to give a meaning for the public sentence 'Kim is not plump'. This does not seem to be much of an advance in understanding, but merely a redescription of the initial problem. The initial problem was to explain how a *non*-combination (there is no combination of the Kim-concept and the Plump-concept) could be said to exist so that it can serve as the meaning of a negative public sentence. And to answer that this non-combination suddenly becomes a combination when the separate and uncombined parts are mixed with the Not-concept does not seem to be much of an explanation. Another way of putting this objection to the miraculous invocation of a Not-concept is to say that the notion of "not" cannot straightforwardly be invoked in a semantic theory which alleges that the meanings of the unnegated sentence is an *object*—regardless of whether this object is a piece of "the world" (as in the original naïve semantics) or whether it is a piece of one's mind (as in cognitivist theories). The negation of an *object* is not an independently well-defined notion; and it needs to be further explicated before it can be used. Negation is defined semantically only for truth-conditions: a negation is true if and only if the positive is false. But cognitivists of the sort we are considering deny that this truth-conditional aspect of the public language is relevant to their viewpoint. So, any cognitivist theory...even one that posits a Language of Thought...is required to give some explanation of their negation to show what sort of function it is, and what sort of values it takes when applied to the objects that the theory holds to be meanings. The mere *naming* of a piece of the mental machinery as 'NOT' or as '¬' simply gets us nowhere until we know how such items actually function in the mental economy...or indeed, whether it is even distinct from any other concepts. They do *not* work like the identically-named apparatus of traditional externalist semantic language, and it is an inadequate cognitivist theory that does not offer any account of the operation of such a sign.

A second attempt to introduce something to be the referent for negations of public language sentences would be simply to increase the number of concepts or primitive terms in the mental language. As before, each positive predicate term of the public language is correlated with some mental item, but now each negation of a predicate term of the public language finds an independent mental item correlated with it, a term which is unrelated to the positive one. There is a mental item (concept, term, etc.) corresponding to 'plump' and likewise one corresponding to 'not-plump'. Positive sentences such as 'Kim is plump' and negative ones like 'Kim is not plump' do *not* make use of the same predicate concept. Rather the positive predicates and the negative predicates are correlated with entirely distinct and logically unrelated mental items. It is to be emphasized that this theory does not posit *any* specific relationship between a positive and (what we would intuitively think of as) its negative counterpart, for this view wishes to evade the task of showing how it is that a mental item correlated with negation operates on a concept to form the correlated negative concept.

It seems clear that this last attempt to (not) answer the problem generated by negative predications is a desperate one, and should only be embraced if no other satisfactory account of the interaction of negation with mental items can be found. For one thing it seems perfectly plain that ordinary people *do* think of their positives and negatives as being related to each other; and it is well known that semantic priming effects can be elicited for a positive by priming with the negative, and conversely. The present proposal in effect says that the mental operation of negation has no systematic result when it is applied to different mental items. And this is simply a view that we should hope not to have to adopt. We would want there to be a "negation" operation that applies to predicates, but what can it be in cognitivist theories? As we've seen, the traditional notion of negation does not apply to objects—even if they are objects that are correlated with predicates.

5. Possible Mental Negations

It seems to me that there are two general directions that cognitivist theories might take in their quest to give some sort of theoretically adequate grounding to the problem of predicate negation. Recall that one of the difficulties with invoking a mental NOT operator and expecting it to do duty as a mental correlate for the public language negation is that the items of the mental language are by hypothesis objects, and that the operation of negation in the public language is just not defined to be applied to objects. So we need to posit some mental operation that *does* apply to objects, and which we can use to generate the appropriate behavior of negation. (The behavior we want to model is given by its operation in the public language.)

One relation that holds between pairs of objects is the relation of *nonidentity*, and I propose to use it to give one type of account of predicate negation. It might be thought that it is somewhat suspect for a theory of mentalese to help itself to such a concept, for (it might be asked) isn't this just once again some sort of miraculous invocation of negation? Well, perhaps it is miraculous, but at least it is a possible property of (pairs of) mental items...arguably even the most basic one, as Locke said in my opening quotation...unlike the impossible NOT. I here offer it to cognitivists who wish to give some adequate account of predicate negation. There is still some work to be done, because (mental) ≠ is not the same as predicate negation. To use ≠ in an explanation of predicate negation, the cognitivist theory also needs to have the resources of quantification. This is perhaps not so much of a miraculous invention, because any adequate mentalese must be able to accommodate quantification in one way or another. In the formulations I give below I will not dwell on how a cognitivist theory should do this. I expect that different styles of cognitivist theories will find different ways to bring quantification into their theory. Instead I will just write a formula that looks rather like quantified logic with the intent that the quantification that is indicated in the formula will have to be suitably accounted for in the cognitivist theory. Recall also that our different cognitivist theories invoke different types of mental structures to correspond to items of public language. In order to stay neutral as to what these mental items are, I will use boldface to stand for whatever mental item the public language term stands for. Thus, if 'F' or 'a' are terms of the public language, then '**F**' and '**a**' are their correlates in the mental theory being developed.

There are in fact two different ways that a cognitivist theory could invoke ≠. The first way is to claim that a (simple) negative sentence of the public language having the form "a is not F" is correlated with this mental structure:

(1) $\forall x(\mathbf{F}x \supset x \neq \mathbf{a})$

That is, the predicate negation amounts to saying that whatever manifests **F** is distinct from **a**. One should be wary about the use of the phrase '**F**x' in this formulation, because '**F**' here stands for some concept (or other mental item) whereas the universally quantified '**F**x' stands for all the concepts (or other mental items) in which something is being **F**. And it is not immediately obvious that the simple F-concept will necessarily play a role in the more complex concepts that involve also a subconcept of an individual. But this is an issue that must be faced by any cognitivist theory: how are items that correspond to complex pieces of public language constructed? Are they made in a compositional manner, being constructed out of the mental items that correspond to the public language parts of the public language whole? This is indeed a central issue for cognitivist theories to face, but for the purposes of the present discussion I will assume that they have somehow answered these questions so that the formula in (1) makes sense, indeed, the "natural" sense that was stated in the sentence immediately after the formula. In this natural sense, it appears that (1) will do perfectly well as a mental correlate of a simple predicate negation.[3] Of course there are other types of negations, such as negations of the quantifiers and other types as well, which need to be given some sort of plausible representation, but we will not consider them now.

The public language sentence that most naturally corresponds to (1) is "a is distinct from all those things which are F". This is not the only way to employ non-identity in an analysis of predicate negation. One could instead say "every property that a exhibits is distinct from F":

(2) $\forall G(Ga \supset G \neq F)$

Although this appears to express a formula of a second-order language in its quantification over predicates, we should remember that in cognitivist theories the predicates are in fact (mental) objects: concepts or images or symbols, etc. Once again, the non-identity is said to hold between *objects*, making it well-formed and a suitable candidate to replace the inappropriate NOT operator that does not hold of objects. The real mystery in both (1) and (2) comes from the quantification. In (1) we need to make sense, somehow, of "all the objects that manifest F" while in (2) we need to make sense, somehow, of "all the properties that **a** manifests." And in the mentalese of various theories these notions will be given different explanations; the explanation of these quantified phrases will in turn depend on how the theory analyzes simple positive predications. But this is not an issue to be discussed here. The issue here is: if they had simple positive predications and quantification, how would they handle predicate negation?

The second direction that cognitivist theories might move in seeking an analysis of predicate negation is to employ a primitive notion of "incompatibility" rather than of "nonidentity". Perhaps incompatibility is not as basic a notion as nonidentity, and perhaps critics might think the cognitivist who employs incompatibility as a primitive notion is unfairly availing him- or herself of negation under some other name. But at least incompatibility, like nonidentity but unlike negation, is a relation that can hold of objects. Of course, it does not hold of *all* objects, but in the sense to be employed, sense can be given to its holding of the type of objects required for the analysis of negation.

The fundamental idea here is that mental entities that correspond to predicates come in "applicability groups." This means that there groups of these mental entities such that, for any (mental correlate of an) object, at most one member of that group can be manifested by that object. A simple example might be the mental concepts corresponding to the public language color predicates. They form such an applicability group, so that given any (mental item corresponding to an) object, it can manifest at most one member of this group—that is, it can have at most one (overall) color.[4]   Other applicability groups might include the shape-concepts, or the size-concepts, or the location-concepts. It seems clear that a cognitive theory would be entitled to adopt such an organization of its mental economy.

Let us use the symbol $\otimes$ to signify belonging to the same applicability group, so that $F \otimes G$ means that F and G are incompatible. Then we could paraphrase "a is not F" of the public language as

(3) $\exists G(G \otimes F \ \& \ Ga)$

or in other words that there is some concept which **a** manifests that is incompatible with F. Once again, it seems that this analysis captures the semantic features of negation in the public language, and does it without invoking an incoherent notion of NOT in a mental theory. As with analysis (2), it appears that (3) is a second-order formulation involving quantification over predicates. But again I remark that the mental correlates of the predicates are *objects* in these cognitivist theories; and so, looks to the contrary notwithstanding, (3) does not in fact involve quantification over second order properties, but only over ordinary (mental) objects.

6. Conclusion

I have presented three possible analyses of predicate negation that a cognitivist theory of language could avail itself of. Each of the analyses avoids the mistake of trying to directly import the public language NOT, which is not applicable to the mental items of a cognitivist theory. Yet each of them accounts for the basic features of the negation in public language, and each of them avoids the puzzles brought out by naïve semantics. For, none of them tries to ground a negation in the non-existence of the very object that is required to give it meaning.

Which of the analyses (1), (2), and (3) that is adopted by any given cognitivist theory will depend on other features of the theory that determine whether one or another of them better meshes with what else is in the theory. But one evaluative comment seems easy to make: analyses (1) and (2), unlike analysis (3), make it difficult to "verify" whether a negation is true. For, in order to do that one needs to determine whether a universally-quantified statement is true...and that could potentially involve an exhaustive search of all the relevant mental items. For example, analysis (1) says that to determine whether "a is not F" is true, one needs to inspect all the mental items that manifest F and determine that they are distinct from **a**. Analysis (2) says that to determine whether "a is not F" is true, one needs to inspect all the (mental) properties that **a** manifests (all the concepts in which it appears?) and determine that they are all distinct from **F**. On the other hand, analysis (3) instructs one to look only to the applicability group of concepts that **F** is a member of, and determine whether **a** manifests one of them. Assuming, as seems reasonable, that an applicability group is a set of concepts relatively limited in size, this would appear to be a much more plausible task to perform than the exhaustive searches suggested by analyses (1) and (2).[5]

It seems to me that cognitivist theories that postulate an internal, mental economy which is to account for the meaning of public language should do more toward addressing these foundational issues. Even if one postulates a mental theory which is just another language having more or less the same syntactic form as the public language, there are differences between the two that need to be carefully considered. Such theories are *not* free just to adopt semantic devices from the public language, for the public devices were designed to apply to a different aspect of the world than is available in a strictly internalist cognitive theory. A theorist who claims that the mental items in his/her mental economy are semantically akin to items in public language, so that notions such as NOT can be directly incorporated, is not employing a strictly internalist account of issue. Such theories are not considered in this article, but one wonders whether the miraculous invocation of semantic properties to mental items doesn't just make the mental items otiose. Why duplicate what is already in the public language?

Notes

[1] Again, we do not pause here to consider the critiques leveled by realists against this view of meaning. My goal here is instead to explain the theory.

[2] The puzzle goes even further. Consider any two positive sentences, S_1 and S_2, that have been given some meaning by correspondence to a combination of mental items. These two sentences correspond to different mental combinations if and only if the sentence "S_1 does not mean the same as S_2," is true. Yet this is a negative sentence, and therefore cannot be true by the argument mentioned in the text. So S_1 and S_2 cannot correspond to different mental items, and so they mean the same thing. But this is true for *every* positive sentence. So therefore, all meaningful sentences correspond to the same mental item, and they all mean the same thing! Cognitivists really must solve the "problem of predicate negation" if they are to have any logically coherent theory.

[3] At least in finite cases. The formula presupposes that we can always find "those things that are different from **a**." But the complement of a set, here the complement of the set containing just **a**, is not always well-defined in a setting of an infinite number of items. But I presume most cognitivist theories would hold that the mental inventory is finite, and so that this is a well-defined notion.

[4] It does not *have* to manifest any member of the group at all, for the object in question may be, for example, a number. And then the entire applicability group is inapplicable. But *if* some member of the group applies to the object, then no other member of that same group can apply.

[5] Of course, people *do* find negations more difficult to deal with (especially in reasoning) than positives, and perhaps this would argue against analysis (3) and in favor of analysis (1) and analysis (2).

THE METAPHORICAL CONCEPTION OF EVENTS AND CAUSES: SOME IMPLICATIONS OF COGNITIVE SCIENCE FOR PHILOSOPHY

G. LAKOFF
University of California at Berkeley
USA

1. First and Second Generation Cognitive Science

My early work was part of the first generation of Cognitive Science. First generation Cognitive Science assumed Putnam's Functionalism, the idea that the mind could be studied independent of the body in terms of its functions, and that the mind's functions could be represented using formal symbol systems. The meanings of the symbols were to be given by interpreting them as referring to things in the world, without any use of human imaginative capacities (e.g., metaphor, mental imagery, and prototype structure). Mind, on this conception, happened to be embodied, but embodiment played no essential role in characterizing Mind. Functionally, mind was disembodied. And imaginative capacities did not enter the picture at all. In short, First Generation Cognitive Science was the Cognitive Science of the Disembodied and Unimaginative Mind.

In the first generation, the following ideas came together in Cognitive Science: Classical Artificial Intelligence, Information Processing Psychology, Generative Linguistics (which used the Language as Symbol System metaphor) and those forms of Anglo-American Philosophy that used the Reason-as-Logic metaphor. My early work on Generative Semantics, dating from 1963, fit perfectly into this paradigm: it took underlying linguistic structure within generative linguistics as being logical form. In the mid-1970's, these ideas coalesced to form first generation Cognitive Science.

Anglo-American Philosophy played a leading role in this enterprise, sanctioning the view of reason as formal logic, thought as symbol manipulation, and meaning as the relationship of symbols to things in the world. The disembodied, unimaginative view of mind that came out of Anglo-American philosophy became the standard for the developers of cognitive science who were educated in that philosophical tradition—the developers of linguistics, artificial intelligence, and cognitive psychology.

The Second Generation of Cognitive Science emerged in the late 1970's with the empirical demonstration that Mind is essentially embodied and that it uses imaginative mechanisms. Some of that research includes:

X. Arrazola et al. (eds.), Discourse, Interaction and Communication, 49–83.
© 1998 *Kluwer Academic Publishers. Printed in the Netherlands.*

- **Color Concepts**

    The Berlin-Kay-McDaniel research on color categorization, paired with the results of DeValois and his colleagues on the neurophysiology of color vision, showed that color categories are grounded by the nature of color cones in the retina plus neural circuitry in the LGN and elsewhere. Color categories are not out in the world, but are formed through an interaction of the retina and brain with reflectances of objects.

- **Basic-level concept**

    Berlin and Rosch and their co-workers discovered that there is a fundamental collection of concepts defined by certain optimal level at which our bodies interact with the world. These concepts are cognitively basic in a number of ways: they are defined in terms of (i) motor programs for interacting with objects, (ii) gestalt perception, (iii) the capacity to form mental images, and (iv) memory structure. Basic-level concepts are learned earlier that either higher level ("superordinate") concepts or lower-level ("subordinate") concepts.

    Antonio Damasio has shown, though work with brain-damaged patients that basic-level categorization is neurally real. Indeed, he has show that concepts that make use of motor+visual properties use different brain structures than concepts that make use of visual information alone.

- **Image-schemas, and their neural foundations**

    Len Talmy, Ron Langacker, Claudia Brugman and others discovered that systems of spatial relations in the world's languages all appear to use a single set of "primitive" images-schemas, whose fundamental properties are topological and orientation in nature. Examples include containers, paths, links, force dynamics, contact, balance, center-periphery, orientations (above-below; front-back), etc. As Mark Johnson observed in *The Body in the Mind*, these are recurring structures of our bodily interactions in the world, both perceptual and motor. These image-schemas define spatial inference patterns.

    Terry Regier has since demonstrated that image-schemas can be modelled using structured connectionism. Regier uses connectionist models of neural structures in the brain: topographic maps, center-surround receptive fields, orientation-sensitive cells, etc.). Topographic maps yield the topological properties of spatial concepts, orientation-sensitive cells yield the orientational properties of spatial concepts, and center-surround receptive fields characterize notions like contact. Such modelling indicates that spatial relations concepts can be characterized neurally (that is, with no symbols), and that their peculiar properties arise from the neural structures peculiar to our brains.

- **Types of prototype structure in categories**

    Wittgenstein pointed out that certain concepts are structured in terms of family resemblances, have best examples, and are extendable from central to peripherical cases. Empirical research by Rosch and others has verified these precise details of category structure. There are many types of best examples, or "prototypes", each with a different cognitive function: typical cases, ideal cases, social stereotypes, well-known exemplars, end-points on scales, and central members of categories to which peripherical members are systematically related.

    There are many types of prototypes, each with a different mode of inference:

Typical Cases, used for default reasoning.
Ideal Cases, used for standards of comparison.
Social Stereotypes, used for snap judgments; overrideable.
Well-Known Exemplars, used for making probability judgments.
End-points On Scales, defines full membership in graded category.
Central Members Of Radial Categories, used as the basis for category extensions.

Antonio Damasio has also shown that prototypes make use of different brain structures than non-prototypes, hence confirming the biological reality of conceptual prototypes.

● **Conceptual metaphor**

There is a vast system, in long-term memory, of thousands of fixed conventional mappings across conceptual domains that permit us to understand more abstract concepts in terms of more concrete concepts. These mappings preserve image-schemas, and therefore allow us to use the logic of physical space as the basis for abstract inference. They also permit abstract inference by mapping knowledge about concrete domains onto abstract domains. Conceptual metaphors are not arbitraty, but are motivated in significant ways by the nature of our bodies.

These are some (by no means all) of the empirical results that define the Second Generation of Cognitive Science. Its view of the mind is fundamentally embodied and imaginative: Color concepts, basic-level concepts, spatial relations concepts, and metaphorical concepts are grounded in the peculiarities of the body. Metaphorical concepts and prototypes are imaginative.

These empirical results are not consistent with First Generation views, in particular, the view that Reason is Logic. All of these basic aspects of human reason go beyond what formal logic is capable of.

1.1. HOW SECOND GENERATION COGNITIVE SCIENCE CHANGES PHILOSOPHY

To many philosophers, philosophy is concerned with the way the world is, not with how human beings happen to conceptualize the world. For them, philosophy's concern with concepts and reason is a concern with transcendental concepts and reason that are not in any way limited by the details of human psychology.

But human beings, including philosophers, can conceptualize the world only using human concepts and human reason. If transcendental concepts and transcendental reason exist, they can only be grasped through human concepts and human reason. The traditional way out of this problem has been for philosophers to assume the human concepts and (correct) human reason were instances of transcendental concepts and transcendental reason.

The results of Second Generation Cognitive Science rule out this possibility. Since the human conceptual system is fundamentally metaphoric, since its concepts have various kinds of prototype structure, and since concepts are grounded in the peculiarities of the way the body happens to be structured, it follows that:

(1) Human concepts and human reason are not transcendental, that is, they do not transcend the human body and human psychology.

(2) Conceptual structure and reason can no longer be characterized adequately by formal logic.

And (3), philosophy can no longer claim that human concepts and human reason provide access to the transcendental, to the world independently of human psychology.

To the extent that philosophy is concerned with concepts and with reason, it must now be concerned with human concepts and human reason, as they have been explored empirically. The empirical study of conceptual systems and of reason is a central part of Cognitive Science. Therefore, much of philosophy rests on empirical results from Cognitive Science.

What emerges from Second Generation Cognitive Science is not Quine's naturalized epistemology, or anything like it. The Quinean metaphor that a language is a system of formal logic is shown by these results to be grossly inadequate. The Quinean program is to keep formal logic, with its classical predicate-argument structure, variables, and quantification, plus its characterization of meaning by interpreting the values of the predicates and the variables as referring to entities in the external world. The only thing added to make it "naturalized" is a commitment to determine, via empirical methods, what the values of the predicates and the variables are.

Quine's naturalized epistemology has no room for the real discoveries about the mind that have come from Second Generation Cognitive Science: conceptual metaphor, basic-level categories, mental images and image-schemas, various types of prototypes, etc. Naturalized epistemology is a creature suited only to First Generation Cognitive Science: It is an attempt to define Cognitive Science to fit traditional philosophical dogmas and to maintain philosophy's fundamental independence from really new discoveries about the nature of mind. The second Generation results make naturalized epistemology a thing of the past.

This paper is concerned with the details of this new dependence of philosophy on Cognitive Science. It asks how central philosophical concepts, like Time, Events, Causation, the Self, and the Mind are changed by Second Generation Cognitive Science, in particular by the range of recent research on conceptual metaphor.

2. Conceptual Metaphor

Most traditional philosophy saw itself as providing a set of basic, literal (nonmetaphorical) concepts for systematically describing the "objectively correct" nature of reality. The particulars of this extensive system of conceptual metaphor undermine the possibility of such a literalist program. It turns out that our most fundamental concepts —such as Time, Events, Causation, Purpose, and even the Self and the Mind—are defined by multiple metaphors that are typically inconsistent with one another.

2.1. KINDS OF EVIDENCE FOR CONCEPTUAL METAPHOR

All of our claims about conceptual metaphor rest on empirical details—on the evidence we have. The evidence for the existence of a system of conventional conceptual metaphors in the mind is of six types:

Generalizations governing polysemy, that is, the use of words with a number of related meanings.

Generalizations governing inference patterns, that is, cases where a pattern of inferences from one conceptual domain is used in another domain.

Generalizations governing novel metaphorical language (see, Lakoff & Turner, 1989).

Generalizations governing patterns of semantic change (see, Sweetser, 1990).

Psycholinguistic experiments (Gibbs).

Gesture studies (McNeill).

I will begin by discussing the first three of these sources of evidence, since they are most robust, and turn to the others afterward.

2.2. LOVE IS A JOURNEY: AN EXTENDED EXAMPLE

Imagine a love relationship described as follows:

Our relationship has hit **a dead-end street**.

Here love is being conceptualized as a journey, with the implication that the relationship is stalled, that the lovers cannot keep going the way they've been going, that they must turn back, or abandon the relationship altogether. This is not an isolated case. English has many everyday expressions that are based on a conceptualization of love as a journey, and they are used not just for talking about love, but for reasoning about it as well. Some are necessarily about love; others can be understood that way:

Look how **far** we've **come**. It's been **a long, bumpy road**. We can't **turn back** now. We're at a **crossroads**. We may have to **go our separate ways**. The relationship isn't **going anywhere**. We're **spinning our wheels**. Our relationship is **off the track**. The marriage is **on the rocks**. We may have to **bail out of** this relationship.

These are ordinary, everyday English expressions. They are not poetic, nor are they necessarily used for special rhetorical effect. Each of the boldface expressions is from the domain of travel, of journeying. And in each case the same expression can be used to speak of love as well as travel. Take the word **crossroads**, which can be used of both travel and love relationships. As a linguist, I ask the question a good linguist must ask: Is there a generalization relating the travel domain meaning of **crossroads** to the love domain meaning of **crossroads**? We must ask the corresponding questions about each of the expressions, **spinning our wheels, going anywhere, a long bumpy road**, etc. Finally, an empirical linguistic researcher must ask:

Is there a single generalization that covers all of the cases given?

A linguist must also ask a second empirical question:

Is there a general principle governing how our patterns of inference about journeys are used to reason about love when expressions such as these are used?

The answer to both is yes. Indeed, there is a single general principle that answers both questions. But it is a general principle that is neither part of the grammar of English, nor the English lexicon. Rather, it is part of the conceptual system underlying English: It is a principle for understanding the domain of love in terms of the domain of journeys.

The principle can be stated as a mapping:

Lovers are Travelers

Love Relationships are Vehicles

Common Life Goals are Destinations

Difficulties are Impediments to Motion

The mapping applies to a certain travel scenario:

The travelers are on a journey together in a vehicle, with common destinations. The vehicle fulfills its purpose as long as it allows them to make progress toward their destinations. The journey isn't easy. There are impediments to motion, and there are places (crossroads) where as decision has to be made about which direction to go in and whether to keep traveling together.

The mapping yields a certain love scenario:

The lovers are in a love relationship with common life goals. The relationship fulfills its purpose as long as it allows them to make progress toward their life goals. The course of the relationship isn't easy. There are difficulties, and there are situations (crossroads) where a decision has to be made about which common goals to pursue and whether to stay in the relationship.

The metaphorical mapping involves understanding one domain of experience, the *source domain* of love, in terms of a very different domain of experience, the *target domain* of journeys. The mapping is tightly structured. There are ontological correspondences, in which entities in the domain of love (e.g., the lovers, their common goals, their difficulties, the love relationship, etc.) correspond systematically to entities in the domain of a journey (the travelers, the vehicle, destinations, etc.).

To make it easier to remember what mappings there are in the conceptual system, Johnson and I (Lakoff and Johnson, 1980) adopted a strategy for naming such mappings, using mnemonics which suggest the mapping. Mnemonic names typically (though not always) have the form: TARGET-DOMAIN IS SOURCE-DOMAIN, or alternatively, TARGET-DOMAIN AS SOURCE-DOMAIN. In this case, the name of the mapping is LOVE IS A JOURNEY. When I speak of the LOVE IS A JOURNEY metaphor, I am using a mnemonic for the set of ontological correspondences that characterize the mapping. It is a common mistake to confuse the *name* of the mapping, LOVE IS A JOURNEY, for the mapping itself. The mapping is the set of correspondences. Thus, whenever I refer to a metaphor by a mnemonic like LOVE IS A JOURNEY, I will be referring to such a set of correspondences.

If mappings are confused with names of mappings, another misunderstanding can arise. Names of mappings commonly have a propositional form, for example, LOVE IS

A JOURNEY. But the mappings themselves are not propositions. If mappings are confused with names for mappings, one might mistakenly think that, in this theory, metaphors are propositional. They are, of course, anything but that: metaphors are mappings, that is, sets of conceptual correspondences that map lexical items and inference structure in the source domain onto lexical items and inference structure in the target domain. The mappings are partial. Not all source domain lexical items, nor all source domain conceptual structure is mapped.

Such correspondences permit us to reason about love using the knowledge we use to reason about journeys. Let us take an example. Consider the expression, "We're stuck", said by one lover to another about their relationship. How is this expression about travel to be understood as being about their relationship?

"We're stuck" can be used of travel, and when it is, it evokes knowledge about travel. The exact knowledge may vary from person to person, but here is a typical example of the kind of knowledge evoked. The capitalized expressions represent entities in the ontology of travel, that is, in the source domain of the LOVE IS A JOURNEY mapping given above.

Two TRAVELLERS are in a VEHICLE, TRAVELING WITH COMMON DESTINATIONS. The VEHICLE encounters some IMPEDIMENTS and gets stuck, that is, makes it nonfunctional. If they do nothing, the will not REACH THEIR DESTINATIONS. There are a limited number of alternatives for action:

They can try to get it moving again, either by fixing it or getting it past the IMPEDIMENT that stopped it.

They can remain in the nonfunctional VEHICLE and give up on REACHING THEIR DESTINATIONS.

They can abandon the VEHICLE.

The alternative of remaining in the nonfunctional VEHICLE takes the least effort, but does not satisfy the desire to REACH THEIR DESTINATIONS.

The set of ontological correspondences that constitute the LOVE IS A JOURNEY mapping maps the ontology of travel onto the ontology of love. In doing so, it maps this scenario about travel onto a corresponding love scenario in which the corresponding alternatives for action are seen. The target domain entities that are mapped by the correspondences are capitalized:

Two LOVERS are in a LOVE RELATIONSHIP, PURSUING COMMON LIFE GOALS. The RELATIONSHIP encounters some DIFFICULTY, which makes it nonfunctional. If they do nothing, they will not be able to ACHIEVE THEIR LIFE GOALS. There are a limited number of alternatives for action:

-They can try to get it moving again, either by fixing it or getting it past the DIFFICULTY.

-They can remain in the nonfunctional RELATIONSHIP, and give up on ACHIEVING THEIR LIFE GOALS.

-They can abandon the RELATIONSHIP.

The alternative of remaining the nonfunctional RELATIONSHIP takes the least effort, but does not satisfy the desire to ACHIEVE LIFE GOALS.

This is an example of an inference pattern that is mapped from one domain to another. It is via such mappings that we apply knowledge about travel to love relationships.

Metaphors are not mere words.

What constitutes the LOVE-AS-JOURNEY metaphor is not any particular word or expression. It is the ontological mapping across conceptual domains, from the source domain of journeys to the target domain of love. The metaphor is not just a matter of language, but of thought and reason. The language is secondary. The mapping is primary, in that it sanctions the use of source domain language and inference patterns for target domain concepts. The mapping is conventional, that is, it is a fixed part of our conceptual system, one of our conventional ways of conceptualizing love relationships.

This view of metaphor is thoroughly at odds with the view that metaphors are just linguistic expressions. If metaphors were merely linguistic expressions, we would expect different linguistic expressions to be different metaphors. Thus, "We've hit a dead-end street" would constitute one metaphor. "We can't turn back now" would constitute another, entirely different metaphor. "Their marriage is on the rocks" would involve still a different metaphor. And so on for dozens of examples. Yet we don't seem to have dozens of different metaphors here. We have one metaphor, in which love is conceptualized as a journey. The mapping tells us precisely how love is being conceptualized as a journey. And this unified way of conceptualizing love metaphorically is realized in many different linguistic expressions.

It should be noted that contemporary metaphor theorists commonly use the term "metaphor" to refer to the conceptual mapping, and the term "metaphorical expression" to refer to an individual linguistic expression (like **dead-end street**) that is sanctioned by a mapping. We have adopted this terminology for the following reason: Metaphor, as a phenomenon, involves both conceptual mappings and individual linguistic expressions. It is important to keep them distinct. Since it is the mappings that are primary and that state the generalizations that are our principal concern, we have reserved the term "metaphor" for the mappings, rather than for the linguistic expressions.

2.3. GENERALIZATIONS

The LOVE IS A JOURNEY metaphor is a conceptual mapping that characterizes a generalization of two kinds:

Polysemy generalization: A generalization over related senses of linguistic expression, e.g., dead-end street, crossroads, stuck, spinning one's wheels, not going anywhere, and so on.

Inferential generalization: A generalization over inferences across different conceptual domains.

That is, the existence of the mapping provides a general answer to two questions:

Why are words for travel used to describe love relationships?

Why are inference patterns used to reason about travel also used to reason about love relationships?

Correspondingly, from the perspective of the linguistic analyst, the existence of such cross-domain pairings of words and of inference patterns provides evidence for the existence of such mappings.

Novel Extensions

The fact that the LOVE IS A JOURNEY mapping is a fixed part of our conceptual system explains why new and imaginative uses of the mapping can be understood instantly, given the ontological correspondences and other knowledge about journeys. Take the song lyric,

We're driving in the fast lane on the freeway of love.

The traveling knowledge called upon is this: When you drive in the fast lane, you go a long way in a short time and it can be exciting and dangerous. The general metaphorical mapping maps this knowledge about driving into Knowledge about love relationships. The danger may be to the vehicle (the relationship may not last) or the passengers (the lovers may be hurt emotionally via the metaphor that EMOTIONAL HARM IS PHYSICAL HARM). Our understanding of the song lyric is a consequence of the pre-existing metaphorical correspondences of the LOVE-AS-JOURNEY metaphor. The song lyric is instantly comprehensible to speakers of English because those metaphorical correspondences are already part of our conceptual system.

3. Some General Issues Concerning Metaphor: Evidence, Inference, and Constraints

The analysis just given uses three kinds of evidence:

Generalizations over polysemy.

Generalizations over inference patterns.

Generalizations over novel extensions.

Three other kinds of evidence are commonly used in establishing metaphorical mappings:

Generalizations over historical semantic change.

Psycholinguistic experiments.

Gesture studies.

Eve Sweetser (Sweetser, 1990) traced the KNOWING IS SEEING metaphor back to Indo-European, where **wit** and **vision** have the same Indo-European root. She observed that, in language after language, in a wide variety of branches of Indo-European, as a new word came into the language meaning **see** it soon acquired the meaning **know**.

Ray Gibbs, in a range of experiments designed to test the psychological reality of conceptual metaphor, has gotten not merely positive, but robust results in case after case. For example, Kövecses and I have worked out the system of conceptual metaphors for anger. The most prominent of these is ANGER IS HEATED FLUID IN A CONTAINER, with examples such as **You make my blood boil, He's steaming, He's letting off steam, I blew my top, He flipped his lid, She hit the ceiling.** Gibbs and O'Brien found that for each such metaphorical idiom, speakers had mental images from the source domain of the metaphor (heated fluid in a container), and that source domain knowledge about causation, intentionality and manner was preserved in the target domain (anger).

Finally, David McNeill, in his classic study of gestures, found that there were metaphoric gestures that were instances of more general conceptual metaphors.

What we have here are six sources of evidence—and they all converge! On the whole, the evidence for conventional conceptual metaphor is overwhelming.

3.1. INFERENCE

With such evidential questions settled, we can now turn to the issue of inference. One of the traditional arguments for accepting formal logic as a model for human reason is that there are certain very general valid inference patterns that people use. Here is an account in terms of conceptual metaphor of how some of them work.

3.2. CATEGORIES

Classical categories are understood metaphorically in terms of bounded regions, or "containers". Thus, something can be in or out of a category, it can be put into a category or removed from a category, etc. The logic of classical categories is the logic of containers (see figure 1).

If X is in container A and container A is in container B, then X is in container B.

This is true not by virtue of any logical deduction, but by virtue of the topological properties of containers. Under the CATEGORIES ARE CONTAINERS metaphor, the logical properties of categories are inherited from the logical properties of containers. One of the principal logical properties of classical categories is that the classical syllogism holds for them. The classical syllogism,

Socrates is a man.

All men are mortal.

Therefore, Socrates is mortal.

is of the form:

If X is in category A and category A is in category B, then X is in category B.

Thus, the logical properties of classical categories can be seen as following from the topological properties of containers plus the metaphorical mapping form containers to categories. As long as the topological properties of containers are preserved by the mapping, this result will be true.

In other words, there is a generalization to be stated here. The language of containers applies to classical categories and the logic of containers is true of classical categories. A single metaphorical mapping ought to characterize both the linguistic and logical generalizations at once. This can be done provided that the topological properties of containers are preserved in the mapping.

The joint linguistic-and-inferential relation between containers and classical categories is not an isolated case. Let us take another example.

3.3. QUANTITY AND LINEAR SCALES

The concept of quantities involves at least two metaphors. The first is the well-known MORE IS UP, LESS IS DOWN metaphor as shown by a myriad of expressions like Prices rose, Stocks skyrocketed, The market plummeted, and so on. A second is the LINEAR SCALES ARE PATHS. We can see this in expressions like:

John is far more intelligent than Bill.

John's intelligence goes way beyond Bill's.

John is way ahead of Bill in intelligence.

The metaphor maps the starting point of the path onto the bottom of the scale and maps distance traveled onto quantity in general.

What is particularly interesting is that the logic of paths maps onto the logic of linear scales. (See figure 2.)

Path inference: If you are going from A to C, and you are now at in intermediate point B, then you have been at all points between A and B and not at any points between B and C.

Example: If you are going from San Francisco to N.Y. along route 80, and you are now at Chicago, then you have been to Denver but not to Pittsburgh.

Linear scale inference: If you have exactly $50 in your bank account, then you have $40, $30, and so on, but not $60, $70, or any larger amount.

The form of these inferences is the same. The path inference is a consequence of the cognitive topology of paths. It will be true of any path image-schema. Again, there is a linguistic-and-inferential generalization to be stated. It would be stated by the metaphor LINEAR SCALES ARE PATHS, provided that metaphors in general preserve the cognitive topology (that is, the image-schematic structure) of the source domain.

Looking at the inferential structure alone, one might suggest a nonmetaphorical alternative in which both linear scales and paths are instances of a more general abstract schema. But when both the inferential and lexical data are considered, it becomes clear that a metaphorical solution is required. An expression like "ahead of" is from the spatial domain, not the linear scale domain: "ahead" in its core sense is defined with respect to one's head-it is the direction in which one is facing. To say that there is no metaphorical mapping from paths to scales is to say that "ahead of" is not fundamentally spatial and characterized with respect to heads; it is to claim rather that "ahead" is very abstract, neutral between space and linear scales, and has nothing to do with heads. This would be a bizarre analysis. Similarly, for sentences like "John's intelligence goes beyond Bill's" the nonmetaphorical analysis would claim that "go" is not fundamentally a verb of motion at all, but is somehow neutral between motion and a linear relation. This would also be bizarre. In short, if one grants that "ahead of" and "go" are fundamentally spatial, then the fact that they can also be used of linear scales suggests a metaphor solution. Indeed, there could be no such neutral sense of "go" for these cases, since "go beyond" in the spatial sense involves motion, while in the linear scale sense, there is no motion or change, but just a point on a scale. Here the neutral case solution is not even available.

Categories and linear scales are extremely general conceptual structures, and the metaphorical analyses of these conceptual structures shows how conceptual metaphor can account for very general inference forms without the mechanisms of formal logic.

3.4. THE INVARIANCE PRINCIPLE

In the examples we have just considered, the image-schemas characterizing the source domains (containers, paths) are mapped onto the target domains (categories, linear scales). This observation leads to the following hypothesis, called "The Invariance Principle".

Metaphorical mappings preserve the cognitive topology (that is, the image-schema structure) of the source domain, in a way consistent with the inherent structure of the target domain.

What the Invariance Principle does is guarantee that, for container-schemas, interiors will be mapped onto interiors, exteriors onto exteriors, and boundaries onto boundaries; for path-schemas, sources will be mapped onto sources, goals onto goals, trajectories onto trajectories; and so on.

To understand the Invariance Principle properly, it is important not to think of mappings as algorithmic processes that "start" with source domain structure and wind up with target domain structure. Such a mistaken understanding of mappings would lead to a mistaken understanding of the Invariance Principle, namely, that one first picks all the image-schematic structure of the source domain, then one copies it onto the target domain unless the target domain interferes.

One should instead think of the Invariance Principle in terms of constraints on fixed correspondences: If on looks at the existing correspondences, one will see that the Invariance Principle holds: source domain interiors correspond to target domain interiors; source domain exteriors correspond to target domain exteriors; etc. As a consequence it will turn out that the image-schematic structure of the target domain cannot be violated: One cannot find cases where a source domain interior is mapped onto a target domain exterior, or where a source domain exterior is mapped onto a target domain path. This simply does not happen.

3.5. TARGET DOMAIN OVERRIDES

A corollary of the Invariance Principle is that image-schema structure inherent in the target domain cannot be violated, and that inherent target domain structure limits the possibilities for mappings automatically. This general principle explains a large number of previously mysterious limitations on metaphorical mappings. For example, it explains why you can give someone a kick, even if they don't have it afterwards, and why you can give someone information, even if you don't lose it. This is just a consequence of the fact that inherent target domain structure automatically limits what can be mapped.

For example, consider that part of your inherent knowledge of actions that says that actions do not continue to exist after they occur. Now consider the ACTIONS ARE

TRANSFERS metaphor, in which actions are conceptualized as objects transferred from an agent to a patient, as when one gives someone a kick or a punch. We know (as part of target domain knowledge) that an action does not exist after it occurs. In the source domain, where there is a giving, the recipient possesses the object given after the giving. But this cannot be mapped onto the target domain since the inherent structure of the target domain says that no such object exists after the action is over. The target domain override in the Invariance Principle explains why you can give someone a kick without his having it afterward.

3.6. ABSTRACT INFERENCES AS METAPHORICAL SPATIAL INFERENCES

Spatial inferences are characterized by the topological structure of image-schemas. We have seen cases such as CATEGORIES ARE CONTAINERS and LINEAR SCALES ARE PATHS where image-schema structure is preserved by metaphor and where abstract inferences about categories and linear scales are metaphorical versions of spatial inferences about containers and paths. The Invariance Principle hypothesizes that image-schema structure is always preserved by metaphor.

The Invariance Principle raises the possibility that a great many, if not all, abstract inferences are actually metaphorical versions of spatial inferences that are inherent in the topological structure of image-schemas. What I will do now is turn to other cases of basic, but abstract, concepts to see what evidence there is for the claim that such concepts are fundamentally characterized by metaphor.

4. Time

It has often been noted that time in English is conceptualized in terms of space. The details are rather interesting.

Ontology: Time is understood in terms of things (i.e., entities and locations) and motion.

Background condition: The present time is at the same location as a canonical observer.

Mapping:
Times are entities.
The passing of time is motion.
The present time is where the observer is.
The future is in front of the observer; the past is behind the observer.
One entity is moving, the other is stationary; the stationary entity is the deictic center.
Entailment:
Since motion is continuous and one-dimensional, the passage of time is continuous and one-dimensional.
Special case 1:
The observer is fixed; times are entities moving with respect to the observer.

Times are oriented with their fronts in their direction of motion.

Entailments:

If time 2 follows time 1, then time 2 is in the future relative to time 1.

The time passing the observer is the present time.

Time has a velocity relative to the observer.

Special case 2:

Times are fixed locations; the observer is moving with respect to time.

Entailment:

Time has extension, and can be measured.

An extended time, like a spatial area, may be conceived of as a bounded region.

This metaphor, TIME PASSING IS MOTION, with its two special cases, embodies a generalization that accounts for a wide range of cases where a spatial expression can also be used for time. Special case 1, TIME PASSING IS MOTION OF AN OBJECT, accounts for both the linguistic form and the semantic entailments of expressions like:

The time will come when... The time has long since gone when... The time for action has arrived. That time is here. In the weeks following next Tuesday... On the preceding day, ... I'm looking ahead to Christmas. Thanksgiving is coming up on us. Let's put all that behind us. I can't face the future. Time is flying by. The time has passed when...

Thus, special case 1 characterizes the general principle behind the temporal use of words like come, go, here, follow, precede, ahead, behind, fly, pass, accounting not only for why they are used for both space and time, but why they mean what they mean.

Special case 2, TIME PASSING IS MOTION OVER A LANDSCAPE, accounts for a different range of cases, expressions like:

There's going to be trouble down the road.

He stayed there a long time.

His stay in Russia extended over many years.

He passed the time happily.

He arrived on time.

We're coming up on Christmas.

We're getting close to Christmas.

He'll have his degree within two years.

I'll be there in a minute.

Special case 2 maps location expressions like down the road, for + location, long, over, come, close to, within, in, pass, onto corresponding temporal expressions with their corresponding meanings. Again, special case 2 states a general principle relating spatial terms and inference patterns to temporal terms and inference patterns.

The details of the two special cases are rather different; indeed, they are inconsistent with one another. The existence of such special cases has an especially interesting theoretical consequence: words mapped by both special cases will have inconsistent readings. Take, for example, the come of Christmas is coming (special case 1) and We're coming up on Christmas (special case 2). Both instances of come are temporal, but one takes a moving time as first argument and the other takes a moving observer as first argument. The same is true of pass in The time has passed (special case 1) and in He passed the time (special case 2).

These differences in the details of the mappings show that one cannot just say blithely that spatial expressions can be used to speak of time, without specifying details, as though there were only one correspondence between time and space. When we are explicit about stating the mappings, we discover that there are two different-and inconsistent-subcases.

The fact that time is understood metaphorically in terms of motion, entities, and locations accords with our biological knowledge. In our visual systems, we have detectors for motion and detectors for objects/locations. We do not have detectors for time (whatever that could mean). Thus, it makes good biological sense that time should be understood in terms of things and motion.

4.1. DUALITY

The two special cases (location and object) of TIME PASSING IS MOTION metaphor is not merely an accident feature of our understanding of time. As we shall see below, there are other metaphors that come in such location-object pairs. Such pairs are called "duals," and the general phenomenon is which metaphors come in location-object pairs is referred to as "duality."

4.2. SIMULTANEOUS MAPPINGS

It is important to recall that metaphorical mappings are fixed correspondences that can be activated, rather than algorithmic processes that take inputs and give outputs. Thus, it is not the case that sentences containing conventional metaphors are the products of a real-time process of conversion from literal to metaphorical readings. A sentence like The time for action has arrived is not understood by first trying to give a literal reading to arrive, and then, upon failing, trying to give it a temporal reading. Instead, the metaphor TIME PASSING IS MOTION is a fixed structure of existing correspondences between the space and time domains, and arrive has a conventional extended meaning that makes use of that fixed structure of correspondences.

Thus, it is possible for two different parts of a sentence to make use of two distinct metaphorical mappings at once. Consider a phrase like, Within the coming weeks. Here, within makes uses of the metaphor of time as a stationary landscape which has extension and bounded regions, while coming makes use of the metaphor of times as moving objects. This is possible because the two metaphors for time pick out different aspects of the target domain. The comings weeks conceptualizes those weeks as a whole, in motion relative to the observer. Within looks inside that whole, conceptualizing it as a bounded region with an interior. Each mapping is used partially. Thus, while the mappings-as wholes-are inconsistent, there are cases where parts of the mappings may be consistently superimposed. The Invariance Principle allows such parts of the mappings to be picked out and used to characterize reasoning about different aspects of the target domain.

Simultaneous mappings are very common in poetry. Take, for example, the Dylan Thomas line "Do not go gentle into the good night." Here "go" reflects DEATH IS DEPARTURE, "gentle" reflects LIFE IS A STRUGGLE, with death as defeat. "Night" reflects A LIFETIME IS A DAY, with death as night. This one line has three different, metaphors for death, each mapped onto different parts of the sentence. This is possible since mappings are fixed correspondences.

There is an important lesson to be learned form this example. In mathematics, mappings are static correspondences. In computer science, it is common to represent mathematical mappings by algorithmic processes that take place in real time. Researches in information processing psychology and cognitive science also commonly represent mappings as real-time algorithmic procedures. Some researches from these fields have mistakenly supposed that the metaphorical mappings we are discussing should also be represented as real-time, sequential algorithmic procedures, where the input to each metaphor is a literal meaning. Any attempt to do this will fail for the simultaneous mapping cases just discussed.

5. Event Structure

I now want to turn to some research by myself and some of my students (especially Sharon Fischler, Karin Myhre, and Jane Espenson) on the metaphorical understanding of event structure in English. What we have found is that various aspects of event structure, including notions like states, changes, processes, actions, causes, purposes, and means, are characterized cognitively via metaphor in terms of space, motion, and force.

The general mapping we have found goes as follows:

The Event Structure Metaphor

States are locations (bounded regions in space).
Changes are movements (into or out of bounded regions).
Causes are forces.
Actions are self-propelled movements.
Purposes are destinations.
Means are paths (to destinations).
Difficulties are impediments to motion.
Expected progress is a travel schedule; a schedule is a virtual traveler who reaches pre-arranged destinations at pre-arranged times.
External events are large, moving objects.
Long term, purposeful activities are journeys.

This mapping generalizes over an extremely wide range of expressions for one or more aspects of event structure. For example, takes states and changes. We speak of being **in** or **out** of a state, of **going into** or **out of** it, of **entering** or **leaving** it, of **getting to** a state or **emerging from** it. The persistence of a state is seen as **staying**, or **remaining, in** it.

This is a rich and complex metaphor whose parts interact in complex ways. To get an idea of how it works, consider the submapping "Difficulties are impediments to motion." In the metaphor, purposive action is self-propelled motion toward a destination. A difficulty is something that impedes motion to such a destination. Metaphorical difficulties of this sort come in five types: blockages; features of the terrain; burdens; counterforces; lack of an energy source. Here are examples of each:

Blockages:
He got over his divorce. He's trying to get around the regulations. He went through the trial. We ran into a brick wall. We've got him boxed into a corner.

Features of the terrain
He's between a rock and a hard place. It's been uphill all the way. We've been bogged down. We've been hacking our way through a jungle of regulations.

Burdens
He's carrying quite a load. He's weighed down by lot of assignments. He's been trying to shoulder all the responsibility. Get off my back!

Counterforces
Quit pushing me around. She's leading him around by the nose. She's holding him back.

Lack of an energy source
I'm out of gas. We're running out of steam.

To see just how rich The Event Structure Metaphor is, consider some of its basic entailments:

Manner of action is manner of motion.
A different means for achieving a purpose is a different path.
Forces affecting action are forces affecting motion.
The inability to act is the inability to move.
Progress made is distance traveled.

We will consider examples of each of these one by one, including a number of special cases.

Aids to Action are Aids to Motion.
It is smooth sailing from here on in. It's all downhill form here. There's nothing in our way.

A Different Means of Achieving a Result is a Different Path.

Do it this way. She did it the other way. Do it any way you can. However you want to go about it is fine with me.

Manner of Action is Manner of Motion

We are moving/running/skipping right along. We slogged through it. He is flailing around. He is falling all over himself. We are leaping over hurdles. He is out of step. He is in step.

Careful Action is Careful Motion
I'm walking on eggshells. He is treading on this ice. He is walking a fine line.

Speed of Action is Speed of Movement
He flew through his work. He is running around. It is going swimmingly. Keep things moving at a good clip. Things have slowed to a crawl. She is going by leaps and bounds. I am moving at a snail's pace.

Purposeful Action is Self-propelled Motion To a Destination.

This has the following special cases:

Making Progress Is Forward Movement
We are moving ahead. Let's forge ahead. Let's keep moving forward. We made lots of forward movement.

Amount of Progress is Distance Moved
We've come a long way. We've covered lots of ground. We've made it this far.

Undoing Progress is Backward Movement
We are sliding backward. We are backsliding. We need to backtrack. It is time to turn around and retrace our steps.

Expected Progress is a Travel Schedule; A Schedule is a Virtual traveler, who reaches pre-arranged destinations at pre-arranged times.
We're behind schedule on the project. We got a head start on the project. I'm trying to catch up. I finally got a little ahead.

Starting an Action is Starting out on a Path
We are just starting out. We have taken the first step.

Success Is Reaching The End of the Path
We've reached the end. We are seeing the light at the end of the tunnel. We only have a short way to go. The end is in sight. The end is a long way off.

Lack of Purpose is Lack of Direction

He is just floating around. He is drifting aimlessly. He needs some direction.

Lack of Progress is Lack of Movement

We are at a standstill. We aren't getting any place. We aren't going anywhere. We are going nowhere with this.

External Events Are Large Moving Objects

Special Case 1: Things

How're things going? Things are going with me. Things are going against me these days. Things took a turn for the worse. Things are going my way.

Special Case 2: Fluids

You gotta go with the flow. I'm just trying to keep my head above water. The tide of events... The winds of change... The flow of history... I'm trying to get my bearings. He's up a creek without a paddle. We're all in the same boat.

Special Case 3: Horses

Try to keep a tight rein on the situation. Keep a grip on the situation. Don't let things get out of hand. Wild horses couldn't make me go. Hold your horses. "Whoa!" (said when things start to get out of hand)

5.1. DUALITY IN THE EVENT STRUCTURE SYSTEM

In our discussion of time metaphors, we noted the existence of an object-location duality. There were two related time metaphors. In both, the passage of time was understood in terms of relative motion between an observer and a time. In the object-dual, the observer is fixed and times are moving objects. In the location-dual, the opposite is true. The observer moves and times are fixed locations in a landscape.

The event structure system that we have seen so far is based wholly on location. But there is another event structure system that is the dual of the one we have just discussed—a system based on objects rather that locations. In both systems, CHANGE IS MOTION and CAUSES ARE FORCES that control motion. The difference is this:

In the location system, change is the motion of the thing-changing to a new location or from an old one.

In the object system, the thing-changing doesn't necessarily move. Change is instead the motion of an object to, or way from, the thing-changing.

In addition, the object in motion is conceptualized as a possession and the thing-changing as a possessor. Change is thus seen as the acquisition or loss of an object. Causation is seen as giving or taking. Here are some examples:

-I have a headache. [The headache is a possession.]

G. LAKOFF

-I got a headache. [Change is acquisition—motion to]
-My headache went away. [Change is loss—motion from]
-The noise gave me a headache. [Causation is giving—motion to]
-The aspirin took away my headache. [Causation is taking—motion from]

We can see the duality somewhat more clearly with a word like "trouble":
-I'm in trouble. [Trouble is a location]
-I have trouble. [Trouble is an object that is possessed]

In both cases, trouble is being attributed to me, and in both cases, trouble is metaphorically conceptualized as being in the same place as me (co-location)—in one case, because I possess the trouble-object and in the other case, because I am in the trouble-location. That is, attribution in both cases is conceptualized metaphorically as co-location. In "I'm in trouble, " trouble is a state. A state is an attribute that is conceptualized as a location. Attributes (or properties) are like states, except that they are conceptualized as possessable objects.

Thus, STATES ARE LOCATIONS and ATTRIBUTES ARE POSSESSIONS are duals, since possession and location are special cases of the same thing—co-location— and since states and attributes are also special cases of the same thing—what can be attributed to someone.

Given this, we can see that there is an object-version of the Event Structure Metaphor:

Attributes are possessions

Changes are movements (of possessions, namely, acquisitions or losses)

Causes are forces (controlling the movement of possessions, namely giving or taking away)

These are the duals of:

States are locations

Changes are movements (to or from locations)

Causes are forces (controlling movement to or from locations)

Similarly, ACTIONS ARE SELF-PROPELLED MOVEMENTS (to or from locations) has as its object-dual ACTIONS ARE SELF-CONTROLLED ACQUISITIONS OR LOSSES. Thus, there is a reason why one can "take" certain actions—you can take a shower, or take a shot at someone, or take a chance.

The submapping PURPOSES ARE DESTINATION also has a dual. Destinations are desired locations, and so the submapping can be rephrased as PURPOSES ARE DESIRED LOCATIONS, and ACHIEVING A PURPOSE IS REACHING A DESIRED LOCATION. Replacing "location" by "object", we get the dual PURPOSES ARE DESIRED OBJECTS, and ACHIEVING A PURPOSE IS ACQUIRING A DESIRED OBJECT (or ridding oneself of an undesirable one).

Here are some examples:

ACHIEVING A PURPOSE IS ACQUIRING A DESIRED OBJECT

They just handed him the job. It's within my grasp. It eluded me. Go for it. It escaped me. It slipped through my hands. He is pursuing a goal. Reach for/grab all the gusto you can get. Latch onto a good job. Seize the opportunity. He found success.

There is also a hierarchical structure in the object version of the Event Structure Metaphor. A special case of getting an object is getting an object to eat. Hence,

ACHIEVING A PURPOSE IS GETTING SOMETHING TO EAT
He savored the victory. All the good jobs have been gobbled up. He's hungry for success. The opportunity has me drooling. This is a mouth-watering opportunity.

Traditional methods of getting things to eat are hunting, fishing, and agriculture. Each of these special cases can be used metaphorically to conceptualize achieving (or attempting to achieve) a purpose.

TRYING TO ACHIEVE A PURPOSE IS HUNTING
I'm hunting for a job. I bagged a promotion. The pennant is in the bag.

The typical way to hunt is to use projectiles (bullets, arrows, etc.)

I'm shooting for a promotion. I'm aiming for a career in the movies. I'm afraid I missed my chance.

TRYING TO ACHIEVE A PURPOSE IS FISHING
He's fishing for compliments. I landed a promotion. She netted a good job. I've got a line out on a good used car. It's time to fish or cut bait.

TRYING TO ACHIEVE A PURPOSE IS AGRICULTURE

It's time I reaped some rewards. That job is a plum. Those are the fruits of his labor. The contract is ripe for the picking.

A more modern way to acquire a desired object is to go to shopping for it.

TRYING TO ACHIEVE A PURPOSE IS SHOPPING
He's shopping around for a new job.

5.2. FIVE VARIATIONS

In addition to duality, there are also variations on the Event Structure Metaphor. We will consider five of them—four variations on the location branch and one on the possession branch. Each variation "inherits" the rest of the overall event structure mapping.

Changing is Turning

Expressions: He **went on** talking. It **stopped** raining. The milk **turned** sour. As before, Causation is Forced Motion, only here it is forced turning: He **turned** the lead **into** gold.
Mapping:

Remaining in a State is Going in the Same Direction
Ceasing to be in a State is Stopping
Changing is Turning

States Are shapes

Expressions: What **shape** is the car in? He's in rare **form** tonight. He's **in shape**. He's got a **twisted** mind? He's physically **fit**. It is **fitting** that he lost. He wants to **reshape** the government. She's a **reformer**. I will **conform** to the prevailing standards. Meditation **transformed** him into a saint.
Mapping:
States are Shapes
An Ideal State is a Canonical Shape
An Abnormal State is an Abnormal Shape
Appropriateness of a State is Fittingness

Change is Replacement

Expressions: I'm a **different** man. After the experiment, the water was **gone** and hydrogen and oxygen were **in its place**. Under hypnosis, the sweet old lady was **replaced** by scheming criminal.
Mapping:
A Thoroughly Changed Entity is a Different Entity in the Same Place
Change is Replacement.

A Change of Entities is the Same Entity Changed

Examples: His house gets bigger every time he moves. Each time he remarries, his wife gets younger.
Mapping:
A Change of Entities is the Same Entity Changed
    Consider the submapping: Purposes are Desired Objects. The mapping given above assumes that the desired objects exist. Only then is acting causally to achieve a purpose conceptualized as taking the desired object. But what if the desired object does not exist? The way to get a desired object that doesn't exist is to make it. This is the basis for metaphor:

Causing Is Making

Examples: I made him leave. He made lead into gold.
Mapping:
Causing is Making
Effects are Objects Made

Conclusion

The philosophical point to all this linguistic analysis is that events are mostly, if not entirely, conceptualized, reasoned about, and talked about in terms of metaphor. The evidence is overwhelming. Event structure as we know it is a product of human imaginative capacities. We structure events in a variety of related ways using a system of metaphor with a highly articulates structure. Any account of what an event is for a human being must take this metaphorical structure into account.

This account of the conceptualization of event structure goes far beyond any prior philosophical analysis in scope and detail. It explains not only the language used, but also the inference patterns that accompany the language. Without conceptual metaphor, it is hard to imagine a philosophical analysis that could account for the generalizations governing both the language used in these examples and for the inference patterns that come with the linguistic forms.

6. The Basic Causation Metaphor: Causes Are Forces

The study of event structure reveals the basic metaphor for causation (first pointed out by Len Talmy), namely that Causes Are Forces. As we shall see, it is not the only metaphor for causation, but it is the most prevalent and most fundamental one. Here is a schematic overview of the basic range of variants on Causes Are Forces, looking at the Event Structure metaphor and the variations on it.

The Event Structure Metaphor:

Causes are Forces
Causation is Forced Movement
Changes are Motions

Location Branch:

States are Locations
Purposes are Desired Locations
External Events are Large, Moving Objects

Causation is the forced movement of affected party to a new location (e.g., bringing the water to a boil)

Object Branch:

Properties are Possessions
Purposes are Desired Objects
Causation is the transfer of an effect to or from an effected party (e.g., the noise gave me a headache and the aspirin took it away).

Nature is a Force
When a person is exerting a force to move an object, it is the person who determines where the object moves, since the person can choose how to direct the force. But when Nature or External Events are conceptualized as forces acting on objects, they cannot, by themselves, determine where the object moves to. What determines where the object will wind up, given natural or external forces, is either the object's initial location or a constrained path the object happens to be on. In such a case, the location or the path can stand for the force, and hence the cause.

The Causal Location Metonymy:
A Initial Location can stand for a Force (and hence, for a Cause).
Example: He died from pneumonia.

The Causal Path Metonymy:
A Path can stand for a Force (and hence, for a Cause).
Example: Smoking marijuana **leads to** drug addiction.

Variations on Causes are Forces

1. **Causes are Forces + Changing is Turning**
   He **turned** lead **into** gold.
2. **Causes are Forces + States are Shapes**
   He wants to **reshape** the government. She's a **reformer**. Meditation **transformed** him into a saint. He wants to **mold** the new government.
3. **Causes are Forces + Change is Replacement**
   The people want to **replace** the totalitarian regime with a democratic government.
4. **Causing is Making (a special case of Causes are Forces)**
   I **made** him leave. I **made** lead into gold.

6.1. CAUSATION IS PROGENERATION AND EMERGENCE

These metaphorical analyses explain exactly why the following expressions are all causal and exactly how the causality is understood in terms of force: **bring, give, take, send, lead to, from, mold, transform, replace, make, turn,** and so on. At this point a further issue arises. Turner, in *Death Is The Mother of Beauty* (Turner, 1987), observed that causation is commonly conceptualized in terms of progeneration, that is, giving birth, fathering, and plant propagations. Some examples include:

Necessity is the **mother** of invention. Our nation was **born** from a desire for freedom. Teller was the **father** of the H-bomb. The **seeds** of War World II were **sown** at Versailles.

There is also a metaphor that Causation Is Emergence, as in:

He shot the mayor **out of** desperation. American democratic institutions **emerged** from British colonial rule.

How are these metaphors linked to Causes Are Forces? The answer, I believe, lies in the birth subcase of Causation is Progeneration. In birth, the child is forced out of the mother. Birth involves forced motion to a new location, and hence, birth is a subcase of Causes Are Forces. Birth is an instance of emergence, which makes emergence a natural candidate for the source domain of a causation metaphor. And since both a father and a mother are required for the creation of a child, we can see why fathering should be natural as a causation metaphor, given that birth is. Since plant propagation creates new plants, just as human procreation creates new people, plant propagation is linked to fathering and giving birth as a natural causation metaphor. Conceptual links of this sort provide an answer to the question of why all these very different concepts map onto causation. There is a collection of metaphors for causation centering on Causes Are Forces and extending to Giving Birth, Fathering, Plant Propagation and Emergence. These Causation metaphors form a radial category (see Lakoff, 1987) with Causes Are Forces as the prototype at the center, and Fathering, Plant Propagation, Emergence, Initial Location, and Paths as conceptual extensions. Metaphor analysis reveals that causation is not a single unified concept with a single common conceptualization. Rather it is radial category of naturally related concepts.

6.2. THE VERB "CAUSE" VERSUS THE CONCEPT OF CAUSATION

The verb "cause" is not linguistically metaphorical, in that it does not have a central sense that names a concept in another conceptual domain. But that does not mean that the concept of causation, the concept named by the verb "cause" is not conceptually metaphorical. For example, it could be the case that, in the sentence, **John caused Bill to leave**, the causation is conceptualized as forced motion. There is no direct linguistic evidence that this is true. But there is also no evidence that it is false.

The Causes Are Forces metaphor certainly exists in our conceptual system. If we give that sentence a metaphorical semantic analysis in terms of Causes Are Forces, all the right inferences follow. Indeed, since the appropriate conceptual metaphor exists in our conceptual system independently of this sentence, it might well be the most parsimonious overall analysis of the language to use that metaphor, rather than some literal definition, to characterize the semantics of the sentence. This case is particularly interesting in that it reminds us that the analysis of a language is based on generalizations over the language as a whole, and is not a sentence-by-sentence matter.

7. Probabilistic Causation

The concept of probabilistic causation is also metaphorical in nature. Indeed, it is a composition of two independently existing metaphors in our everyday conceptual systems.

Metaphor 1: Uncertainty is Gambling

Examples: His chances are 50-50. It's a toss-up as to whether he'll live or die. He's got one chance in 20 of pulling through. The odds are against me. The stakes are high. You've gotta play the hand you're dealt.

Mapping:

Source Domain: Gambling   Target Domain: Events

A gamble --> An Event with an uncertain outcome
The outcome of a gamble --> The outcome of an event
The **distribution** of X in the **past** for a **population** --> The **probability** of X in the **future** for **an arbitrary individual in that population.**

This metaphor is motivated by an important truth about gambling games, namely:

The **distribution** of X in the **past** for a **population** = The **probability** of X in the **future** for **an arbitrary individual in that population.**

For example, consider a roll of the dice. Suppose that in a sufficiently large population, seven has been rolled P percent of the time. Then the probability that a given individual will roll a seven on future roll is also P.

Gambling is a particular kind of event with an uncertain outcome. The Uncertainty Is Gambling metaphor allows one to understand any kind of event with an uncertain outcome in terms of gambling. For example, suppose that one-half of the people who test positive on a certain blood test develop leukemia. Then if you test positive, you will most likely believe that you have a 50-50 chance of developing leukemia. That is, you will understand the future probability of an occurrence of X for a single individual— you—in terms of the past distribution of X over a relevant population. Here X = developing leukemia, given a positive blood test.

To see that this inference is metaphorical, compare gambling games and leukemia. In gambling games, the odds are independent of who is doing the gambling. It doesn't matter whether you roll the dice a thousand times or a thousand people roll the dice once. The same percentage of sevens will come up. But leukemia may very well depend on differences among people. Thus, future probability may not be equal to past distribution for leukemia.

Nonetheless, because the Uncertainty Is Gambling metaphor is so pervasive in our culture, that metaphor will lead on to understand future probability in terms of past distribution—despite the fact that leukemia is not like gambling. It is an extremely deep and powerful metaphor in our everyday conceptual system.

The second metaphor that goes into making up the concept of probabilistic causation is another everyday metaphor:

Metaphor 2:
Causation is Correlation

Consider the following instances of this metaphor:

Examples: An increase in pressure **accompanies** an increase of temperature. Pressure goes up **with** an increase in temperature. Homelessness **came with** Reagonomics.

Each example literally states a correlation—accompanying or going with something. Yet these statements are understood metaphorically as causal statement, e.g., that an increase in temperature causes an increase in pressure.

This metaphor has an obvious motivation: If Y causes Z, then Z is correlated with Y. That is, there is a systematic relationship between causation and correlation. The mapping is stated as follows:

Y is **correlated** with a change Z --> Y **causes** a change Z

We are now in a position to see how these two common everyday metaphors combine to yield the concept of probabilistic causation.

Probabilistic Causation:

Uncertainty Is Gambling + Causation is Correlation

Let us form the composition of these two mappings:

Mapping 1: Uncertainty Is Gambling; Probability is Frequency
A gamble--> An event with an uncertain outcome
The outcome of a gamble--> The outcome of an event
The **frequency** of X in the **past** for a **population**--> The **probability** of X in the **future** for **an arbitrary individual in that population.**

Mapping 2: Causation is Correlation:

Y is **correlated** with a change is Z --> Y **causes** a change in Z

The composite mapping is structured as follows:

In the source domain.

Z(in 2) = the **frequency** of X **in the past in a population as a whole** (in 1)

In the target domain:

Z(in 2) = the **probability** of X **in the future for an arbitrary member of that population** (in 1)

The resulting mapping is:

The Probabilistic Causation Metaphor

A gamble--> An event with an uncertain outcome
The outcome of a gamble--> The outcome of an event
Y is **correlated** with a change in the **frequency** of X **in the past in a population as a whole**--> Y **causes** a change in the **probability** of X **in the future for an arbitrary member of that population.**

This metaphor is the basis for the attribution of causation on the basis of correlation throughout the social sciences. Because its component metaphors are a natural part of our conceptual systems, this metaphor is so natural that it is often taken as an obvious truth.

8. Is Causation An Inherently Metaphorical Concept?

Many philosophers assume that causation exists in the world independent of human beings, and independent of the imaginative capacities of human minds. Such a mind-free Causation concept must therefore be (1) literal, not metaphorical (2) not prototype-based, since both metaphors and prototypes are products of the mind. Indeed, philosophers regularly produce definitions of causation that are neither metaphorical, nor prototype-based. Perhaps the most common of these is the following:

    A causes B if and only if A entails B and A precedes B and A is contiguous to B and B wouldn't have happened without A.
    But such characterizations in terms of literal necessary and sufficient conditions have never been shown to characterize the full range of causal expressions. For example, the definition just given fails to characterize **leads to**, since, if A leads to B, it doesn't follow that A entails B. For example, smoking may lead to getting cancer, but it

doesn't entail getting cancer. Similarly, **sowing the seeds of** does not necessarily entail contiguity. Indeed, philosophers regularly revise and re-revise their favorite causation definitions to cover their favorite range of cases. To my knowledge, no literal and non-prototype-based definition of causation exists that covers all and only the causation concepts in English and correctly characterizes the inferential properties of those causation concepts.

The evidence given above shows that most expressions of causation in English are metaphorical, and that a collection of related causation metaphors accounts for both the inferential and linguistic character of those causal expressions. In short, there is evidence backing up the metaphorical analyses presented. But there is no evidence I know of backing up the claim that causation is nonmetaphorical and non-prototype based. Most philosophers just seem to take it for granted.

But now that philosophy has entered the Age of Cognitive Science, evidence becomes relevant. What evidence is there, or could there be, to show that causation is a purely literal concept defined by necessary and sufficient conditions? Until that question is answered, what we know is that the vast majority of causal expressions are conceptualized via metaphor. And it is an open question whether causation is purely a metaphorical concept, or whether it can be characterized meaningfully in literal terms, even in part.

Incidentally, it would by no means be a strange result were causation to turn out to be purely metaphorical, conceptualized in terms of forces, progeneration, emergence, and gambling+correlation. As soon as one realized that it is the norm to conceptualize abstract concepts metaphorically in terms of more concrete concepts, it becomes natural to think of a concept as abstract as causation as being conceptualized purely by metaphor.

At this point, I must ask the following questions:

If causation is purely a metaphorical concept, does that mean that there is no causation objectively in the world and that only impose causation upon the world?

If human concepts of causation are purely metaphorical, it would not follow that there could be no objective causation in the world. There might be an objectively existing causation that we comprehended using causation metaphors.

However, if our comprehension of causation is always metaphorical, then we might not be able to conceptualize objective causation, even if it existed.

Is it possible that objectively existing causation is an illusion, and that we project causation onto the world via our metaphors?

Yes, that it possible. After all, laws of physics are equations that only state constraints; they do not mention causation. For example, $e = mc^2$ states a constraint on energy and mass, it says nothing about causation. It could be that we impose the concept of causation on the world.

But that sounds ridiculous. If I knock over a glass of water with my arm, I have caused the glass to fall over. Surely you are not saying that I haven't. Surely you are not saying that no one can cause anything.

Using our human conceptual system with its (perhaps metaphorical) concept of causation, we would certainly, and perhaps necessarily, conceptualize your knocking over the glass as causation.

But, outside the human conceptual system, the world might only be structured by constraints like those in physical equations, with no objective causation. But if human conceptual systems always categorized knocking over a glass as causation—whether or not there was objective causation in the world.

From inside the human conceptual system, we would certainly conceptualize the world in terms of causation. Since I can only use a human conceptual system, I would certainly conceptualize occurrences of knocking over a glass as causation. But I can nonetheless imagine that the world is structured independent of the human mind only in terms of physical constraints with no objective causation.

Conclusion

There is lots of evidence that we conceptualize abstract causation metaphorically, and no evidence that I know of that also conceptualize causation literally, without understanding causation in terms of forced movement, progeneration, etc.. The fact that we conceptualize causation metaphorically tells us nothing about whether or not the world is objectively structured via some transcendent causation concept. And if we do always understand causation metaphorically in some way, then it is not even clear what a transcendent, nonmetaphorical concept of causation would be. We are simply ignorant about whether abstract causation is or not an objective feature of the world as it exists independent of human beings.

9. Metaphor and Belief

Once we realize that much of ordinary everyday thought is metaphorical, the question arises as to whether we can have metaphorical beliefs. The answer is yes. Indeed, they are very common, though, like everyday metaphorical thought in general, metaphorical beliefs tend not be noticed as such. Indeed, most people with metaphorical beliefs will take them as being literal.

Consider the following newspaper article:

The Great Employee Time Robbery

Employees across the nation this year will steal $150 billion worth of time from their jobs in what is termed by an employment specialist as the "deliberate and persistent abuse" of paid working hours.

The study, released by Robert Half International, Inc., reported that the theft of working time is America's No. 1 crime against business, surpassing employee pilferage, insurance fraud, and embezzlement combined.

Robert Half, president of the firm bearing his name, said that time is the most valuable resource to business because it "cannot be replaced, recovered, or replenished."

He defined time theft as leaving work early or arriving late, extended lunch hours, excessive personal phone calls, conducting personal business during company hours, unwarranted sick days and nonstop chitchat at the proverbial water cooler.

The study showed that the average weekly time theft per employee amounted to four hours and 22 minutes.

This is an extreme example, but only because it is a novel extension of an otherwise conventional metaphor: the TIME IS MONEY metaphor, in which time is seen as a money-like resource. Everyday expressions exemplifying this metaphor are:

She *wasted* an hour of my time this morning. I'm having trouble *budgeting* my time. I *lost* a lot of time on that project. This gadget will *save* you time. You're *spending* too much time on that project.

Note that any of these sentences can be believed: I can believe that you wasted an hour of my time this morning. I can believe that I need to budget my time, or that you spent too much time on silly projects, and so on. These are, of course, metaphorical beliefs—beliefs in which time is conceptualized metaphorically as a money-like resource. Of course, time in itself is no such thing. But when we conceptualize time metaphorically as a money-like resource, that conceptualization can be used in a belief, making the belief metaphorical, like Robert Half's belief that his employees are stealing time from him.

There is nothing exotic about metaphorical beliefs. You can believe, for example, that time passes rapidly. If you do, you are using the common metaphor for time, that TIME IS A MOVING OBJECT, exemplified by expression like:

The time for reducing the deficit has *arrived*. The time will *come* when you'll be sorry. Every Tuesday *follows* a Monday. The time has long since *gone* when you could buy a nice house for $25,000.

If you believe any of these sentences, you have a metaphorical belief—a belief that uses a metaphorical conceptualization of time.

Or take some other fairly obvious cases. Many people believe that marriage is a partnership, or a journey through life together, or that a marriage must be built with a firm foundation. These are beliefs that use metaphorical conceptualizations about marriage. Many people believe that if someone does something nice for you, then you are *in their debt*, that you *owe* them something and should *pay* them *back*. Such beliefs conceptualize ethics metaphorically as a form of accounting. They too are metaphorical beliefs.

What exactly does it mean to have a metaphorical belief? What happens in these cases is that a conventional metaphorical mapping is used automatically and unconsciously to conceptualize one domain in terms of another. Inferences from the source domain are carried over to the target domain, and those inferences fit experience well. If the inferences fit well enough, we will believe the metaphor and take the metaphor as expressing a truth. Given a conceptualization of time as a money-like resource, I can consider it true that you wasted an hour of my time this morning, or that I owe you a favor. And given that such metaphors can structure our social life, it can *be* true that you wasted an hour of my time or that I owe you a favor. If a conceptual metaphor provides the normal way to conceptualize a situation, then a statement based on that conceptual metaphor may be taken as true.

The cases given above are for the most part fairly obvious, since the source and target domains are so distinct. Time is obviously not, in itself, literally money. Nor is the "passage" of time literally motion through space. Marriage is not literally a journey or a building. Ethical conduct is not literally accounting. When the source domains are so obviously different from the target domains, we can recognize consciously that we are metaphorically conceptualizing time, marriage, and morality, even though we are most often not conscious of doing so.

The result is an interesting phenomenon. Our unconscious, automatic, conventional metaphors are so deeply entrenched in our minds that we normally don't notice when we use them. Moreover, they may be the normal way that we conceptualize some subject matter. We formulate our thoughts in terms of those conceptual metaphors, without realizing we are doing so. We reason in terms of those conceptual metaphors, without realizing we are doing so. When those conclusions fit our experience as we conceptualize it using those unconscious metaphors, then we take the conclusions as truths. We believe them. But we may not know that we have the conclusions as truths. After all, if those unconscious metaphors provide the normal way of conceptualizing, reasoning about, and talking about some domain, then from the perspective of what we are consciously aware of, we take ourselves to be thinking, reasoning, and talking literally.

But this raises an issue: If I believe that I am thinking, reasoning, and talking literally, what right does anyone else have to say that I am not. Am I not the final arbiter about my own mind? Similarly, Robert Half, the billionaire corporate raider, may really believe that his employees are literally stealing time from him. Isn't he the final arbiter of his own beliefs? Who are we to say that stealing time is metaphorical, not literal?

Cognitive Science, as the scientific study of the mind, makes an implicit claim: you are not the final arbiter of your mind. Consider any of the classical results in cognitive science: Color categories, for example, do not exist in the external world, independent of human bodies and brains. Color categories are constructed by the eye and brain, and a great deal has been discovered about just how it is done—a story that involves kinds of color cones in the retina and neural circuitry in the LGN. None of us is aware that our bodies and brains are creating color categories, yet they are. One's intuitions on the matter are irrelevant. You simply do not have conscious access to the mental processes involved in color vision and color categorization. Or take one of the most basic results in phonology: Speakers of English aspirate initial consonants, without exercising conscious control or having any awareness that they are doing it. It can be shown in sound spectrographs, or if one prefers a low-tech demonstration, by lighted matches. Phonological rules operate well below the level of consciousness, and are not accessible to consciousness, and yet are real. We simply do not have conscious awareness of the real cognitive principles governing how we pronounce words. You can say all you want that the "p" in "pot" and the "p" in "spot" are the same sound, but if you're a normal speaker of English, they aren't.

The same is true in the case of metaphor. We normally do not have conscious access to metaphorical processes, but we know that they are real. We know from all the standard sources of evidence:

Generalizations over polysemy
Generalizations over inference patterns.
Generalizations over extensions to novel cases.
Historical semantic change. (Sweetser, 1990)
Psychological experiments. (Gibbs)
Gesture research. (McNeill)

In short, no matter how much Robert Half may say that it is literally true that his employees are stealing time from him—and that this is form of literal stealing—it is still the case that his belief is a metaphorical belief. The reason is this: metaphoricity has to do with the way the mind operates, not with how you think is operates. If there is a mapping across different conceptual domains, then metaphor is at work. Time and stealing are in distinct domains. Of course there is knowledge that involves both domains at once: People commonly get paid in proportion to the time they work. That knowledge links two domains that are distinct in our experience. As long as they are distinct and one is conceptualized in terms of the other, there is a conceptual metaphor at work.

One reason why people resist the idea that beliefs are metaphorical is that metaphor, on the traditional analysis, has gotten a bad rap. It is commonly assumed that metaphors cannot be true, and hence that one's metaphorical beliefs cannot be true. If that were the case, no one (especially a philosopher!) would want to be caught having metaphorical beliefs.

But as we saw above, metaphorical beliefs are extremely common and are often true. As I pointed out, it can be true that I am wasting an hour of your time right now. Just as it can be true that time passes rapidly and that I have a marriage with a solid foundation.

The problem lies not with conceptual metaphor or metaphorical beliefs, but with the concept of truth. As Johnson and I observed (1980), the fact that metaphorical beliefs can be true requires bringing cognition into the notion of truth. What was previously left out was that, whenever we take an expression or idea as being true of the world, we can only take it as being true of the world as we conceptualize it. If we conceptualize the world via conceptual metaphor, then we can have metaphorical beliefs about the world. And if our beliefs fit world as we conceptualize it, we will take them as being true beliefs.

Thus, if we conceptualize time as a money-like resource, and if, according to the metaphor, you are the judge as to the efficient use of that resource, then it can be true that I am wasting your time right now.

The point is that every judgment of truth about the world can only be about the world-as-conceptualized, not the world-in-itself. And we so commonly use metaphorical concepts to conceptualize the world that it is anything but rare to have metaphorical beliefs that you judge to be true.

Metaphorical beliefs are at least as common in the academic world as they are in everyday life. We saw above that THE MIND IS A COMPUTER is a common metaphor for mind, and that it is motivate by other common conventional metaphors: THOUGHT IS OBJECT MANIPULATION, THOUGHT IS CALCULATION, THOUGHT IS LANGUAGE, and THE MIND IS A MACHINE. The metaphor that THOUGHT IS COMPUTATION is taken very seriously, and is widely believed. Indeed, in certain circles in artificial intelligence and cognitive science, it is taken as an obvious truth.

It is worth going over just what makes THOUGHT IS COMPUTATION a metaphor rather than just a literal belief. Thought is a domain of human experience. We experience it as something not very clearly structured. Computation, in the technical sense, is a very different domain. There is a precise mathematical theory of it, and the computer industry has led to enormous development of the details of computation. The THOUGH IS COMPUTATION metaphor allows one to conceptualize the abstract and not very clearly structured domain of thought in terms of the very precise and well studied domain of computation.

Philosophy also has its metaphors, as Mark Johnson has been pointing out. There is a common metaphor in philosophy of language, namely, that A LANGUAGE IS A SYSTEM OF FORMAL LOGIC. This is the basis for philosophical views as divergent as those of Richard Montague and W.V.O. Quine. A related metaphor occurs in generative linguistics, namely, A LANGUAGE IS A FORMAL SYMBOL SYSTEM. These too are widely believed metaphors, and it is important to be aware of just why they are metaphors. Language is something we all experience, but our experience of it is abstract and amorphous. Systems of formal logic, and more generally, formal symbol systems, are mathematical objects that can be precisely characterized and that have been studied extensively. Language is experienced by just about every human being, while systems of formal logic and formal symbol systems are mathematical constructions that very few people ever have experience with. They are very different domains. These metaphors take language, the universally, but amorphously experienced domain and conceptualize it in terms of certain mathematically precise domains. Again, one domain is being conceptualized in terms of another, quite different domain.

The THOUGHT IS COMPUTATION metaphor is not only taken as literal and self-evidently true within much of artificial intelligence; it is also taken by many people as defining the field. When this happens, its metaphorical character is overlooked. Similarly, A LANGUAGE IS A FORMAL SYMBOL SYSTEM is the metaphor that defines the field of generative linguistics, and is taken in that discipline as an obvious truth. And A LANGUAGE IS A SYSTEM OF FORMAL LOGIC is taken by many practitioners to be definitional of the field of Philosophy of Language. Those practitioners do not see it as a metaphor, and take it as an obvious truth.

In my Generative Semantics days, back in 1963-75, I believed both of these metaphors for language. I put them together by claiming that the underlying structure of language was a system of formal logic. I have since recognized that discoveries in cognitive science are very much at odds with these metaphors. Discoveries like basic-level categories, prototypes, image-schemas, and conceptual metaphors are at odds with these views. For example, the phenomenon of conceptual metaphor is as odds with the metaphor that A LANGUAGE IS A SYSTEM OF FORMAL LOGIC. Since formal logic does not permit metaphor within it, the fact that metaphor is pervasive in language shows that logic is grossly inadequate as the basis for a discipline that claims to study language seriously. In other words, the very phenomenon of conceptual metaphor is inconsistent with one of the most dominant conceptual metaphors in Philosophy of Language.

Conclusion

Philosophical theories are themselves inescapably metaphorical. When we believe a philosophical theory, we believe the metaphors that comprise it. There is nothing strange about this, since metaphor is a major mechanism in all theorizing. If we are to understand the conceptual structure of our theories, we must understand the metaphors that comprise them.

The Second Generation of Cognitive Science has changed forever the nature of philosophical inquiry. Philosophy must accommodate itself to the new empirical results about the mind—to conceptual metaphor, prototypes, image schemas and all the rest. Philosophy must be consistent with what has been discovered about the mind if it is to continue to address the deepest and most important questions of human existence.

References

Lakoff, G. (1987). *Women, Fire, and Dangerous Things*. Chicago: University of Chicago Press.
Lakoff, G. and Johnson, M. (1980) *Metaphors We Live By*. Chicago: University of Chicago Press.
Lakoff, G. and Turner, M. (1989) *More Than Cool Reason: A Field Guide to Poetic Metaphor*. Chicago: University of Chicago Press.
Sweetser, E. (1990) *From Etymology to Pragmatics*. Cambridge: Cambridge University Press.
Turner, M. (1987) *Death is the Mother of Beauty*. Chicago: University of Chicago Press.

FORMAL SEMANTICS, GEOMETRY, AND MIND

J. E. FENSTAD
Institute of Mathematics
University of Oslo
Norway

Standard theory of grammar postulates the existence of two modules, one being a conceptual module which includes what is often referred to as knowledge of the world, one being a computational module which is concerned with the constraints on our actual organization of discrete units, such as morphemes and words, into phrases. Much of current theory is a theory of the syntax/semantics interface, i.e. a theory of how to connect grammatical space (the computational module) with semantical space (the conceptual module). In addition there has always been much work on the structure of grammatical space. However, remarkably little work has been devoted to the structure of semantical space. Even the Montague grammarians rarely make any use of the structure of their models; it is almost always possible to stay at the level of lambda-terms.

Let me proceed to fill in a few details in this account. A major part of current linguistic theory has been focused on the investigation of grammatical space. There is no need to review this work here; I assume that the reader is familiar with current representational forms, either as tree-like structures or as attribute-value structures. There is a continuing discussion of how many subunits one needs to recognize within the combinatorial component—of phonological, morphological and/or syntactical nature—and how to determine their exact interdependence; this is not our concern in the present discussion. As to the nature of the conceptual component I shall at this point only make one preliminary assumption, that it has—at some level—a standard model-theoretical core. This claim is not uncontroversial; it is one of the aims of this paper to argue that model theory—correctly understood—is a necessary link between grammar and mind.

It remains to add a few comments on current theories of the syntax-semantics interface. There exists a large and sometimes bewildering number of proposals. In the framework proposed by Chomsky in *Aspects of the Theory of Syntax* (see Chomsky 1965) the connecting sign between grammatical deep structure and semantical representation was basically an arrow decorated with a name (a so-called projection rule)—but with no particular content. In R. Montague's theory as presented e.g. in his *Proper Treatment of Quantifiers in English* (see Montague 1974), the connecting sign was a logical formula in a system of higher order intensional logic. The connecting sign may also take the shape of an attribute-value structure. *Lexical-functional grammar* (LFG) is an important example of such a theory (see R. Kaplan and J. Bresnan, 1982).

X. Arrazola et al. (eds.), Discourse, Interaction and Communication, 85–103.

This format was extended to also include semantical attributes in the work on situation schemata; see the exposition in *Situation, Language and Logic*, Fenstad et al 1986.

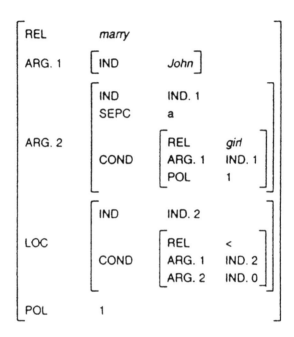

Figure 1

The situation schema is a representational from computable form linguistic structure; in this case from the sentence *John married a girl*. One key point of the analysis is to rewrite a noun phrase as a generalized quantifier; see the ARG.2 attribute. We also see how the tense marker PAST of traditional LFG analysis is rewritten as a space-time attribute LOC; this is of crucial importance in the analysis of locative prepositional phrases (see Colban, 1986).

A further example of the use of an attribute-value structure as a connecting sign is the theory of *Head Driven Phrase Structure Grammar* developed by C. Pollard and I. Sag (see Pollard and Sag, 1987). H. Kamp's theory of *Discourse Representation Structures* (see the recent exposition in Kamp and Reyle, 1993) gives another example of a connecting sign bearing some similarities to attribute-value theories. Within AI research we have seen a variety of proposals in the form of trees, frames, scripts, etc. We need not enter into further details concerning the syntax of the connecting sign since our standing assumption is that at some level there is a model-theoretic core; the structure of this core is our concern.

Every theory of language has as its ultimate goal an account of the link between linguistic structure and meaning. Some theories, e.g. Chomsky's model in *Aspects*, are biased toward the combinatorial component; others, such as the HPSG account, are more balanced between the combinatorial and conceptual modules. From our point of view Montague's theory is primarily a theory of "the connecting sign"; his grammar is simple and he makes remarkable little use of the structure of his semantical component; the discussion can in almost all cases be carried out at the level of lambda-terms. The model theory is in an indirect sense necessary; it allowed him to draw several relevant linguistic distinctions, e.g. between a *de re* and a *de dicto* reading of noun phrases.

Cognitive grammar is an interesting exception. Here we see—against Chomsky— that the center of theoretical gravity has moved towards the conceptual end of the theoretical spectrum. The theory has been extensively developed by R. W. Langacker (see his two volumes *Foundation of Cognitive Grammar*, 1987 and 1991). In its original form the theory still recognizes two modules, one phonological and one semantical. In addition there is also a connecting symbolic structure, which is closely related in form to an attribute-value matrix. But in more extreme versions of the theory we see that the phonological component is subsumed under the semantic one; " ... phonological space should instead be regarded as a subregion of semantic space (Langacker, 1987, p 78)".

We may have some sympathy with the cognitive grammarian's revolt against the combinatorial dominance within current theoretical linguistics. But at the same time we are surprised to see the rather primitive formal apparatus used by Langacker. There seem at first to be few connections between the hand-drawn representations in *Foundation of Cognitive Grammar* and other parts of cognitive science. We shall return to this issue in our discussion of conceptual spaces. Our first and preparatory task, however, will be a critical review of standard logical semantics and its ontology. This is necessary—even urgent—since we have already proposed that model theory is the "core" of any theory of natural language understanding.

1. Formal semantics and its ontology

First order logic—seen from a proof-theoretic perspective—is a system of remarkable strength. It has a complete proof procedure, i.e. every universally valid formula is provable. And all of mathematics, dressed in its set theoretic garb, is formalizable within the system. Yet this strength is illusory; we shall explain why.

Logic, as well as language in general, has two sides; one is syntax and proofs, the other is semantic and validity. In first order logic we seem to have a perfect balance between the two. On the syntactical side we have notions such as proof and theorem, on the semantical side we have the notions of model and validity. These notions are in the general theory of first order logic perfectly matched through the celebrated Gödel completeness theorem: a formula is provable, i.e. is a theorem of first order logic, if and only if it is universally valid, i.e. true in all models. Gödel's theorem is primarily a technical result, but also is an insight with broader explanatory power.

In a sufficient wide sense, logic is a natural science: We have a preformal idea of truth and, hence, of a correct argument. Logic converts this preformal idea into two distinct technical notions, the syntactical notion of proof and the semantical notion of validity in a model. Informally we may convince ourselves that what is provable is necessarily true in the preformal sense, and what is true in the preformal sense is, in particular, true in all models. Thus the preformal notion of truth is caught between the two technical notions of proof and validity. Gödel's completeness theorem, which asserts that validity in all models implies provability, closes the circle and seems to show that the preformal notion of truth has a correct and adequate analysis in terms of the technical notions of proof and validity in all models. This is an exemplary piece of applied science; a natural phenomenon has been given a sound and comprehensive theoretical analysis. We can even go one step further. The notion of proof, being a finite combinatorial structure, is algorithmic. The notion of being provable is not: a formula is provable if and only if it has a proof—but we cannot effectively decide in general if a proof exists or not. However, fragments of logic have effective proof procedures; it is a valid scientific strategy to explore the limits of effective computability and to combine the search for algorithms with various heuristic and probabilistic recipes. From this perspective reasoning and understanding seems to be reduced to the search for ever more sophisticated proof procedures. But, despite the successes, the strength is illusory.

The reason is ontological. The true ontology of first order logic is an ontology of lists; we explain why: A model for first order logic is a set-theoretic structure consisting of a non-empty set, the domain A, and a collection of relations, R_1, R_2, ... , defined on the domain A. We use the word set-theoretic to emphasize that an n-ary relation at this level of explanation is nothing more than a set of n-tuples over the domain. An n-ary relation R on A can be represented in the form of two lists. One a list of basic or atomic positive facts, i.e. a list of all

(i). $Ra_1 ... a_n$

such that $(a_1, ..., a_n)$ belongs to the relation R; and a supplementary list of basic or atomic negative facts,

(ii). $not\text{-}Rb_1 ...b_n$

for $(Rb_1 ...b_n)$ not belonging to the relation R. The lists, which may be infinite if the domain A is infinite, are complete, i.e. any n-tuple over A defines an item in either list (i) or (ii). The important thing to recognize is that the model structure is "flat". All objects of A have the same ontological status, there are no structurally defined hierarchies. Of course, a relation R may in a specific structure impose a hierarchy on its domain. But to prove deductive completeness theorems we must necessarily speak of all models. This means, e.g. in applications to set theory, that the semantical interpretation is a coding of a possibly rich structure into a flat domain. This may be adequate for book-keeping purposes, even for linguistic engineering applications, but not for understanding, in particular, for natural language understanding.

This limitation of first order logic has always been recognized, and several extensions have been studied. We mention briefly:

higher types and partiality,

possible worlds and situations,
order/time/events and episodic logic,
masses and plurals.

The literature on extensions of first order logic is vast; we can only mention a few references of special relevance for our current purposes. Partiality and higher types is reviewed in Fenstad, 1996. Situation theory, partiality and the relational theory of meaning is the topic of Barwise and Perry, 1983. The theory of mass nouns and plurals have been studied by G. Link and J. T. Lönning; for general references see Lönning, 1987 and 1989.

The extensions are, however, "tame"; all of them rest on the ontology of lists. A partial model corresponds to partial lists, which means that if the relation R in a structure A is partial, then there are n-tuples over A which occur neither in (i) nor in (ii) above. In a similar way structures of higher types correspond to lists of lists, and possible world structures correspond to collections of indexed lists. A small extension occurs with order and time. In these cases the domain A has a fixed order relation, but since theories of linear, partial, and other types of order are algebraic and easy axiomatized, we remain with the same ontology. We should be careful to note that this ontology is adequate and productive for many technological applications. We have recently seen a fruitful merging of ideas from data base theory and logic. This is not the place to review current advances in relational and deductive data base theory and to see how data base theory is becoming more and more intertwined with finite model theory. We shall, however, indicate the connection by presenting a simple example of a Q-A (i.e. question-answer) system.

The system has the following architecture (Vestre 1987; see also the exposition in Fenstad, Langholm and Vestre, 1992):

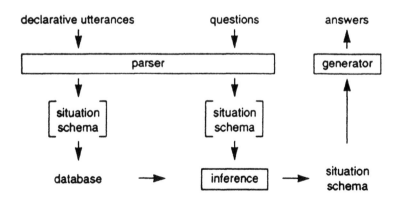

Figure 2

The system stores factual information is a data base. This data base can be updated by accepting input sentences within a natural language fragment. The parser rewrites such sentences in the format of a situation schemata, which is a particular kind of an attribute-value structures (Fenstad et al, 1986). The system automatically extracts from the attribute-value structures basic fact- positive or negative—and stores these facts in the data base. A question is rewritten   as an incomplete situation schemata. The inference module accepts these incomplete structures and tries deductively to transform the incomplete sign into a complete attribute-value structure, using information from the data base as admissible hypotheses for the proof. Finally, the generator transforms the completed sign into a grammatically correct answer. The architecture of the system is open. The system can be extended to accept a larger class of sentences and questions by extending the syntactical component. The domain of application can be extended by reading into the system more information. The system can also be made more efficient by further development of the inference subpart. Seen in this perspective the system is successful as an example of language engineering. But there are limitations.

A sufficiently precise question will receive a correct and exhaustive answer. But if the question is more open and searching, it may signal that we are interested in answers which are "relevant" and "informative" rather than just "correct" in a strict logical sense. This may be the case when a question is part of a larger dialogue situation. An adequate analysis of dialogues is, however, not a matter of grammar alone. If this point is granted, we immediately see the limitations of the system, viz. the conceptual module, i.e. meaning and understanding, is reduced to a data base which is nothing more than a list of basic facts. The equation "model = data base" has useful technological applications, but it cannot serve as a basis for an analysis of the flow of meaning in a natural language dialogue.

To analyse the situation in some more details we need to review a few facts from cognitive development theory. This is a domain of many theories, often at odds with each other. What we need will only to a small degree be touched by these controversies. With some justification we shall therefore concentrate on only one account—the story as told in M. Donald, *Origin of the Modern Mind* (Donald, 1991 and 1993).

According to Donald we can recognize four stages in the evolution of culture and cognition: *episodic culture, mimetic culture, mythic culture, and theoretical culture*. The episodic culture was characterized by the ability to react to a fixed situation in which the individual was placed. In a certain sense one "understood" the significance of this situation and could react accordingly. But this insight could not be used to understand when placed in other analogous situations. The transition to mimetic culture extended the limited mode of understanding found in episodic culture. The individual was now able to decompose the meaning of a specific situation into components and to recombine these in order to develop effective patterns of reaction in other, but similar situations. A rudimentary communication system between the members of a tribe also developed. According to Donald this was pre-linguistics and exclusively composed of gestures and other mimetic elements. The transition from mimetic to mythic culture was above all characterized by the acquisition of language. We now see an emerging communication system—a possibility for dialogue—which is a combination of gestures and speech. Donald is very careful to ground his theories in anthropological data on anatomical and cultural development. He stresses, in particular, how the development is cumulative, e.g. in a dialogue we have both mimesis and speech, the latter stage has not suppressed the former—a dialogue is not reducible to a text.

In the third transition, from mythic to theoretical culture, there are no anatomical changes. We see a transition to a stage where we have access to external symbolic storage. The development of written language was an early stage in this transition; present day information technology represents another. For the philosophically informed it may be instructive to compare Donald's analysis of the third transition to Popper's theory of the so-called World III (see Popper 1972); another and compatible story is the anthropological analysis of the concept of culture (see White 1947). There are many comments that one could want to make; I shall only emphasize one crucial new element occurring at stage four, viz. the possibility of an external memory without an anatomical foundation, or—expressed in a more colorful language—the possibility of a "collective mind" independent of the individual brains of the species. This explains why certain applications of linguistics to engineering are successful and why other fails.

A limited Q-A system can be completely located within the fourth cultural stage, i.e. theoretical culture with the possibility of external symbolic storage. None of the previous stages need to be involved; semantical space is therefore reducible to lists and data bases, as was the case in the system described above. But a real-life dialogue lives at the intersections of many cultures, in particular, the mimetic and mythic. The dialogue is a combination of gestures and speech and is therefore not reducible to an external text. The dialogue is seen to pose other and more intractable challenges to the conceptual module; the successful analysis of dialogues, beyond a few stereotypes, is not a matter of incremental extensions of current linguistic technology. On the other hand, limited translation systems do belong to the fourth stage, which means that an ontology for translation is an ontology of external objects, and hence reducible to an ontology of lists and lexicons; for an interesting example of a limited and interactive translation system see the PONS system developed by Dyvik 1993.

The situation will be radically changed if we want to build a system for combined speech and vision. As a starting point we may be looking for something very simple— e.g. a system which shall recognize objects simply by name. To simplify even further the domain of application may be severely restricted, but we shall insist on a system which will model the task in the "correct" human way. This is challenge almost totally within episodic culture, with a modest component of mythic culture, but with no component from mimetic culture. The task is, however, far from trivial—and not yet convincingly solved. The difficulty lies with the conceptual module. Meaning can no longer be reduced to a list or a data base; to succeed we need geometry.

Remark

Current philosophy of language distinguishes three aspects of language, syntax, semantics, and pragmatics which is also the current dogma of applied and computational linguistics (with the necessary addition of a phonological module to deal with speech). This is harmless for simple applications, such as ticket reservation systems, which operate entirely within the phonological-syntactical-semantic range. In more complicated applications, such as dialogue systems, current approaches foresee added pragmatic features—however, in an incremental way. We have suggested a different perspective based on a four-stage evolution of culture and cognition, where the stages are cumulative. Granted the correctness of this evolutionary history we would explain the success of limited systems, such as the PONS translation system, by the fact that such systems live almost totally within the fourth theoretical stage. In this perspective, "pragmatics" is not an addition to the syntax-semantics division in order to deal with a number of "rest factors", but a label which masks a number of radically different phenomena. There is a need for a new analysis of "pragmatics" within the broader context of a theory of cognitive development.

2. Model Theory and Geometry

In a historical perspective logic and geometry were partners from the beginning, the paradigm being the Euclidean axiomatization of geometry. But today logic and model theory seem to be in a much closer partnership to algebra and arithmetic. The reason for this has both historical and systematical explanations. From Descartes we saw a coordinatization of geometry; in the late nineteenth century we saw an arithmetization of analysis; Hilbert wanted to prove the consistency of geometry through a reduction to number theory; and Dedekind and Peano gave penetrating logical analyses of the systems of natural and real numbers. At the same time we saw the formalization of logic through the work of Frege, Russell and Whitehead. This line of development culminated in the first order formalization of set theory by Skolem around 1920. Thus everything conspired to give first order logic its prominence.

A model for first order logic is in essence an algebraic structure; and a fruitful partnership between algebra, arithmetic and logic has been established, starting from the Gödel completeness theorem. Natural axiomatizations of geometry and topology would seem to use higher order logic. Since such systems lack the compactness property with respect to the class of intended models, time was not ripe for further collaboration between logic and geometry. There was, however, some activity in the first order model theory of elementary geometry, see Tarski 1959. And a first start on a topological model theory was made by Flum and Ziegler 1980. But geometry was basically missing from model theory.

Interestingly, the link between logic and geometry survived in other fields of study. One example is measurement theory. From the 1950s on there developed links between logic and foundational studies in measurement theory. The starting point was quite algebraic in spirit, scales being seen as systems with an ordering relation. But with multi-dimensional scales the geometric content necessarily becomes more prominent. Studies of perception and measurement led to the notion of a perceptual space, where the prime example is the theory of color space; for an account of these developments, see Suppes et al 1989.

The need for a richer structure on the conceptual component was convincingly argued in the work on mental models by P. J. Johnson-Laird 1983. He was able to show how a simple geometrical representation of knowledge combined with the use of symmetry and invariance properties gave better (i.e. psychologically more plausible) models of reasoning than the standard deductions of formal logic. This insight was carried further by J. Barwise and J. Etchemendy in a paper from 1991, *Visual Information and Valid Reasoning*. In this paper we see a first presentation of the "hyperproof" program which is a system for combined visual and logical reasoning. This has sparked a rich development of systems for heterogeneous reasoning; for further references see the contribution by Barwise in this book. We should also within the same circle of ideas mention the work of Habel on representation of spatial knowledge; see Habel 1990. He also argued for a dual coding for the processing of the spatial expressions, with both a propositional and a depictorial representation. This is closely linked to the theory of mental models and ideas concerning heterogeneous reasoning. In all approaches the inspection of "mental models" combined with rule-based deductions are seen as essential ingredients in spatial reasoning.

We remarked above that even within Montague grammar, where the model theory seems to be given a prominent role, one almost never sees in an actual analysis any geometrical structure. Most of the work can be carried out at the level of lambda-terms. But linguistic analysis sometimes forces one to pay attention to geometry; this was a point which I argued in an early paper on Montague grammar; see Fenstad 1979. We shall mention some examples. Our first example concerns the meaning of reciprocals; the geometry of "each other" is quite different in the two examples:

> The men were hitting each other.
> Five Boston pitchers sat alongside each other.

An interesting classification of the geometry of reciprocals, using the apparatus of generalized quantifiers, has been carried through by S. Peters and co-workers; see Dalrymple et al 1994.

Locative prepositional phrases present another example where geometry is necessary for the semantical analysis; see E. Colban 1986. We cannot enter into the details of his theory but restrict attention to one simple example. In this case the prepositional phrase has an adjunct reading:

> Peter ran to the school.

The semantical analysis proposed by Colban of this sentence makes a reference to a path or trajectory in space-time ending at the school, such that Peter is in the state of running on the curve. Colban's study presents a full fragment, connecting syntax and semantics through an implemented system.

Much of the work that we have reported on in this section can be conveniently brought under the notion of a *conceptual space* introduced by P. Gärdenfors in a number of recent papers; see Gärdenfors 1991, 1993 and 1994. We conclude this section with a review of this work, showing in particular its connection to theories of natural kinds, to prototype theory (see Rosch 1978) and cognitive grammar (see Langacker 1987 and

1991, Lakoff 1987). A crucial geometrical notion in this work is the concept of convexity; we shall explain why.

A conceptual space S is given by a number of qualitative dimensions, D_1, ..., D_n; a point in S is a vector $v = (v_1, ..., v_n)$, where each v_i is an element of D_i. Perceptual spaces in the sense of measurement theory (see Suppes et al 1989) are typical examples of conceptual spaces. As a cognitive construct color space has three dimensions, hue, saturation and brightness, where hue is represented by a circle, saturation and brightness are linear.

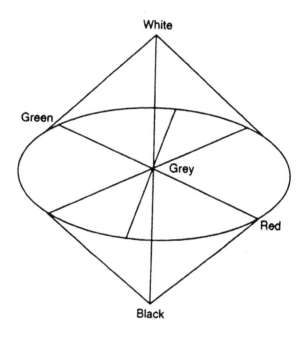

Figure 3

The dimensions determining a given conceptual space may either be inborn or culturally acquired. However this may be, the crucial fact is that each dimension comes equipped with a geometrical or, more generally, topological structure. In color space we have a metric structure defined by measuring length along the appropriate curve (a circle or a straight line). But conceptual spaces can be more abstract than perceptual spaces, one example is the two-dimensional conceptual space generated by the first two formants of vowels frequencies, see Gärdenfors 1991.

P. Gärdenfors has applied the notion of a conceptual space to an analysis of "natural kinds". In traditional model theory a property is interpreted as a subset of the domain. In the theory of conceptual spaces we have access to geometrical notions. A natural property is constructed as a convex subset of the model space. This is obviously the correct way in the case of colors; take any two points in the red sector of the color circle, then any point between is also red, i.e. red as a property is a convex subset of color space. More remarkably, the construction fits the facts in the conceptual space used for the phonetical identification of vowels. How far this assumption is valid, remains to be seen; we shall return to the point in our discussion of geometry and mind.

Here we point out one pleasing application, viz. a valid principle of induction for conceptual spaces: Let P be a natural property in the conceptual space S and let a_1, ... , a_n be points of S belonging to P. Then the convex hull of a_1, ... , a_n, i.e. the least convex subset of S containing all points a_1, ... a_n, is a subset of P; see the discussion in Gärdenfors 1994.

The proposal has also applications to theories of prototypes; see Rosch 1978. In traditional logic properties has been identified with subsets of the domain of interpretation. Granted no further structure there has been no end to the philosophical discussion of what are the "natural" properties and how do we determine when two objects share the same property—when is a tiger a tiger, what exactly are the necessary and sufficient conditions for a chair to be a chair ? Prototype theory has developed as an alternative to the logical approach which was based on lists of necessary and sufficient conditions. Natural properties form convex sets in a suitable conceptual space, certain exemplars are more central or typical as examples of the property, i.e. they may serve as prototypes, and the extent of the concept is a convex neighborhood of the accepted prototypes; see Rosch 1978, Mervis and Rosch 1981, Lakoff 1987 and Gärdenfors 1993. Conversely, if we are given a set of categories and have decided on a set of prototypes p_1, ... p_n for them, then the prototypes determine the categories as a convex partition of the space:

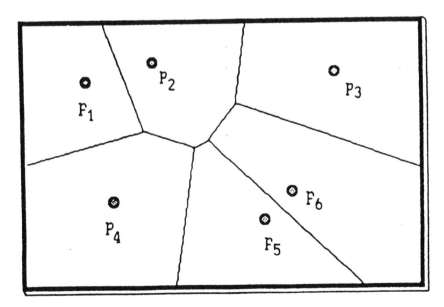

Figure 4

This partition procedure is an example of a Voronoi tessellation; for a comprehensive review of this technique see Okabe et al 1992. We shall continue this discussion in the next section, translating the discussion into the language of dynamic processes. Here it remains to add a few comments on cognitive grammar.

We expressed in the introduction to this paper some sympathy for the revolt of the cognitive grammarians. But we also noted with some surprise the rather primitive apparatus used by Langacker 1987 in his exposition of the basic ideas. P. Gärdenfors has in *Conceptual Spaces as a basis for Cognitive Semantic* (see Gärdenfors 1993) shown how model theory with a geometric extension may serve as a basis for cognitive grammar. He agrees that meaning is conceptualization in a cognitive model, not truth conditions in possible worlds. He notes that cognitive models are mainly perceptually determined and that semantical elements are based on spatial or topological objects. He argues in agreement with the cognitive grammarians that semantics is primary to syntax and that concepts show prototypical effects. All of this leads to the conclusion that conceptual spaces define a "correct" framework for cognitive grammar. We agree—but only up to a point. At this juncture we will only recall that "cognitive space" is the end result of a complex development. This means that conceptual space and linguistic engineering need not live in the same region of cognitive space. However, in order to draw the correct distinctions we need to proceed from grammar and geometry to mind.

3. Geometry and Mind

We have so far made a journey from grammar via semantics to geometric structure. In this part we will start out with some remarks on brain dynamics and explain how the associated processes lead to certain geometric structure spaces. The main suggestion of this lecture is the proposal to identify the geometric structure space derived from brain dynamics with the geometric model theory discussed in the last section, the link being the identification of the notion of a "natural property" seen as a convex region of logical model space with the property of being a domain of attraction of an attractor of the brain dynamics; we shall briefly discuss both color space and prototype theory from this point of view to highlight the connection. A theory of mind would then be founded on the theory of this class of geometric structure spaces, and granted the identifications mentioned above, we would have a seamless connection from grammar via geometry to mind. Such are the ambitions; we shall see how far they are able to withstand the complexities of the real world.

The affirmative side of the story is presented in a recent review article by J.-P. Changeux and S. Dehaene, *Neuronal Models of Cognitive Functions* (Changeux and Dehaene 1989). They give a survey of current work at the interface between cognitive science and neuroscience, hoping to build bridges rather than enlarge on differences. "The real issue becomes the specification of the relationship between a given cognitive function and a given physical organization of the human brain. From an experimental point of view, our working hypothesis (rather than philosophical commitment) is that levels of organization exist within the brain at which a type-to-type physical identity might be demonstrated with cognitive processes (op. cit)". In their article they review, in particular, work done on short-term and long-term memory and the recognition, production and storage of time sequences. They deliberately pass by a discussion of complex cognitive functions such as problem solving and language processing, since at this stage of development of the theory the neurobiological basis is too complex and the relevant data too few for fruitful mathematical modeling activity. But this is almost a temporary restriction; their final conclusion is that "it is timely to approach cognition in a synthetic manner with the aim to relate a given cognitive function to its corresponding neural organization and activity state (op. cit)". We shall have more to say about the strong assumption of one-to-one correspondence between cognition and anatomy as claimed by Changeux and Dehaene. But first we shall briefly recall another, but related approach to cognitive modeling.

Our next example is the theory of *attractor neural networks* developed by D. J. Amit; see his book *Modeling Brain Function* (Amit 1989). An attractor neural network consists of a finite set N of nodes or neurons, a_1, ..., a_N, each of which can in the simplest case be in one of two possible states, $s_i = 0$ or $s_i = 1$. Each pair (a_i, a_j) of neurons is connected through a function J_{ij} which measures the influence or the synaptic efficacy which the node a_i may have on the node a_j. We assume that the process is a discrete time process; its dynamics will be given by the two equations:

(i) $s_i(t + 1) = ch(h_i(t + 1) - T_i)$

(ii) $h_i(t + 1) = J_{i1}s_1(t) + ... + J_{iN}s_N(t)$

The system operates as follows: At time t the system is in stage $s = (s_1, ... s_N)$. At each node there is defined a local field h_i. This local field is at stage $t + 1$ determined by the current stage s and the channel weight functions J_{ij} according to equation (ii). The function T_i represents a threshold level at node a_i. If the field h_i at a_i at time $t + 1$ is greater than T_i then neuron a_i fires, i.e. the value of $s_i(t + 1)$ is set to 1; if h_i is less than T_i, then neuron a_i is inactive, i.e. the value of $s_i(t + 1)$ is set to 0. The function ch formalizes this description, i.e. ch(n) is 1 or 0, depending upon whether n is positive or negative; this is the content of equation (i).

The dynamic behavior of such systems can be quite complicated; we recommend Amit's book as an excellent guide to the field. The analogy to spin-glass theory in non-linear statistical mechanics is striking. Assuming full connectivity, i.e. J_{ij} is defined for each pair i, j, and symmetry, i.e. the validity of the set of equations $J_{ij} = J_{ji}$, the full force of mean field theory comes into play and it is possible to analyze the dynamics of an attractor neural network in great details, in particular, to give a rather full description of the set of attractors of the system. From a neurobiological point of view, the assumption of full connectivity and symmetry is suspicious, if not outright false. But as Amit argues, they form a convenient starting point; through some further "robustness studies" it is also possible to see how the assumptions may be relaxed in order to obtain models more faithful to neurobiological fact.

For the moment let us play with the simplified version of an attractor neural network. It is easy to see how a system defined by the equations in (i) and (ii) can be made memorize certain patterns: In fact, let p^1, ..., p^K be K prescribed patterns, i.e. each p^k is an N-tuple of 0's and 1's, $p^k = (p_1^k , ... p_N^k)$. Define the synaptic connectivity by the equations:

(iii) $J_{ij} = (p_i^1 \, p_j^1 + ... + p_i^K \, p_j^K) / N$

Then a simple argument shows that the patterns p^1, ..., p^K are the fixed point attractors of the dynamics defined by the set of equations (i), (ii), and (iii). With all our simplifying assumptions the system also has an energy function defining a suitable geometric phase space of the system. The configurations p^k, being the attractors of the system, determines both the local minimum locations on the energy surface, as well as their domain of attraction. It is tempting to see such geometric space as the proper starting point for a phenomenological theory of mind.

In the previous section we saw how the notion of a color space could be reconstructed as a conceptual space. Colors correspond to convex regions in the space; let us for the moment think of hues only, i.e. focus on the color circle. According to E. Rosch colors have prototypical properties, thus the geometry of color space is determined by a Voronoi tessellation based on a finite set of prototypical exemplars. In a similar way color prototypes can be interpreted as a fixed set of patterns to be stored by a suitable attractor neural network. In this case the prototypes are the attractors of the system and the concept of color corresponds to a domain of attraction in the energy surface of the system; for a related discussion of prototypes and neural networks see J. A. Anderson 1995. This would give a reasonable dynamics for color perception. The correspondence between convex geometry and the dynamics of attractors is quite close; granted sufficient regularity assumptions the claim is that the two accounts tell basically the same story. In this way we see a connection between grammar and mind—the link being geometry.

Remark

The storage and retrieval of temporal sequences is a first important step beyond the "passive" networks described by equations (i) an (ii) above. D. J Amit has constructed an attractor neural network that is able (in a precise technical sense) to count chimes; see Amit 1989. Amit sees this as a tentative step into abstract computation. His suggestion should be reviewed in the context of a theory of cognitive development. Recognizing and reacting to a fixed number of chimes may be an activity of episodic mind only. But theoretical arithmetic, e.g. the recent proof of Fermat's theorem, is beyond any doubts an activity of the fourth stage of cognitive development. It is therefore a questionable exercise to attempt an account of mathematics in terms of neural networks, i.e. as an activity of an individual mind. The act of doing mathematics is rather a subtly shared activity involving several cognitive stages; see the discussion on the changed role of biological memory in Donald 1993.

Returning to our main theme we would like the picture drawn by Amit to be true, and it may, in principle, be so as an account of individual mind. But what we today know about actual cognitive processes in the brain, tells us that the simple and sometimes one-to-one connection between cognition and neuronal activities postulated by current work in neural network theory is currently far off the mark. Let me briefly point to some of the facts. On the positive side we have the wealth of results obtained through such techniques as PET scanning; see e.g. Kosslyn and Koenig 1992 and Posner and Raichle 1994. This has made possible quite detailed models of cognitive functions, models which are well grounded in anatomical facts. But they also points to the complexity of the link between cognition and anatomy. One striking example is a study of lexical access which is reported in Posner and Raichle 1994; see chapter five of their book. In this chapter they study a hierarchy which starts with the act of passively viewing displayed words, through the gradually more complex tasks of listening, speaking and generating words. Each task in this hierarchical experiment is seen to activate distinct set of brain areas. The information is precise but true understanding is complex and still far away. I shall only make two comments: PET studies do identify brain areas active in a given cognitive task, but they tell us little about the mechanism involved. Typically, Kosslyn and Koenig have in their book a chapter on computations in the brain, but little use is made of this chapter in later parts of the book—simply because the "true" computational structures are not known; for a reasonably current review see Churchland and Sejnowski 1992. My second comment is that while there certainly is a correspondence between cognitive function and neural structure and activity states, the correspondence is not necessarily one-to-one; different activity areas with different architectures may generate similar geometries.

Both reasons argue for an independent phenomenological theory of mind. This means a study of the geometry without presupposing a detailed knowledge of the underlying dynamic behavior. This is not an unusual situation in science; to mention one example we know that we in equilibrium thermodynamics are—at least in principle—able to reduce the phenomenological theory of heat to molecular motion, but that we in non-equilibrium theory are still largely ignorant of the dynamics and therefore must introduce separate equations for the phenomenological level. A beautiful example of this strategy is found in A. Turing's study of the chemical basis of morphogenesis, see Turing 1952. He assumed the existence of two active chemical substances—so-called concentrations of morphogenes in his language—which generate a non-linear dynamics governed by a pair of coupled diffusion-reaction equations. Within this model he was able to show how the geometry generated by the process could explain certain morphological phenomena, one example being the process of gastrulation. One reason for mentioning this work is that Turing's model is not only a beautiful example in itself, but that it may also teach a lesson how to model the connection between geometry and mind; for a recent exposition on pattern formation and diffusion-reaction equations see Meinhardt 1995.

This modeling task was attempted by R. Thom around 1970; see his papers *Topologie et Linguistique* (Thom 1970) and *Langage et Catastrophes: Eléments pour une Sémantique Topologique* (Thom 1973). The geometric locus for Thom is also an "energy surface" which is supposed to be derived from an underlying brain dynamics. Thom, however, does not explicate the dynamics. His discussion proceeds at a purely geometrical or phenomenological level. In the 1970 paper he classifies spatio-temporal verb phrases in terms of singularities in the energy surface, and derives a "natural classification" of such verb phrases in terms of his classification of singularities into seven classes. This should be seen in connection with the classification of "natural kinds" in terms of convex region and domains of attraction which was discussed above. In the second paper he develops a more systematic discussion. It would be beyond the scope of this paper to survey this work here. Suffice it to say that he claims, in complete agreement with our previous discussion, that a noun phrase is described by a potential well in the dynamics of mental activities and a verb phrase by an oscillator in the unfolding space of a spatial catastrophe. However, Thom's work has not had the influence on theoretical linguistics which it merits. There seems to have been an incompatibility of minds. Thom severely criticised Chomsky for his combinatorial approach as being totally inadequate as a theory of linguistic meaning. Linguists, unfamiliar with the mathematics, saw little relationship between Thom's "speculations" and their science. One early attempt to bridge the gap can be found in my paper on Montague grammar, *Models for Natural Languages* (Fenstad 1979). I argued with reference to Thom's work for a link between him and Chomsky based on a geometrization of the model theory of Montague. But I did not pursue the topic further at that time.

In conclusion I would like to discuss some current work on sentence processing which fits into the picture drawn here. This is work done by G. Kempen and T. Vosse (see Kempen and Vosse 1990). They have developed an attribute-value approach to grammar called segment grammar :

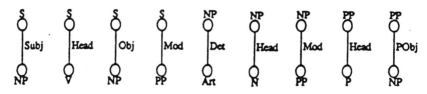

Figure 5

The grammar has two kinds of signs. One type—the so-called syntactic segments exhibited in the figure above—has a purely structural function. The other type—the lexical signs—are signs which carry linguistic meaning; see the following example taken from the same paper:

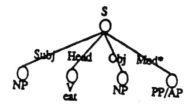

Figure 6

The authors introduce the notion of unification space, which to use their words is a kind of "test tube" filled with a mixture of syntactical and lexical signs. The structural signs are always assumed to be present in the tube; from time to time lexical signs are added and the tube well shaken. A reaction occurs and complete sentential signs are crystallized.

The pictorial language has a complete algorithmic interpretation. Signs combine through a unification procedure; see Kempen and Vosse 1990:

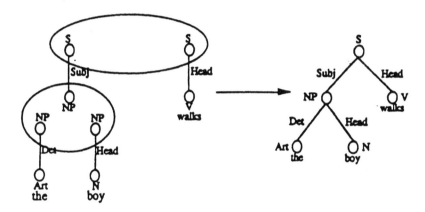

Figure 7

The dynamical behavior of the unification process is defined by a simulated annealing algorithm. Such algorithms, which have their root in statistical mechanics and material science, have become very popular in the field of combinatorial studies. In a sense they are very universal in nature, but not always efficient in execution. Since such algorithms are well known, we shall not give any details but rather suggest another possibility for the dynamics of unification spaces.

In a number of recent works W. J. Freeman and co-workers at Berkeley have developed an alternative approach to neural modeling; for a convenient survey see the papers Skarda and Freeman 1987 and 1990. Their particular concern is the olfactory system, but the aim is a general model of brain dynamics. They—of course—recognize a neuronal level of description but claim that it is not the right level for a general theory of brain dynamics. They find a philosophical alibi in the work of the French phenomenologist Merleau-Ponty and describe the dynamics as examples of non-linear and, hence, self-organizing systems; they could as well have made a reference to the work of Turing 1952. They argue for a chaotic dynamics, in particular, in order to account for the speed in the recognition of smells. In the Behavioral and Brain Sciences paper (Skarda and Freeman 1987) there is the usual critical review section. There may be critical comments, but the validity of a description at a phenomenological level cannot be denied. This was a point we also argued above. The complexity of brain mechanisms in the execution of cognitive tasks is so intricate that we are in any case forced back to a phenomenological level of description. It remains to be seen whether this is a matter of convenience or of principle—J. P Changeux and W. J. Freeman would probably differ on this point.

We have in this lecture traced a line from grammar to mind, the link being geometric model theory. Current computational linguistics concentrate to a large extent on the syntax/semantics interface. In most of this work the meaning component—the conceptual module—is reduced to a data base. This is adequate as long as we restrict attention to the final and theoretical stage of cognitive development, which is characterized by external symbolic storage, and which forms the base for current developments in language engineering. But it is not adequate as a basis for a theory of linguistic behavior in human beings. This is why we have insisted on including all stages of cognitive development in our account in order to appreciate the complexities involved. This perspective led to a geometrization of model theory as a basis for a phenomenological model of mind.

But mind could also be the starting point in our quest for understanding the connection between language and meaning. Our working hypothesis would then be that a phenomenological theory of "mind" is nothing but a branch of geometric model theory. The geometry is the basic object which introduces the lexical items, the rest— grammar, logic and mathematics—are formal tools used in the study of its structure. In particular, it seems possible to take a modified notion of unification space as a starting point for an account of language and speech, but in order to do so we need to explore a wider range of possible dynamics going beyond the simulated annealing algorithm used by Kempen and Vosse 1990. This is why we have made a reference to the work of Skarda and Freeman 1987; the reader should also consult the recent book by J. A. Scott Kelso 1995. This could lead to an account compatible with the architecture of cognitive systems as found e.g. in Kosslyn and Koenig 1992. It may also suggest different strategies for computational praxis.

References

Anderson, J.A. (1995) *An Introduction to Neural Networks*, MIT Press, Cambridge, Mass.
Amit, D.J. (1989) *Modeling Brain Function*, Cambridge University Press, Cambridge.
Barwise, J. and Etchemendy, J. (1991) Visual Information and Valid Reasoning, in W. Zimmenmann and S. Cunningham (eds.), *Visualization in Mathematics*, Math. Ass. America, Washington DC.
Barwise, J. and Perry, J. (1983) *Situations and Attitudes*, MIT Press, Cambridge, Mass.
Changeux, J.P. and Dehaene, S. (1989) Neuronal Models of Cognitive Functions,*Cognition* 33.
Chomsky, N. (1965) *Aspects of the Theory of Syntax*, MIT Press, Cambridge, Mass.
Churchland, P.C. and Sejnowski, T.J. (1992) *The Computational Brain*, MIT Press, Cambridge, Mass.
Colban, E. (1987) Prepositional Phrases in Situation Schemata, Appendix A of Fenstad et al (1987).
Dalrymple, M., Kanazawa, M., Mchombo, S., and Peters, S. (1994) What Do Reciprocals Mean?, in *Proceedings of the Fourth Semantics and Linguistics theory Conference*, Cornell University Working papers in Linguistics.
Donald, M. (1990) *Origin of the Modern Mind: Three Stages in the Evolution of Culture and Cognition*, Harvard University Press, Cambridge, Mass.
Donald, M. et al (1993) Precis and Discussion of Origin of the Modern Mind, *Behavioral and Brain Sciences* 16.

Dyvik, H. (1993) Exploiting Structural Similarities in Machine Translation, Institute of Linguistics, University of Bergen.

Fenstad, J. E. (1979) Models for Natural languages, in J. Hintikka et al (eds.), *Essays in Mathematical and Philosophical Logic*, D. Reidel Publ. Comp., Dordrecht.

Fénstad, J.E., Halvorsen, P.K., Langholm, T., and van Benthem, J. (1987) *Situations, Language and Logic*, D. Reidel Publ. Comp., Dordrecht.

Fenstad, J.E., Langholm, T., and Vestre, E. (1992) Representations and Interpretations, in M. Rosner and R. Johnson (eds.), *Computational Linguistics and Formal Semantics*, Cambridge University Press, Cambridge.

Fenstad, J.E. (1996) Partiality, in J. van Benthem and A. ter Meulen (eds.), *Handbook of Logic and Linguistics*, North-Holland, Amsterdam.

Flum, J. and Ziegler, M. (1980) *Topological Model Theory*, Springer Lecture Notes in mathematics, Springer-Verlag, Heidelberg.

Gärdenfors, P. (1991) Framework for Properties, in L. Haaparanta et al (eds.), Language, Knowledge and Intentionality, *Acta Philosophica Fennica* 49, Helsinki.

Gärdenfors, P. (1993) Conceptual Spaces as a Basis for Cognitive Semantics, Department of Philosophy, Lund University, Lund.

Gärdenfors, P. (1994) Three Levels of Inductive Inference, in D. Prawitz et al (eds.), *Logic, Methodology and Philosophy of Science IX*, North Holland, Amsterdam.

Habel, C. (1990) Propositional and Depictorial Representation of Spatial Knowledge : The Case of Path-Concepts, in R. Studer (ed.), *Natural Language and Logic*, Lecture Notes in Artificial Intelligence. Springer-Verlag, Heidelberg.

Johnson-Laird, P.J. (1983) *Mental Models*, Cambridge University Press, Cambridge.

Kamp, H. and Reyle, U. (1993) *From Discourse to Logic*, D. Reidel Publ. Comp., Dordrecht.

Kaplan, R. and Bresnan, J. (1982) Lexical-Functional Grammar, in J. Bresnan (ed.), *The Mental Representation of Grammatical Relations*, MIT Press, Cambridge, Mass.

Kempen, G. and Vosse, T. (1990) Incremental Syntactic Tree Formation in Human Sentence Processing, *Connection Sciences* 1.

Kosslyn, W. and Koenig, O. (1992) *Wet Mind*, The Free Press, New York, NY.

Lakoff, G. (1987) *Women, Fire and Dangerous Things*, Chicago University Press, Chicago, Ill.

Langacker, R.W. (1987 and 1991) *Foundation of Cognitive Grammar*, vols 1 and 2, Stanford University Press, Stanford, CA.

Lönning, J.T. (1987) Mass Terms and Quantification, *Language and Philosophy* 10.

Lönning, J.T. (1989) Some Aspects of the Logic of Plural Noun Phrases, Cosmos-Report No. 11, University of Oslo, Oslo.

Meinhardt, H. (1995) *The Algorithmic Beauty of Sea Shells*, Springer-Verlag, Heidelberg.

Mervis, C. and Rosch, E. (1981) Categorization of Natural Objects, *Annual Review of Psychology* 32.

Montague, R. (1974), *Formal Philosophy* (edited by R. Thomason), Yale University Press, New Haven, Ct.

Okabe, A., Boots, B., and Sugihara, K. (1992) *Spatial Tessellations, Concepts and Applications of Voronoi Diagrams*, J. Wiley, New York, NY.

Pollard, C. and Sag, I. (1987) *Information-Based Syntax and Semantics*, vol 1, CSLI Lecture Notes, Stanford University, Stanford, CA.

Popper, K. (1972) *Objective Knowledge*, Clarendon Press, Oxford.

Posner, M. Y. and Raichle, M.E. (1994) *Images of Mind*, Scientific American Library, New York, NY.

Rosch, E. (1978) Prototype Classification and Logical Classification, in E. Scholnik (ed.), *New Trends in Cognitive Representation: Challenges to Piaget's Theory*, Lawrence Erlbaum Ass., Hillsdale, NJ.

Scott Kelso, J.A. (1995) *Dynamic Patterns: The Self-Organization of Brain and Behavior*, MIT Press, Cambridge, Mass.

Skarda, C.A. and Freeman, W.J. (1987) How Brain Make Chaos in order to Make Sense of the World, *Behavioral and Brain Sciences* 10.

Skarda, C.A. and Freeman, W.J. (1990) Chaos and the New Science of the Mind, *Concepts in Neuroscience* 1.

Suppes, P., Krantz, D.H., Luce, R.D., and Tversky, A. (1989) *Foundations of Measurement*, vol 2, Academic Press, New York, NY.

Tarski, A. (1959) What is Elementary Geometry, in L Henkin et al (eds.), *The Axiomatic Method*, North-Holland, Amsterdam.

Thom, R. (1970) Topologie et Linguistique, in *Essays on Topology*, Springer-Verlag, Heidelberg.

Thom, R. (1973) Langage et Catastrophes: Eléments pour une Sémantique Topologique, in J. Palis (ed.), *Dynamical Systems*, Academic Press, New York, NY.

Turing, A.M. (1952) *The Chemical Basis of Morphogenesis*, Philos. Trans. R.Soc. London Ser. B., London.

Vestre, E. (1987) Representasjon av Direkte Sporsmal, Cand. Scient.Thesis, Department of mathematics, University of Oslo, Oslo.

White, L.A. (1947) The Locus of Mathematical Reality: An Anthropological Footnote. *The Philosophy of Science Journal*.

INFORMATIONAL SEMANTICS AND EPISTEMIC ARROGANCE

S. SILVERS
Clemson University
South Carolina
USA

1. Introduction

An adequate epistemology of human knowledge should explain what is assumed to be distinctive about that knowledge. The assumption that human knowledge is distinct in kind is challenged by various forms of naturalized epistemology. Tradition has it that it's the propositional character of human knowledge that distinguishes it from all other kinds. This suggests that if we can explain how the human mind entertains propositions we will have explained human cognition, rational action (behavior under the causal control of logically coherent thought patterns), and gained insight into human cognitive hegemony. A naturalistic explanation of human knowledge and cognition cannot permit itself the metaphysical luxury of Descartes' dualistic ontology. Descartes' discontinuity thesis explains the distinctiveness of human knowledge by severing it and, especially the minds that have it, from everything else. It is the urge to naturalize that creates the tension with what we identify as the human cognitive advantage, namely, rational thought.[1] One part of the argument for the propositional character of human knowledge rehearses Descartes' discontinuity thesis that distinguishes human linguistic capacity as sui generis and locates the mental outside the natural order. The other part of the argument attempts to show that while thought, *in practice*, is discontinuous with the mental capacities of the beasts, it is nevertheless explainable compatibly with the resources of natural science. This is, of course, precisely what Descartes denied.

A naturalized theory of mind would seem to eradicate the discontinuity thesis once and for all. A bonus would be that epistemology too gets naturalized in its wake. *Contra* the tradition in epistemology of keeping issues of knowledge and cognition discrete, Jerry Fodor (1994) has linked these two projects as part of a larger philosophical package that is designed to preserve Cartesian rationality within a naturalized framework for human mind and knowledge. In a concluding paragraph of his book *The Elm and the Expert* he remarks,

·*X. Arrazola et al. (eds.), Discourse, Interaction and Communication,* 105–120.
© 1998 *Kluwer Academic Publishers. Printed in the Netherlands.*

"There are, increasingly, signs of an emerging naturalist consensus that is Realist in ontology and epistemology, externalist in semantics, and computationalist in cognitive psychology. And what's especially nice about the new naturalism is how much it allows us to retain of our traditional understanding of ourselves as largely rational creatures." (p. 102)

Here I want to consider critically Fodor's proposals for how informational semantics is supposed to elucidate his version of naturalized epistemology of human knowledge while retaining our self-proclaimed human rationality. In section 1, I examine Fodor's arguments for extracting belief content, the stuff of epistemology and rational action, from externalist or informational semantics. I argue that the constraints he imposes on semantic content requires him to adopt the same sort of explanatory apparatus that he decries in his archenemy, meaning holism. In section 2, I turn to the third component of Fodor's naturalism, "computationalism in cognitive science." There my point will be to show that the syntax-driven computational model of mind and its characteristic philosophy of science is too idealized and abstract for a naturalized theory of human rationality. I moralize about the epistemic arrogance of this view in section 3. There is an appendix where I take up some concerns with meaning, denotation, and translation.

2. Informational Semantics, Intentional Psychology, and Rational Belief-fixation

Let's begin by setting out some of the terms in contention.

"Semantics, according to the informational view, is mostly about counterfactuals: what counts for the identity of my concepts is not what I do distinguish but what I could distinguish if I care to (inter alia by exploiting instrument and experts)." (Fodor, 1994, p. 37)

In contrast, meaning holism is the view that the content of beliefs that we ascribe to one another depends upon the context, in particular, the epistemological context, of the ascription and thus on countless other beliefs one is rationally supposed to have in that context. This is the radical interpretation version of meaning holism; something is a mental or intentional state just in case it bears the proper relations to other intentional states. It follows from this view that you cannot have a belief without having lots of them. As Kim (1988, page numbers from 1994) puts it,

"What is crucial is this: for the interpretation and attribution of beliefs to be possible, not only must we assume the overall rationality of cognizers, but also we must continually evaluate and re-evaluate the putative beliefs of a cognizer in their evidential relationship to one another and other propositional attitudes...the point is that belief attribution requires belief evaluation in accordance with standards of evidence and justification." (p. 229)

Here Kim joins the epistemological and transcendental issues, something which external semantics tries to keep strictly asunder. Informational semantics, being "mostly about counterfactuals," is a modal theory about what truth condition tokening here and in nearby possible worlds causally occasions by way of symbol tokening in the appropriately structured denizens of those worlds. The proximity of the possible worlds is constrained by the laws here holding there too. Very briefly, "mice" means mice because (instantiations of) mice cause, or are reliably correlated with, or are nomologically sufficient for the tokening of mice-representations. Token mice-representations refer to the mice (instantiations) that ceteris paribus cause them. Mutatis mutandis for mice pictures, etc. This is the case, moreover, because in any nearby possible world in which mice failed to cause mice tokenings, "mice" would not mean (not represent, not refer to) mice in those worlds. Mutatis mutandis for mice pictures, etc. In short, on the external semantics view, you can have a belief with the content "mice" without any other beliefs because the information you have carries that meaning. "It is, to put the point starkly, the heart of externalism that semantics isn't part of psychology. The content of your thoughts (/utterances), unlike, for example, the syntax of your thoughts (/utterances), does not supervene on your mental processes." (Fodor. 1994, p. 38)

Informational semantics isn't psychology but it is a resource since it provides psychology the (naturalistic) means to explain behavior by showing how an agent's mental states are connected to the external environment. Following Fodor, we want, for example, to explain (a) Oedipus's behavior (marrying Jocasta), in terms of (b) his desire to marry Jocasta (and understandably his desire not to marry his mother, M), and (c) his (false) belief that Jocasta is not the same person as M.   Such cases are problematic for informational semantics since the same set of truth conditions (the person Jocasta) causes Oedipus to desire and not desire to marry her. That is, Oedipus' mental state content *desire to marry Jocasta* is very different from his mental state content *desire to marry M* yet the identical informational source, Jocasta, causes Oedipus to have them. That's not the kind of counterfactually based causation any empirical science can use.[2] The idea is to make plausible the common sense explanations of actions by counterfactually supported psychological laws that refer to the contents of the agents' mental states. The key problem for informational semantics is that a single thing can inform mental state content differentially, as in Frege's morning star-evening star cases. Or, as we have just seen, the Jocasta and Oedipus's mother case.

Fodor's (Language of Thought) solution to this problem distinguishes between belief content and variably informational modes of presentation. These modes of presentation "... are sentences (of Mentalese), and sentences are individuated by their syntax." (1994, p. 47) Therein lies the solution to two problems: One is that Oedipus' desire to marry Jocasta and his desire to marry his mother are different desires and it's the syntactical differences in the modes on which our inferences and actions depend. That's why we find it plausible that Oedipus acts positively vis-à-vis his marry-Jocasta-desire but negatively vis-à-vis his marry-mother-desire. This solution also comports nicely with the Turing-computation thesis that mental processes are syntactical, a sine qua non of the Language of Thought's thesis. However, there is the objection that since it's the modes of presentation that are different, it's the syntactical relations and not the counterfactuals that do the work of distinguishing the modes of presentation. This objection would discredit another important component of informational semantics, namely, the idea that mental state content is causally broad. For insofar as the syntactical relations are taken to (co)-determine content, such content is not externally and atomistically established. The objection is thus antithetical to Fodor's project, for it leaves content narrowly and holistically determined. This is bad for Fodor because it's his view that "Meaning holism is the idea that the identity—specifically, the intentional content—of a propositional attitude is determined by the totality of its epistemic liaisons." And "Meaning holism looks to be entirely destructive of the hope for a propositional attitude psychology." (Fodor, 1987, p. 56) And furthermore that "meaning holism is simply preposterous." (Fodor & Lepore, 1992, p. xii)

Meeting the objection requires Fodor to amend the semantic externalism he wants and needs to defeat meaning holism. He undermines his own efforts with an argument that concedes to holism a critical feature that he denies it has. Furthermore, he supports the argument on grounds that are at best speculative and at worst, question-begging.

The debilitating concession has to do with a central point in the external semantics project. External semantics rejects the "radical interpretation" arguments (of Dennett, 1971, Davidson, 1980, and Kim, 1994, among many others) that ascribing belief content to an agent presupposes the agent's other beliefs that are its logical consequences. This is the idea that belief content cannot be divorced from the normative context of ascription. For otherwise, as Dennett (1971, p. 11) puts it, we have "no predictive power at all" regarding an agent's behavior in light of her beliefs.

To frustrate this line of reasoning Fodor asks us to consider a population that counts as "a natural domain for psychological explanation because the conditions for successful water-directed behavior are fairly uniform across the ecology that the creatures occupy, and because each has beliefs about water sufficient for reliable success of its water-directed actions." (1994, p. 51.) The trouble is that "water-directed behavior" looks like the description we would give to an agent's motion were we to ascribe watery-beliefs to her. The "success" in successful water-directed behavior is a red-herring since success criteria, as we might treat them, are equally suffused in the normative context of belief content ascription. For example, my aversion to PCB polluted water seriously affects the success of my water-directed behavior. Fodor's maneuver does not beg the question against radical interpretation so much as it concedes to it the very idea that he rejects in holistic theories, viz., that we ascribe to agents belief content that rationalizes their behavior within observed contexts. He uses the notion of water-directed actions to underwrite the ascription of water as the belief content of the agents in the population. This is precisely what he disallows in his critique of the holism entailed by radical interpretation.

Next Fodor tries to defuse another problem with treating successful actions as reliable indicators of beliefs. In the hypothesized population the contingencies of watery interactions might be radically variant. When we explain successful water-directed behavior by some sort of independent reference to the distinct modes of water presentation, "there need be no Mentalese sentence that all—or even very many—of (the population) reliably have in their heads whenever they think, as it might be, that water quenches thirst." (p. 51) Thus while populations of water-believers need "not all have the *same* modes of presentations of water (we can say) *that water is what they all have modes of presentations of.*" (p. 52)

This way out looks suspiciously behavioristic for it suggests that psychological laws do not generalize over causally efficacious mental state content, after all. The laws can't generalize over different presentational modes without there being some regularity that collects them and that the laws capture; *ex hypothesi*, that's not the case. Of course, what we do infer from the behavior is that the different modes must have water (and thus water-beliefs) as their common feature. But as noted in the previous paragraph, it's doubtful that, given Fodor's context-independent semantics, he has this option available.

The speculation on which this solution is based is that, "for the purposes of psychological explanation" (p. 52) there is the possibility that in "our world" (p. 52), despite the dissimilarity of experience and resultant variety of background information, "we are all much the same sorts of creatures, and we are all causally connected to the world in much the same sorts of ways. No wonder if, de facto, minds that all exhibit the *impress* (my emphasis) of a connection to water do so in ways that regularly overlap." (p. 53) This is to say that all creatures with our kinds of minds when confronted with instances of water (H_2O) reliably represent water in the same way. This "is strictly an empirical issue" (p. 53) but it's surely no less speculative for all that. The evidence that would substantiate this hypothesis requires having the independent access to cognitive operations which we notoriously don't have. For consider that talk of the impress in the relevant representational sense is subjective occurrence in a way that we are not positioned epistemically to acknowledge. But if "impress" means the causal impingement of a stimulus on the sensory cortex then the argument assumes what it set out to establish. The physical occurrence of cortical excitation can be described innocuously and measured as an impress. The mental occurrence, the arrival of the content water in, say, one's belief-box, can also be described properly as impress, but here it's the semantically evaluable notion that plays the explanatory role.

According to Fodor, "It's a fact about the world that the causal properties of our minds are pretty similar, and that the causal chains that connect our minds to the fact that P aren't arbitrarily various." (p. 53) What we can assert at most is that the similarity of our minds' causal properties explains the regulatory functions underlying similarity in behavior. But such mind-world causal chains help us very little in explaining variation in mental content qua qualitative, epistemic, semantically evaluable content across agents. That human neural structure is sufficient for minds is obvious. But, to assume, as Fodor does, that similarity of neural structure is sufficient for similarity of mental content begs the question of how the brain produces mind. We are left with three alternatives: contexts of belief ascription figure essentially in ascribing belief content, *contra* Fodor's repudiation of meaning holism; the syntactically defined modes of presentation determine content, *contra* Fodor's externalism, or mental content plays no role in explaining behavior, *contra* Fodor's abhorrence of behaviorism.

3. Cognitive Management and Our Rationality

As I mentioned in the preceding section, there's a nagging problem with trying to naturalize the epistemology of human knowledge while defending its uniqueness. If our kind of knowledge is part of the "natural order" then it can't really be discontinuous with it. If there is continuity then naturalism needs to establish the case for epistemic modesty, that the universe grows knowers (to appropriate Jay Rosenberg's delightful term) as well as the case for epistemic hubris, that human knowers know better than the others. Efforts to have things both ways might be characterized as an exercise in epistemological chiropractic. Here's Fodor's bold account of matters.

"We are, it seems to me, at an obvious cognitive advantage, not only with respect to rocks and reflex machines, but also with respect to every other kind of creature that we have so far encountered. This is strikingly the case. We are patently far cleverer than anybody else, and that cries out for explanation. Only the most benighted of evolutionary gradualists could be sanguine that the apparently radical intellectual discontinuity between us and the other creatures will prove merely quantitative. Correspondingly, a good theory of the mind might reasonably be expected to say what it is that's so exceptionally good about our minds; in particular, what it is about our minds that allows us, alone among the organisms, to do science. Here again, I think there is much to be learned from an account of mental representation that stresses connections between content and causation." (pp. 91-92)

That gives us the flavor of the account. Notice how easy it is to slide up from talk of causally engendered information to intentional content, to talk of intelligence, to talk of knowledge, and then to the epistemic virtue of the theory of a thus semantically informed mind. A process-product confusion seems to operates here at full tilt.

On Fodor's view, naturalized epistemology has the mind as the organ of experimentation, and it's experimentation that contributes to our cleverness. It's our mind's interaction with its environment that holds the key to the storehouse of ambient information. However, it's one thing to hold the key, unlock the storehouse, and access the information. It's quite another thing to do with it what one is intelligently supposed to. This was, of course the message of the first section; belief-ascription seems inescapably normative. For that matter, it's no idle question what one is supposed to do intelligently with information. Given the diverse contexts in which there are mind-world interactions, the options are virtually limitless and intelligent action is notoriously hard to prototype.

Experimentation is the ability to tinker with truth condition instantiation such that one can determine what sorts of instantiations in the world correlate reliably with token representations of those truth conditions. Intelligence then is the *appropriate* application of mental state content to itself to determine how the world must be for the mental representation of it to be what it is. The metaphysics of the theory of content is etiological (external world instantiations of x cause *ceteris paribus* tokenings of x representations)..."so, if you know the content of a thought, you know quite a lot about what would cause you to have it." (p. 92) Counterexamples such as illusions abound but Fodor would protest that we're violating the ubiquitousness of the *ceteris paribus* provisos. But this is, I think, not only too quick and easy; it reminds us uncomfortably of the behaviorist maneuver to ensure the dubious explanatory force of the law of effect that explains successful actions by their success. There's something distressingly unfalsifiable about this and Fodor's (1968) "logical connection argument" stressed this methodological sin.

Still, the idea is that our cognitive capacity enables us to construct conditions under which we come to believe-true that P. The information caused by the world's effect upon us yields knowledge, in the sense of rational belief, but certainly not by the reliability of the correlation alone. We tinker with the environment (see to it that the world tokens P's truth conditions) because we (already) know what causes us to believe that P. It's because we can think in some appropriate way about our thoughts and what causes them that we have the traditional epistemologists "privileged access position." (p. 92)   Here   again, counterexamples from Descartes to Austin deluge us, but to no avail, thanks to *ceteris paribus* and deference.

The counterpart to semantics being mostly about counterfactuals is Fodor's claim that "epistemology... is mostly about money, about whether I prepared to pay for what it costs to insure that one or another of my beliefs is true, and whether the insurance I can get is worth the coverage." (p. 37) The insurance comes in the form of a policy about to whom to defer, for example, experts, in matters where your tokening a p-representation is mediated by someone else's tokening a p-representation. If I want a true belief about the time I look at a reliable clock or, if there are none in view, I ask someone reliable what time it is. Deference is thus an epistemic concept, but it is a logically independent byproduct of the causal powers of informational semantics. Information begets intelligent application of information management that yields knowledge in the sense that the series of cognitive operations leading to belief fixation is a rational one. Because of their formal properties, the physical operations (in the brain) adhere reliably to principles that instantiate rational inference.

The concept of deference that Fodor deploys is important in what I call experimental epistemology (a term that was once used to describe studies in artificial intelligence). Deference is a disposition to (or perhaps an epistemic policy of) belief fixation. The concept traverses a wide variety of situations. Deference operates in experimentation where you contrive the world to cooperate in tokening truth conditions P so that you will believe that P. It also applies at the other end of the epistemic spectrum where you rely on expert reports and opinions to proxy or serve as surrogates for the causal-informational relation between your belief content and the way some fragment P of the world is.

The most damaging problem for accounts like this is that there's just too much undifferentiated information out there for the mind's mental economy to cope with. Deference in itself does nothing to resolve the problem of there being so much amorphous information. Deference by itself does not decide among informational saliencies. That's why it is crucial to Fodor's thesis to require additionally that one "thus compose one's mind to a state of *judicious* receptivity." (p.93)

Philosophers from Hobbes to Hume to Honoré and Hart convincingly emphasize that there is no judiciousness in the natural order. What judiciousness or the use of good judgment there seems to be is, in Gould's (1989) term, "radical contingency." If by "judicious" Fodor means reducing the likelihood of error by modifying conditions, much more needs to be said. In matters of rational morality where behavior is explained and evaluated at levels that presuppose mind-world correlations, if judiciousness supervenes on that correlation it does so in coherent conspiracy with other non-natural properties. It is the relationship to these other contributory properties, equally supervenient on the nomological sufficiency of the mind-world correlation, that turns veridical representational mental state content into rational belief. In the absence of epistemic justification, the holding of true beliefs doesn't make you smart, it makes you lucky, sometimes, but certainly not always.

The line of defense that Fodor has deployed against this kind of objection is to distinguish between meaning holism and confirmation holism.[3] The latter is an epistemological thesis about scientific methodology. The details of the viability of this distinction is not a concern I pursue here. Instead, I want to grant the distinction and argue that it fails to provide support for the claim that the explanation of human cleverness, in particular, the explanation of how human minds do science, has much to learn "from an account of mental representation that stresses the connections between content and causation." (Fodor, 1994, p. 92)

It seems to me, in light of the meaning/epistemology distinction, that semantic externalism obscures the relations between content and causation. The reason is that semantic externalism is the view that belief content is nomically determined and thus that statements have their semantic properties essentially (Fodor & Lepore, 1992, p. 44). The epistemic gap created between semantic meaning and rational cognitive performance is one that Fodor's view of mind has insufficient resources to close. Fortunately, the elements of the argument have already been previewed in the preceding section. Fodor is adamant that semantics is no part of psychology. But if, *ex hypothesi*, psychological processes operate on suitably instantiated belief contents then belief content cannot be the cognitively impenetrable units that Fodor's modular view of mind requires. It's either the syntax of the modes of presentation that do the inferential (rationally clever) work , as in Stich's syntactic theory of mind, and content is causally inert or belief content is implicated in the explanation of rational action but the explanation is not mechanistic. I argued above that there is a question-begging ambiguity in Fodor's account of the homogeneous impress of water on biologically type-identical mind/brains vis-à-vis the heterogeneous nature of individual experiences. Fodor wants to dismiss the latter as "collateral information." [4] But without some principled, that is, non-question begging, way to distinguish collateral from constitutive information it looks like nothing more than a legislative decision.

It's important to ask what factors tilt Fodor's scale in this direction. The answer, I think, is that it's Fodor's commitment to computationalism that determines his strategy. It brings him to opt for the first (computational) alternative and 'solve' the problem of content by annexing it counterfactually to causal connectivity when it seems that concern with fecundity of theory would make the second alternative more plausible. Of course, that alternative also depreciates the cognitive value of calculation while it obscures the notion of content. (See Appendix)

This raises the question (or should raise it) of the reasons for this Kamikaze-like defense of the computational model of mind. Fodor suggests that rather than beginning with questions about representational fidelity we , "start with the question of how thought can both control behavior *and make contact with the world*, a semantics that reduces content to symbol-world causation is clearly what the case cries out for....It's precisely because semantics *isn't* part of psychology that the content of our thoughts can explain the success of our behavior." (1994, p. 87) It is certainly proper that Fodor concerns himself with local behavioral success since on the evolutionary account that he disparages it's still a bit too soon to start crowing about the success afforded by the rationality of human behavior.

Our minds enable us, "alone among all organisms, to do science." (p. 91)[5] Indeed, but in looking at how we do science, to see how our minds generate it, it's equally important to look at the various ways of limning science and perhaps see other reflections of mental stratagem.

My diagnosis is that Fodor views doing science on the corporate model, and it's very modular. It seems to be something like this: There are the natural resources that the ecology provides us and they are, as the philosopher wisely says, what they are. Then there are the various levels of material and administrative processes that get the raw materials to plants where they get refined in accordance with a vast array of rules for the manufacture of distribution, and sale of goods for consumption and creature comfort. It's important that these various procedures be kept distinct; labor and management have their well-defined domains of operation. This is, of course, good old fashioned rational reconstruction of scientific knowledge now applied to the psychological explanation of human cognitive prowess. It's also a lot of hubris. We get the natural mental resources via externalist semantics. The resources then get processed under the constraints of syntactic rules that operate on mental contents in virtue of the formal structures they instantiate. The resultant is the logically rational consequent of the operations on the resources.

To view the mind in Fodor's way, abstracts away from the facts of the matter for it proceeds rather from the perspective of what a rational processes must be like to yield rational product, to wit, science.[6] Viewing science organized in this way it comes as no surprise that corporate capitalism flatters itself as a natural extension of human rational action. The *invisible hand* in Fodor's analysis of the human cognitive economy lies in the convenient collusion of information, computation, and intentional generalization. You need not "buy into" the (original) Kuhn-Feyerabend radical philosophy of science to acknowledge that "doing science" is a much messier cognitive endeavor than our positivist mentors had us believe. Apart from the contentiousness of each of these notions, the scenario in which they figure is turned upside down in the same way that Darwinian biological theory is a reflection of Malthusian economics. It didn't take long before *laissez faire* economists began appealing to the laws of nature "red in tooth and claw" to *naturalistically* "vindicate" predatory business practices. Fodor's view conjures up a picture of doing science in an atmosphere as carefully regulated as the computer lab.

There is, I suggest, some rather convincing evidence that the tidy picture of mental modules carrying out their teleologically (but for Fodor, not necessarily evolutionarily) assigned tasks to yield intentional behavior and rational action is not as neat and clean as the flow charts have it. One recent and moving account of a very different view of human rationality is developed by Antonio Damasio (1994). He puts forward a bold and compelling case for what he calls the "neurobiology of rationality." (p. 85) His thesis presupposes a neurobiological theory of consciousness and critiques those theories of cognition that characterize human mentality as computation over symbolic representations.

"The 'high-reason' view, which is none other than the common-sense view, assumes that when we are at our decision-making best, we are the pride and joy of Plato, Descartes. and Kant. Formal logic will, by itself, get us the best available solution for any problem. An important aspect of the rationalist conception is that to obtain the best result, emotions must be kept out. Rational processes must be unencumbered by passion." (p. 171)

Damasio is direct in his repudiation of this model. "Now, let me submit that if this strategy is the *only* (his italics) one you have available, rationality, as described above, is not going to work." (p. 172) His *somatic-marker* hypothesis is a neurobiological alternative account of mental processing that involves emotions *essentially*. The hypothesis avoids not only the problem of limited memory capacity ubiquitous in the computer model of mind. It also offers an account of the errors in reasoning that Tversky and Kahneman researched in their experiments on the "devastating ignorance and defective use of probability theory and statistics." (p. 172)

Emotions are bodily states geared ultimately to organismic survival. Primary emotions are innate, hard-wired states of the brain's limbic system, in particular the amygdala, that enables the organism to react emotionally to a varied class of stimuli both environmental and imagined. Secondary emotions are experientially acquired. The somatic-marker hypothesis identifies these emotional states of the body, explains their etiology in the neural states of the brain's limbic system, and explains their functional role in cognitive processing. "The action of biological drives, body states, and emotions may be an indispensable foundation for rationality...Rationality is probably shaped by body signals, even as it performs the most sublime distinctions and acts accordingly." (p. 200)

4. Epistemic Arrogance

Having identified one important alternative explanatory theory of rational control of behavior, it's time to bring the strands of Fodor's account together to see how they are supposed to braid into a theory of rational belief fixation. "We are," it seems to Fodor, "at an obvious cognitive advantage, not only with respect to rocks and reflex machines, but also with respect to every other creature that we have so far encountered...This is *strikingly* the case. We are far cleverer than anybody else, and that cries out for explanation." (1994, p. 91) On the informational semantics view, there are, consistent with Descartes' discontinuity thesis, reflex machines and us.   It's Mother Nature whose tricks ensure that orienting reflexes react as if they believe that P when it is the case that P. This is epistemology at its most banal, since all that's going on there is brute causality. In our case, cognitive self-management is our unique(?) capacity to tinker and/or defer to experts who tinker with nature where we can't. The point of such tinkering is that we come to believe, for example, that it's a mouse because we token a mouse representation and, counterfactually, that we wouldn't token a mouse representation were it not the case that the world is now instantiating mouse truth conditions.

The naturalized philosophy of mind is thus the handmaiden of the naturalized epistemology of rational belief. I think a moment's reflection and then some should disclose that the epistemology of cleverness is pretentious and arrogant. Recall the opening quotation, "And what's especially nice about the new naturalism is how much it allows us to retain of our traditional understanding of ourselves as largely rational creatures." Largely rational creatures indeed, we might scoff. Quite invidiously the issue is reminiscent of the (possibly apocryphal) debate between Wilberforce and Darwin. Wherein lies our human rational superiority? Inductive reasoning? Surely not, Hume reminds us. Abductive inference then: our mechanisms of rational belief fixation that have now been identified as informational semantics plus or minus some other stuff, is the best explanation of our cleverness.

Two responses: First, abductive inference is compatible with an informational semantics based on causally reliable mind-world correlations. However, the causal theory of semantic information together with our fallible mechanisms of information pick-up is compatible with our belief content that P being reliably correlated with that P'. In particular, where the belief that P' (rather than P), is, in this story, of greater epistemic value than our "knowledge" that P.[7]

Second, our cleverness is surely measured, in part, by some of our successes in science. If the claim is that it's our (Aristotelian) ability to "do science" *per se*, that captures the nature of human rationality, regardless of whatever consequences might attend this (our) *telos*, it is a form of rationality both narrow and dangerous. For human cleverness is measured equally by success in life and love, in the abundance of our milk of human kindness, and in the varying degrees of holocaust to which we rationally superior creatures seem increasingly better at becoming inured. Do I make light of our frail rational condition?

Not at all, I lament it. And it is very hard to see how our superior cognitive management is the best explanation of our self-congratulatory cleverness. There is, alas, this dismal side to the story of human rational superiority. But this is not the place to rehearse it.

The fault in the theory lies not in the failure to see the truth and virtue of informational semantics. It's harmless truth in the same way that causation is harmless unless you, by dint of radical contingency, happen to be in its way when its effect upon you is bad. Whether or not the consequences of being part of the causal-information chain are happy ones is quite obviously going to depend upon lots of other collateral information. After all, causal chains in and of themselves are value neutral. The fault is rather in believing that informational semantics can subserve an epistemology of rational belief formation and a rationally moral view of belief and behavior assessment. Informational semantics can certainly help, it helps explain how we and our mental worlds are related to our external environment. It's undeniably part of the process that yields rational belief, but it can't be the product. Informational semantics alone can't be an epistemology of rational belief any more than it can underwrite a theory of rationally moral behavior. And it is thus very hard to see what useful lesson we can learn from "an account of mental representation that stresses the connections between content and causation." That there is a connection is obvious, what the connection might be, is a lesson yet to be learned.

Human cognitive cleverness might very well be orders of magnitude beyond those with which we cohabit the planet, at least as measured by the Church-Turing criteria of computational coordination. Sure, we have causally informed beliefs and perhaps survival value related wants. Rationalization of behavior, given reliable information about beliefs and desires, goes a long way toward explaining our computational acumen. But I'm still puzzled by how anyone can think that this goes any way at all toward explaining our cleverness. I've already alluded to the cross currents of criteria that interface with judgments of cleverness. The point of Fodor's epistemic exercise is, consonant with Descartes' discontinuity thesis, to establish a difference in kind for human rational cognitive management. But what we seem to get is a theory that lumps it together with all such naturalistic theories that explain rationality exclusively as formal inference of behavioral consequences from beliefs and desires unconstrained by any other normative assessment. Well, not quite exclusively for as noted above, Fodor does illicitly and inconsistently require an unexplained place in his scheme for judiciousness. I'll spare you the old saws about the cleverness (if not the judiciousness) of the cockroaches' orienting reflexes that enables them to survive where other species haven't. A similarly popular epistemology of human intelligence was resurrected again a few summers ago. It's the obverse of Forest Gump's mother's theory of stupidity: Clever is as clever does.

5. Appendix: Content, Counterfactuals, and Translation

The mantra of informational semantics, Fodor's style, is "it's the counterfactuals that count."(p. 119)[8] In particular, "Semantics, according to the information view, is mostly about counterfactuals; what counts for the identity of my concepts is not what I do distinguish but what I could distinguish if I cared to (inter alia, what I could distinguish by exploiting instruments and experts.)" (p. 37)

In unpacking the referential meaning of "Aristotle" as Aristotle, Fodor claims that among others, it's a property of Aristotle that he (or some appropriately causally-historically grounded Aristotle-token) is nomically related to occurrences of mental representations with the content Aristotle in Fodor. Of course it can't be only Fodor who figures in this nomic relationship on pain of subject-relative laws and kinds, which he disavows. (p. 31) On the one hand, this is a curious property of Aristotle not because it is modal but because it's not a property of Aristotle in any proprietary sense. It doesn't contribute to individuating Aristotle as distinct from any other distal stimulus that happens into Fodor's visual field and crosses over into his representational space. On this hand, we're concerned, as is Fodor, with nomic relations among elements in causal chains. Here it seems we explain that Aristotle tokens cause token Aristotle-representations as instances of the general principle that the tokening of distal stimulus X ceteris paribus causally produces tokening of X-representations in things having an internal organization sophisticated enough to take as a representational system. In short, token effects are, ceteris paribus, brought about by whatever their token causes are. So this property of Aristotle is peculiar in the sense that it looks like it's a property of anything at all that nomically, counterfactually co-varies with something else. Consider the two side-by-side instantiations, one of Aristotle, the other of Alcibiades. You ask me, "Who's who?" to which I reply, "My token representation of the guy on the left is about the guy on the left and similarly for the guy on the right." This I submit is both true, informationally correct, and counterfactually supported. The content of my representation is something that would be caused by the side-by-side instantiations were they to be appropriately placed vis-à-vis me. It does leave us wondering, however, how we get from causal-informational accounts of representational content to the cognitive-epistemic account; and that does seem to be the critical issue in Fodor's epistemology of human cleverness.

On the other hand, it seems more natural to hold that it's a property of Fodor, rather than Aristotle, that he (Fodor) tokens Aristotle-representations (representations with the content Aristotle) when exposed to instantiations of Aristotle. As Fodor has it, such tokens would cause his Aristotle-representations, were he to be, ceteris paribus, confronted with them. This seems to be no different from the image recorded on the photographic plate when the shutter opens. The molecules of the plate are, by design, moved about and reconfigured by the information in impinging light to yield a representational token of the distal stimulus. On this reading of it being a property of Fodor, it's not going to be a sui generis property of his but a property of a select collection of representers. That is, Fodor and selected persons represent Aristotle, the individual who satisfies Aristotle's truth-conditions, in the cognitive-epistemic sense in virtue of the "cultural baggage" they bring to the perceptual task.

Suppose, again that Fodor and selected persons are presented with two tokenings, one of Aristotle, the other of Alcibiades. Here the cognitive-epistemic issue is distinguishing between the two and the 'success' of the counterfactual test depends on what else is present and available to the representing system. Thus consider the situation in today's high-tech history of ancient philosophy class where the test question might be to identify the two figures projected on the screen. The requisite response, the one that gets you through the course, is that it's Aristotle on the left and Alcibiades on the right.[9] Certainly the projected image is a mode of presentation and, as Fodor argues, what makes it a mode of presentation of Aristotle is what it has in common with (almost all) other modes of Aristotle-presentations. Suppose that the CONCEPT Aristotle is characterized as what you would distinguish were you to be confronted by an Aristotle-instantiation. This provokes a question about the relevant cognitive-epistemic property of concepts. These are properties enabling you to (a) distinguish Aristotle (from say, Alcibiades) in terms of his contributions to Western culture and (b) explain why you (and the rest of us) are wrong if it turns out that (in Kripke-like fashion) the person who in fact wrote *The Poetics*, etc. is not the same as the one credited by the historical record.

Semantics is apsychologistic in that meaning is nomic co-variation of object instantiation (e.g., instantiations of rabbithood) and tokens (e.g., 'rabbit'-tokens). This view is independent of psychology but, as I have argued, for that reason it's also independent of interest in cognitive explanations of behavior. For purposes of psychological explanation, especially explanations requiring translational equivalency (for example, that expression p in L_1 carries the same information and is thus translationally equivalent to expression q in L_2) informational semantics alone is not only insufficient, it's irrelevant. Fodor's solution to Quine's inscrutability of reference puzzle distinguishes 'rabbit' from "undetatched rabbit part" but only on the specification of formal inferential structure, especially "the logico-syntactic apparatus that English makes available to its speakers." (Fodor, 1994, p. 75) He minimizes the significance of inferential norms since that apparatus is "exhaustively 'logico-syntactic;' (and) we've found no reason to suppose that it infects the nonlogical vocabulary." (p. 75)

There are at least two reasons that should make us skeptical of such bravado. One is that the appeal to a logical-nonlogical vocabulary distinction begs the question against the (Quinean) view that this dichotomy is provincial and conventional. The other concerns the supervenience base for a language's ontology. The logico-syntactic apparatus on which ontology partially supervenes is an normative inferential structure. Any successful program of naturalization must, as Fodor notes, include "a naturalistic account of inferring. Since inferences are surely part of the causal structure of the world, this is true whether or not they are constitutive of meaning." (p. 77) It would seem, however, that any such successful account would undermine the logical-nonlogical vocabulary distinction upon which Fodor's pardons his reluctant tolerance of inferential norms.

Finally, even on Fodor's brand of semantic externalism, "all there is to content is denotation" (Fodor, 1992, p. 173), the notion of content remains inscrutable. On the seemingly reasonable assumption that it's intentional content that an adequate translation conveys between languages, the price one pays for a "strictly informational semantic theory" is that "'Gavagai' means gavagai, and that is not something you can say in English." (p. 78) For Fodor, translation traffics not in sameness of meaning across inter-translatable languages qua content but qua belief-states. And it's the belief-states not the content that occupy the functional roles that figure in translational adequacy. So it looks like the assumption that it's content that we translate is not so reasonable after all.

How then does this story explain meaning as content? If you and I believe that P then the truth of our beliefs depends on it being the case that P. You and I come to agree on this because we stand in the same nomic relation to that P. For you, that P is called "gavagai" and in your mind that P is an instantiated undetached rabbit part while for me, that P, is an instantiated rabbit. Fodor is right, translation becomes an exercise in exceedingly subtle adjustments, especially in ignoring information, for which there are no well-defined criteria.[10] But then meaning as content on the externalist's view looks very much like *collateral information* vis-à-vis translation. The denotational meaning of any term is simply the ineffable whatever it is that's instantiated. When content informs meaning in this way Quine's remark about meanings as shadowy entities seems to be right on the mark.

Notes

[1] Kornblith (1994) relates that a colleague of Nisbett and Ross, having read their review of the literature about poor results on Tversky and Kahneman's experiments on human reasoning, asked, "If we're so dumb, how come we made it to the moon?" (p. 83)

[2] Nor is this the kind of issue about which cognitive scientists are concerned. An anonymous cognitive scientist reviewer once remarked indignantly on a paper I had submitted on a theory of Fodor's that cognitive scientists are not seriously influenced by Fodor's work, if they read it at all.

[3] "Meaning Holism and Confirmation Holism" in Fodor & Lepore (1992).

[4] Fodor (1984) previously referred to the "Dreaded Collateral Information Problem." For a extended discussion of the collateral information issue, see his (1986) "Banish DisContent."

[5] See Fodor (1991).

[6] It also recalls the old empiricist principle of "like effects, like causes" about which Philo corrected Cleanthes in Hume's *Dialogue Concerning Natural Religion.*

[7] On one such conceivable scenario (Cornman, Lehrer, and Pappas, 1992) accurate information that P might lead to the confirmation of hypotheses enabling us to construct and inevitably use a doomsday machine. So, knowledge may continue to imply truth but at a potentially disastrous risk. One wonders if any theory of rational belief fixation is prepared to run this risk of being the best epistemology in the cemetery of extinct species.

[8] Cf. Putnam's (1992) critique of Fodor's metaphysics of counterfactuality.

[9] The text for this implausible class might be D. D. Runes' *A Pictorial History of Philosophy* (1963).

[10] Cf. Steiner.

References

Cornman, J., Lehrer, K. & Pappas, G. (1992) *Philosophical Problems and Arguments.* Fourth Edition. Indianapolis, Hackett Publishing Company.

Damasio, A. (1994) *Descartes' Error.* New York, Grossett/Putnam

Davidson D. (1973) "On the very idea of a conceptual scheme." *Proceedings of the American Philosophical Association*, XLVII, 1972-73, 5-20.

Davidson, D. (1980), *Essays on actions and events*. Oxford, Clarendon Press.

Dennett, D.C. (1971) "Intentional Systems" in his *Brainstorms*. Cambridge, MIT Press.

Fodor, J.A. (1994) *The Elm and the Expert*. Cambridge, MIT Press.

Fodor, J.A. (1991) "The dogma that didn't bark. A fragment of naturalized epistemology." *Mind*, 100, 201-220.

Fodor, J.A. (1987) *Psychosemantics*. Cambridge, MIT Press.

Fodor, J.A. (1986) "Banish DisContent." In Butterfield (Ed) *Language, Mind, and Logic*. Cambridge University Press.

Fodor, J.A. (1984) "Semantics, Wisconsin Style" *Synthese*, 59, pp. 231-250.

Fodor, J.A. (1975) *The Language of Thought*. New York, Thomas Crowell.

Fodor, J.A. (1968) *Psychological Explanation*. New York, Random House.

Fodor, J.A. & Lepore, E. (1992) *Holism: A Shopper's Guide*. Oxford, Blackwell.

Gould, S.J. (1989) *Wonderful Life*. New York, Norton.

Kahneman, D., Slovic, P, & Tversky, A. (Eds.) (1982) *Judgment Under Uncertainty*. New York, Cambridge University Press.

Kim, J. (1994) *Supervenience and Mind*. Cambridge, Cambridge University Press.

Kornblith, H. (1994) *Inductive Inference and Its Natural Ground*. Cambridge, MIT Press.

Putnam, H. (1992) *Renewing Philosophy*. Cambridge: Harvard University Press.

Rosenberg, J.F. (1974) *Linguistic Representation*. Boston, D. Reidel.

Runes, D.D. (1963) *Pictorial History of Philosophy*. Paterson, NJ, Littlefield, Adams.

Silvers, S. (1996) "Rational reconstruction and immature science." *Philosophical Psychology*. Vol. 9, No. 1, pp. 93 - 109.

Steiner, G. (1975) *After Babel: Aspects of Language and Translation*. Oxford, Oxford University Press.

Stich, S.P. (1983) *From Folk Psychology to Cognitive Science: The Case Against Belief*. Cambridge, MIT Press.

COLLECTIVE GOALS AND COOPERATION

R. TUOMELA
Academy of Finland
Department of Philosophy, University of Helsinki,
P.O. Box 24, 00014 University of Helsinki, Finland

1. Introducing collective and joint goals

Human cooperation in the fullest sense involves acting towards a collective goal. This is one of the main theses of the theory developed in Tuomela (1997). In particular, cooperative joint action (e.g. carrying a table jointly, singing a duet) involves acting towards an intended joint goal—the one that the presupposed action-generating joint intention involves (cf. also Tuomela, 1993, on this). But cooperative joint action is not the only case of cooperative activity, and in order to be able to deal with the other cases, collective goals in a more general sense will be needed. Thus, for example, we cooperate to keep the city clean. The state of the city's being clean is our collective goal here, and we do not usually act jointly (in the strict plan-based sense of the notion) to achieve it. But our collective action is needed to secure this goal. However, I will not present my arguments for the necessary presence of a collective goal in cooperation in this paper (I have done this in Tuomela, 1997). The present paper will focus on an analysis of collective goals.

There are at least four importantly different notions of a collective goal, of which only one will be properly discussed and analyzed in this paper. Let me list the various core notions I have in mind:

1) collective goal based on shared "we-wants" (or "we-goal")
2) (intended) collective goal
3) (intended) joint goal
4) a collective's (intended) goal.

Of these 1) is the weakest notion, in which the central connecting "social glue" is the participants' mutual belief and which does not even require that the participants intend to achieve the goal but does require that the agent by his or her own actions satisfy the goal-content in question. Thus some people may have as their goal to see a certain opera performance, believing that the others in the collective (or many of them) also have that goal and also believing that this is mutually believed in the collective. The shared goal to see the opera is a shared we-goal requiring for its satisfaction that each goal-holding agent attend the opera performance.

X. Arrazola et al. (eds.), Discourse, Interaction and Communication, 121–139.

The next strongest notion is that of an intended collective goal. It involves the participants' "merely personal" or "private" intention but not their joint intention to achieve the goal, requiring collective activity. Some people can have as their intended collective goal to have an old, historically valuable building restored on the basis of their collective activity. An intended collective goal in this sense is based on the goal-holding agents' intentions to satisfy the content of the intention by acting together. The "Condition of Collectivity" applies to the present notion of satisfaction: If one or more agents satisfy the intention content, then it is on non-contingent, "quasi-conceptual" grounds satisfied for all participants. That is, it is satisfied due to the participants' acceptance of the goal as a collective goal, a goal which is a goal for the collective in question. The notion of intention here is one which can be adequately applied to the collective of agents in question. The individual agents cannot normally intend the content in question in the standard "action-sense" of the notion of intention (requiring basically that they believe that they by their own action can satisfy the content). They can, however, be said to have the content of the collective intention as their goal, they can aim at its satisfaction and be in collective sense committed to it, their basic action-commitment being to their own contributions to the goal at hand.

An intended joint goal in the full-blown sense in turn is based on the participants' joint intention to jointly achieve the goal-state or to jointly perform the goal-action. In the case of a joint intention (to perform something X jointly) each agent intends to perform his part of the joint action. This is a standard kind of action-intention and it involves his basic action-commitment, which is, however, based on the joint intention in question. He is also assumed to we-intend X (or, to be a little more precise, to "group-intend" in the sense of Tuomela, 1995, Chapter 3) and is accordingly committed in a collective sense to the successful joint performance of X by the participants. We-intentions are not action-intentions (but intentions in a broader aiming-sense), although they by practical entailment lead to action-intentions to perform one's part.

A social collective can have as its goal to perform an action X. For example a state can have the goal to conquer a certain territory. Basically, at the level of the members of the collective, this can involve two quite different things, indicating two basically different senses in which a collective can have a goal in an intentional sense. First, and this is the "normative" or group-binding sense, the collective may have a decision-making system (an "authority system" in the terminology of Tuomela, 1995, Chapter 4) in virtue of which the goals are jointly agreed upon for the collective. Secondly, a collective can be said to have as its intended goal to achieve something X if its members—or a majority of them—share a weak we-intention to X (in the sense of our category 1) above).

Over and above collective goals in senses 1)-4) there are what might be called "mere" shared goals—states or actions states which are personal goals of several agents (with or without accompanying mutual belief). In this paper I will concentrate on 2) and make some comments on 3). (As to 1) and 4), see Tuomela, 1995, Chapter 6 and especially 1997.)

Some further introductory comments on intended joint goals and collective goals are still pertinent here. Let us start with some agents' intended joint goal to perform something X jointly. Here they must jointly intend X, and this in standard cases amounts to their sharing a "we-intention" to perform X about which there is mutual, communication-based knowledge. Intended joint goals and joint intentions go together in that intention-contents can be regarded as goals. Such a goal can be a joint action or a state. If you and I we-intend—have the joint intention—to build a house together, building the house can be called our intended joint goal. Alternatively, and often more appropriately, we call the state of the house having been built our intended joint goal. Sometimes a certain kind of activity is inherently involved in an intended joint goal: we may have as our joint goal to jog together or to sing a duet together. In some other cases only the end state matters: we jointly intend to see to it that the house stays warm or that there is beer in the fridge or that nobody steals our luggage. I will below accept both state-goals and action-goals as collective and joint goals. In some cases action-goals are not means to a collective end but are either ends in themselves (without being means to anything else) or are means to personal ends. To rationally have an intended goal presupposes that the intending actor believes that the goal is achievable by some means. In the case of a full-blown collective goal this belief must be a mutual belief of the participants that they by their collective actions can achieve the goal at least with some probability. (All this will be discussed below in some detail.)

As said, intended joint goals in their fullest sense involve shared "we-intentions" or at least "group-intentions", which are dispositions to we-intend; see Tuomela, 1991, 1995, for we-intentions and group-intentions.[1] I will regard all joint goals as collective ones below. To show that there are collective goals which are not full-blown joint goals we consider the following example: Some time ago London underground trains carried a sign urging the passengers to cooperate by refraining from the use of the Victoria Station, which was under reconstruction. Not using the Victoria station can, first, be a *mere personal goal* of many Londoners (something they can satisfy independently of others having this goal). But it can also be their *collective goal* in a sense requiring their collective cooperation. Furthermore, it can be some or all Londoners' *joint goal* in a fuller sense requiring their joint plan to refrain from using the station. In the case of collective goals there will be many persons at least potentially involved (the participants also believe this), and they need only accept the collective goal separately (thus without group discussion and communication of their acceptance to the others). Indeed, their goal-directed action is separate and, furthermore, they may not know—or even have specific beliefs about—which other people have accepted the goal. We might speak of a mere collective goal when we are dealing with the weaker kind of goal and reserve the term 'intended joint goal' for the more specific case which satisfies, at least typically and as default conditions, the *communication of acceptance* condition, *jointness of goal-directed action* condition, and the *knowledge of other participants' acceptance* condition.

An intentionally performed joint action involves a relevant shared we-intention and hence a joint goal, which is we-intended (see Tuomela, 1984, 1995). Given this, it obviously follows that in the case of cooperative joint action there must be a joint goal involved. Even in cases of joint action with conflicting preferences (desires), such as playing tennis, there is a joint goal: playing tennis. As argued in Tuomela (1997), indeed all cases of full-blown cooperation involve if not a joint goal at least a collective goal. If this is true, there will be a collective goal also in various cases involving collective action or "coaction" in a broader sense and also in cases which are expected to involve—or potentially involve—collective action in which the participants can separately (as opposed to jointly) contribute to the goal—cf. conserving energy or helping to keep the city clean. (However, there are cases of interaction or "interactive coaction" with cooperative elements but without an intended collective goal and even without a collective goal, but they are not my present concern.)

2. The ingredients of collective goals

Starting my analytic discussion of collective goals, one may classify goals on the basis of 1) their contents, 2) their "holders" or "carriers" (persons or groups), and on the basis of 3) their carriers' reasons for having them. As to 1), contents can concern either merely personal ("private") or collective matters. In this connection we may ask, for instance, whether a single person can (either on factual or conceptual grounds, as the case may be) satisfy the goal-state or not. In the latter case we speak of an essentially collective or many-person goal, entailing that a single person cannot have it as his "action-goal" but only as his broader "aim-goal". The carrier of this kind of goal can be a single agent, several agents, or a social group. As to 2), the carriers can be single agents, collective agents (e.g. social groups) or several agents jointly. Finally concerning 3), the reason for which a certain carrier has a goal may be collective or may only have to do with the carrier's (a non-collective agent's) well-being. Obviously these distinctions would warrant a long discussion. Here I will be concerned with collective goals that several agents can be taken to have, thus omitting a discussion of single-agent goals and the goals collectives (groups) have. I will later argue that the beneficiaries problem 3) is largely irrelevant to the concerns of this paper.[2]

As partly opposed to collective goals one can also speak of "mere personal" or "private" goals such as a person's goal to achieve a Ph.D. degree, which require that he by his own actions will try to achieve his goal. A mere personal goal can concern also some other persons' or some collective's welfare and in this sense be collective. Thus a person's personal goal that all people on earth live in peace is, in this content-sense although perhaps not in the sense of the Collectivity Condition of this paper, also a kind of collective goal.

I will below be concerned primarily with "intended goals", goals which the carrier intends to achieve. I will first be concerned with what it is for some people to intentionally have—viz., to accept and sustain—a certain collective goal. Let me start with the following schematic suggestion for a partial analysis of a notion of an intended collective goal in the case of you and me, or our dyad (a limiting case):

(CG) You and I have G as our *intended collective goal* only if
a1) I accept G as my goal.
a2) You accept G as your goal.
b1) Part of my reason for a1) is that it is a mutual belief among us that a1) and a2).
b2) Part of your reason for a2) is that it is a mutual belief among us that a1) and a2).

As intentional acceptance of G is at stake I could as well have spoken in a1) of my intention to achieve G. I will take b1) and b2) to entail the intersubjective existence of the mutual belief in question:
*) It is a mutual belief among us that a1) and a2).
(This entailment is valid if a mutual belief—"common" belief in the economist's language—is taken to amount to an open-ended conjunction of hierarchical beliefs; cf. Tuomela, 1995, Chapter 1.) I will later consider the question of what to add to the conditions in the above analysans to make them jointly sufficient for the analysandum—an intended collective goal. I will in effect argue that this requires that G be accepted as a collective goal rather than as a merely personal (or private) goal, although the final analysis be much less circular. We can accordingly say that a correct analysis of collective goals must concern collective preferences and acceptances and not merely personal ones. We will see that it is part and parcel of this idea that a single agent holding a collective goal is required to contribute to the achievement of this goal. His personal action-goal thus is to contribute or participate on the grounds and for the reason that he has the collective goal in question.

Before going on I will make a remark on the notion of reason and adopt a convention in connection with it. When speaking of a reason of action it is customary to distinguish between what might be called *objective* and *subjective* reasons. Suppose I acquire the belief that it will soon start to rain (and desire not to get wet). In this context, my reason for taking my umbrella with me is that it is raining. The fact that it is raining is the objective reason for my action. The subjective reason is that I believe that it is raining. I assume that the external circumstance of raining can be a reason for my action only via my belief that it is raining. Thus we may say technically that the reason for my taking my umbrella with me is the pair (it is raining, I believe that it is raining). But when I mistakenly believe that it is raining and take the umbrella with me this pair shrinks to the belief that it is raining. Analogously with social reasons such as that the reason for my having something G as my goal or intending G due to your having G as your goal or due to some other mental state of yours: I will below use the formulation "I intend G for the reason that (I believe that) you intend G" or even the formulation "I intend for the reason that I believe that you intend G" to cover all the relevant possibilities. When an expected but so far non-existent future state—such as your (future) intending G or your acting towards the achievement of G—is a reason-state it is particularly central to emphasize the belief-aspect. In accordance with my convention, b1) entails that your accepting G as your goal—and thus your intending G—is part of my reason for having G as my goal. Also the fact that there is a mutual belief about our having G as our goal is part of my reason for having G as my goal, and thus also, for instance, your belief that I have G as my goal is part of my reason for maintaining G as my goal.

Let me note in passing that my formulations b1) and b2) may seem problematic in the following sense. They may seem to suggest that one can believe that it is a mutual belief that one has an intention before one has formed that intention. While that perhaps is a weird possibility, it surely is not what is meant in this context. What is meant is basically that my reason for having G as my goal (and intending G) is in part that (I believe that) you also intend G and have it as your goal. Thus, we should rather say that we are here speaking about a condition for maintaining or sustaining an intention rather than a condition for forming one.

If you and I share a joint goal we are jointly responsible for its achievement. In standard cases of intended joint goals we must accordingly have as our personal goals to perform our shares of these joint goals. Let G_1 be the goal corresponding to my share (action) and G_2 be the goal your performing your share is assumed to lead to. Then our accepting G must entail each of us accepting the conjunctive state $G_1 \& G_2$ as a goal—although perhaps with a priority for one's own goal in accordance with our part-division (if there is one). The goals G_1 and G_2 need not always be our private goals—we may already when accepting G as our collective goal have compromised and dropped our original private goals. An example clarifies this. Suppose your private goal is to see a ballet tonight while my goal is to watch a certain movie and I would actually never want to go to the ballet. You again hate the kind of action movies I like. Still we want to be in each other's company. This is an instance of the Battle of the Sexes. We may settle the matter by agreeing to do one thing tonight and the other thing the next time we have the opportunity. In this situation G consists of compromised personal goals: Were you alone you would not accept such a compromise-goal for yourself, and the same goes for me. Furthermore, to be a collective goal rather G must in this case be accepted in a sense satisfying the Collectivity Condition, to be discussed later.

I claim that in the context of full-blown cooperation only intended goals need to be involved—and thus an intention to realize the state (or, in some cases, action) G. Why is this so? It is basically because cooperation—in the standard, full-blown sense of the notion—is inherently intentional: one cannot cooperate with others without being aware that one is cooperating. Thus one cannot unintentionally (e.g., inadvertently) cooperate with others, although one can unintentionally perform a cooperative action (an action which can be regarded as cooperative). One can perform a single-agent action such as closing the window inadvertently (thinking it was a door one closed) but one cannot unintentionally participate in a cooperative collective action. If I conserve energy or refrain from polluting water but am not aware that a collective goal of our group is involved, I am not cooperating in the proper sense but am only acting privately.

In my present analysis b1) and b2) are a kind of non-accidentality conditions. As a matter of fact we might have considered the following conditional instead of b1) and b2):

b1*) Had I not believed that it is a mutual belief among us that a1) and a2), a1) would not have been true of me.

b2*) Had you not believed that it is a mutual belief among us that a1) and a2), a2) would not have been true of you.

We must still ask why a full-blown collective goal must be based on full mutual belief rather than a mere shared belief e.g. in the following sense:

b1#) Part of my reason for a1) is that (I believe that) a2).

What indeed is the argument for b1) and b2) in the first place? Does it show that b1#) and its analog b2#) are not enough? Let us consider the possibilities we are discussing by means of an example. Suppose you and I are both separately considering spending a week's holiday in New York. Also suppose that we enjoy each other's company and would like to be in NY together at the same time. Why is it not enough in general that I intend to go in part because you intend (and analogously for you)? My intention here has a social reason in a weak sense: I intend to go in part because (I believe that) you also intend to go and believe that I will go (maybe only in the weak sense of taking the same flight). These beliefs affect my intention to go to NY together with you and are a part of my total reason both for this intention and its content-action. But in the fullest case we need more: my total reason consists not only of my belief that you will participate and that you believe that I will participate but also in part of the fact that I believe that you believe that I act for this reason. In fact, we must in principle have here the possibility of further iteration—my total reason contains our mutual belief that we intend to go to NY together.[3] Note that the content of my intention in the present kind of example could be simply to go to NY (accompanied by such and such beliefs and having such and being supported by such and such reasons) or it could be to go to NY together with you. This latter kind of content is required (or at least presupposed) of collective goals.

As far as collective goals go, our argumentation shows that we can take b1) and b2) to be warranted for *full-blown intended collective goals*. I do not, and need not, claim that we can have weaker kinds of collective goals in the case of which mutual beliefs are not reasons and may not even exist. Note that intended collective goals in the present strong sense still fall somewhat short of implying that you and I have somehow explicitly or implicitly agreed to go to NY. Let me emphasize that I do not want to legislate about language use in this connection. Rather I am after conceptually and philosophically significant distinctions. Therefore, the weaker possibilities for analyzing collective goals can still qualify as different kinds of collective goals—they do involve collective considerations and social connections of some kinds. Accordingly, a weaker kind of collective goal related to our present discussion would be one which in the two-person case accepts the obvious conditions a1) and a2) but replaces b1) and b2) by a condition simply requiring the agents to believe that the other one will do a certain part of a joint task or contribute to the coming about of a "collective state" (in a sense satisfying clause c) in the analysis (*ICG*) below). A stronger alternative is obtained by imposing the condition *) but accepting the possibility that the mutual belief is not a part of the agents' reason for having the goal in question. (I have in effect argued above that this does not, however, always give a "sufficiently social" notion of a collective goal.) The next stronger notion of collective goal would be one accepting a1) and a2) and replacing b1) and b2) respectively by b1#) and b2#).

Let us further consider the following strengthening of a1):
a1*) I accept G as our collective goal;
and analogously for you.
In clauses a1*) and a2*) collectiveness is circularly built into the content of a collective goal acceptance. I shall below analyze the idea of accepting something as one's group's collective goal basically in terms of the Collectivity Condition and some related conditions about the "indexicalities" and commitments involved. It can be pointed out here that we can strengthen a1*) so as to concern acceptance of G as "our joint goal". Given this, jointness and "we-ness" is built into the content of the intentional acceptances, entailing the existence of a joint intention.

As noted, our (*CG*) only gives a necessary condition for a collective goal. In order to arrive at a satisfactory view of intended collective goals much more must be said. I have distinguished between (intended) joint goals, (intended) collective goals, and goals shared in a sense not requiring intention (and including we-want-based goals). Joint goals in their full intentional sense require the notion of "we" and they also require that the participants accept a joint plan. Intended collective goals are weaker. No plan-acceptance is required, but a weak notion of "we" (or "our group") is required—plus the notion of *acting together* (a weak notion of joint action). This will be seen below. As noted, shared goals can be much weaker than intended collective goals. Going to the same restaurant for lunch can of course be merely an accidentally shared goal even when there is mutual knowledge about this. When there indeed is mutual knowledge (or belief) we are dealing with a shared "we-goal" based on a "we-want" or weak, private "we-intention"—not to be confused with the notion of we-intention clarified in note 1. (Note that both tokens and types of states can be shared—cf. having as repairing the roof of this house versus separately but parallelly singing a certain song on Christmas Eve.)·

If a single or collective agent has a goal, this agent must act towards that goal or must at least be disposed to act so as to satisfy it. Thus an accidental coming about of G when G is some agent's goal which he does not act towards or which does not come about by virtue of his acting towards it cannot be a case of *satisfaction* of the goal, although the agent in such a case will have to drop the goal. What the satisfaction conditions of a collective goal are, depends on what—as I will call it—the *presupposition* of the goal says. The intuitive starting point in my analysis of collective intentions in the sense of intended collective goals is that there must be a collective of persons which has such an intention to achieve a content or goal, say G.[4] This collective, say C, can be, e.g., a society, an informal collection of people, or a social group. Thus we can also speak of a collective in the context of a collective goal. A collective goal can be had by a collective and by any number (even a single one) of its members even if they do not believe that they can alone satisfy the goal. Thus intending a goal G need not be an action-intention by itself, although there must be an action-intention involved here—the intention to contribute to the achievement of G. This conceptual feature of the situation makes it plausible to say that the broad notion of goal (or, more broadly, collectively sharable content or aim or end) is needed when speaking about collective intentions.

As earlier, I will accept the innocuous stipulation that some persons collectively intend something G if and only if G is their intended collective goal. The following discussion will motivate and give reasons for a more detailed account to be given later. When a single agent intends a goal-content in the normal action-intention sense he must, due to the cognitive nature of intention and the factual circumstances concerning the possibilities of achieving the goal, have various relevant beliefs. He must of course believe—on conceptual grounds—that the goal is satisfiable and that he can satisfy it at least with some probability, and he may have various factually grounded beliefs concerning how to satisfy the goal. Analogous remarks can be made in the case of collective goals. Thus, when some persons—members of a collective C—have a collective goal G there must be a mutual belief (or at least a shared belief) saying something about the achievement and satisfaction of G. It can accordingly be proposed that, on conceptual grounds, these persons cannot intentionally have a collective goal unless it is mutually believed by them that they can (or can with some likelihood) collectively achieve the goal—although it is not required that they believe that they can, or for that matter cannot, achieve that goal alone. This is a thesis which obviously is based on the cognitive nature of intention (intended goal): As in the case of ordinary personal action-intentions, intended collective goals can only be satisfied by means of the intenders' activities (although they may make use of other person's activities when trying to satisfy the collective goals in question). The *presupposition* of the collective goal may specify the nature of those activities, but a general underlying presupposition is, anyway, that a collection of persons can (at least with some likelihood) satisfy its collective goals by its collective actions—and in the last analysis can rely only on its members' collective actions, on their somehow acting together to achieve the goals. (If, say, only one person can actually bring about our goal G we, the goal-holders, can ask him to do it.)

A great many collective intentions are of the kind that they require that all or most of the members of the collective participate in some way—similar or different way, depending on the nature of the goal and situation. For instance, one single member cannot factually satisfy the intention or goal of reducing the ozone-hole in the atmosphere. The collective may specify what kinds of collective actions qualify. Thus, there may be a law saying that every man must take part in the defense of the country. There may be a proper social norm—a' socially accepted moral norm—saying that everyone ought to do his share of, say, conserving energy. In some cases, it may be allowed and may even be necessary that only one person act, bringing about the goal state.

As seen, we can say that there must always be an intention-presupposition in the case of any collective intention, and this presupposition is the content of a mutual belief. Moreover, this content is often normative. Thus, typically it would be something like this: it is a mutual belief in C that in order to satisfy a collective intention such and such activities by the members ought to be performed. This 'ought' can be based on a social rule-norm ("r-norm"), a proper social norm ("s-norm"), or agreement-making between the members of C (see Tuomela, 1995, Chapter 1, for these concepts). While these are the basic cases, we must still add that the "ought" may be a technical one e.g. due to the fact that the satisfaction activities for the present intention rely on the factual or conceptual nature of the intention content in question (cf. the collective goal of diminishing human suffering). Thus we can conclude that a collective intention is always normative at least in the minimal sense of involving either a full-blown social norm or normative expectation or a "technical ought" to act towards the goal (viz. in order to achieve the goal the members ought to act collectively in a certain way).

One important feature of a collective intention which follows from the aforementioned considerations is that if the collective intention becomes satisfies for one of the participants it is satisfied for all participants, on quasi-conceptual grounds. I will discuss this important collectivity condition in detail later in the next section.

3. The final analysis of intended collective goals

I can now give a summary analysis of the notion of a collective goal—the full-blown notion of a collective goal based on the participants' intention. I write my analysis for the general case with any finite number of agents taking part in a situation S and being members of some suitable collective (which could even be their society) as follows:

(*ICG*) G is an *intended collective goal* of some persons $A_1,...,A_m$ forming a collective C in a situation S if and only if G is a state or (collective) action such that
a) each member of C has G as his goal in S, entailing that he intends to contribute (at least if "needed"), together with the others—as specified by the mutually believed presupposition of the shared goal G—to the realization of G;
b) part of each member's reason for a), viz. for his having G as his goal, is that there is a mutual belief among them to the effect that a);
c) if G is satisfied for a member A_i of C, then, on quasi-conceptual grounds, it is satisfied for every member of C; and this is mutually believed in C. (Collectivity Condition)

I suggest that this analysis gives the strongest viable notion of an intended collective goal which does not involve full-blown joint intention. It relies on personal (but "non-private") intentions, but does refer to the notion of acting together. It also makes the personal intentions responsive to mutual belief—this is a requirement that we need to impose only on full-blown cases. Furthermore, the analysis (*ICG*) makes the intention (goal) collective not only in the sense of involving acting together but also in the sense (which also joint intentions and joint goals satisfy) of "each for everyone and everyone for each" (cf. clause c)).

In clause a) the notion of acting together is used. Acting together is meant to be understood here as something possibly weaker than proper joint action, understanding proper joint action to be action based on the agents' shared plan to do something together. Let me briefly and roughly indicate what I mean without giving a proper defense (but see Tuomela and Bonnevier-Tuomela, 1997). Consider the simple case of two agents, you and I:

(*AT*) You and I intentionally *act together* in performing X if and only if
1) X is a collective action type (in the sense of a "joint action type" Tuomela, 1984, Chapter 5, viz. an "achievement-whole" divided into A's and B's parts, not necessarily on the basis of an agreement or even a social norm);
2)   a) I intend that we perform X together, and I perform my part of X (or participate in the performance of X) in accordance with and (partly) because of this intention;
        b) you intend that we perform X together, and you perform your part of X (or participate in the performance of X) in accordance with and (partly) because of this intention;
3)   a) I believe that you will do your part of X (or participate in the performance

of X);

  b) you believe that I will do my part of X (or participate in the performance of X);

4) 2) in part because of 3);

5) If my intention that we perform X together is satisfied, then, on quasi-conceptual grounds, also your intention that we perform X together is satisfied, and vice versa (viz. my participation commitment to X is not fulfilled before yours is, and vice versa), and each of us believes so.

  The notion of acting together depends on the participants' intention to act together. Thus the concept of acting together is taken to be possessed by the participants of acting together. We are here dealing with personal collective intentions in the strong sense of intentions with a collective content (specifically: acting together). But in a weak sense the participants collectively intend—based on their beliefs that the other one will participate. The participants must share the presupposition belief that they cannot realize their intentions without the other one participating, and they also have acquired the belief that indeed the other will participate. (Note that not only is our (AT) somewhat circular but so is also our (ICG)—this is what our non-reductive approach gives!)

  Condition b) of (ICG) gives a partial social reason for the agents' having G as their goal, viz. their mutual awareness. Thus the agents can be argued to have as their partial reason to contribute to G that (they believe that) the others take part as well—there would be no motivational point in a person's contributing alone to the achievement of a goal taken to require many contributors; and our agent can take the others to rely on his contribution only if he believes that that the others believe that he will participate (and so on: the belief-loops can be iterated). I will not here dwell longer on this argument and on b) (see Tuomela (1997) for a longer discussion). Condition b) represents the full-blown case. My present notion of acting together can be taken to suggest that responsiveness to mere belief rather than mutual belief might sometimes suffice.

  Let us now consider in some detail c), the *Collectivity Condition*. That it does some work is seen from familiar examples like getting a street lights to our village. When it has been provided (in accordance with the presupposition of the goal) every villager's collective goal of getting street light has been satisfied. The satisfaction of clause c) is an important feature of an intention's being a collective one.[5] I wish to emphasize that the satisfaction of a collective intention requires more than the mere coming about of the content-state: it must come about due to collective action as specified by the presupposition of this collective intention. As noted, the participants' construct collective goals by their conceptual activities, by their collective acceptances and allowances. In our examples of providing street lights, the participants must collectively bring about the goal in order to satisfy it. What if only one of us produces the street lights—brings them about himself or gets somebody to else to perform the task? This process leads to a proper satisfaction of the collective goal only if the participants have somehow authorized the person to do it—or, to use my earlier terminology, only if this is allowed by the presupposition of the collective goal. The fact that a collective goal must be conceptually constructed by the participants (or by some authorities in institutional cases) and accepted as a collective goal (at least in a presystematic sense) can still be illustrated by the following example. Suppose that at an airport the authorities have set up a sign "Do not leave your luggage unattended". This suggests a collective goal. If the passengers accept to obey, not leaving one's luggage unattended becomes a collective goal. Here the collective goal is constructed on the basis of personal ones. To clarify the conceptual situation assume there are only two participants, you and I. I accept as my personal goal not to leave my luggage unattended; and similarly for you. These personal goals are satisfied by our not leaving our luggages unattended. Not leaving one's luggage unattended can also be our collective goal if we have accepted it as such. In this case the Condition of Collectivity is imposed. Not leaving one's luggage unattended is satisfied as a collective goal only if we not only have not left our luggages unattended but also have accepted that our collective effort is required in a sense leading to a satisfaction of the Condition of Collectivity. Thus the collective goal is not satisfied until each person in our collective (here dyad) does not leave his luggage unattended but also accepts that when the goal is satisfied as a collective goal for one of them, it is by its very construction satisfied also for the other members.

In view of the importance of the collectivity condition the following more detailed remarks concerning it are warranted. Let me restate the basic, strong form of the Collectivity Condition:

(CC_s) If G is satisfied for a member A_i of C, then, on quasi-conceptual grounds, it is satisfied for every member of C; and this is (normally mutually) believed in C.

Here the qualification "on quasi-conceptual grounds" involves—to put the matter somewhat circularly—that the collective goal G is collective due to the collective acceptance (and construal) by the members of C as their intended collective goal (understood minimally in a sense entailing (CC_s)). If the analogue of our strong collectivity condition were satisfied on contingent grounds only, G would not be a collective goal but only a shared personal goal with a collective content.

To make some further points, let us consider an example where the members' goal is to take part in a departmental meeting. What could the members' goal be? Consider any member's acceptance of one or more of the following conditions:

i) I take part in the meeting requiring at least m participants.
ii) We (the members of our department) collectively take part in the meeting.
iii) The departmental meeting will take place.

The shared state-goal iii) should in our present context be understood as an action-entailing collective goal; that it is equivalent to ii). Accordingly, iii) and ii) satisfy (CC_s). This does not require that all persons with the goal ii) or iii) actually need to participate in a literal sense, but they must be disposed to contribute to its satisfaction, making allowance for being somehow thwarted in their contribution attempt. There are at least two cases to be considered here. First, they may have some acceptable excuse— an acceptable social "revocability" condition may apply to them. The second case is to have a prudential subjective excuse (whether socially acceptable or not) such as that they think they are not, after all, needed for the achievement of the collective goal, as there will be enough contributors in a particular situation anyway. Nevertheless, if the meeting is held, the goal is satisfied for them: we can indeed use the notion of satisfaction in this liberal way. Alternatively, we might use the stricter notion requiring that the goal is satisfied only for those who actually succeed in taking part in the meeting. This liberal usage requires that (CC_s) be modified accordingly to apply only to those members who actually take part or contribute to the goal. I shall adopt the liberal reading of the Collectivity Condition below.

One can say that the conceptual content of a collective goal is basically "we-indexical" in that the satisfaction of the goal is assumed to rely on "our" collective activities. Due to the involved requirement that *prima facie* every person accepting the collective goal (or, indeed, who ought, *qua* a member of the relevant collective accept it) is required to contribute—by his own activities—to the goal. This introduces "I-indexicality". Accordingly, there is an indexical personal element "I" in i) and another indexical element "we" in ii) and, although only implicitly, in iii). Goal i) cannot be satisfied unless both ii) and iii) are satisfied and, in addition, I personally take part in the meeting (rather than only somehow unsuccessfully try obtain my goal, viz. taking part in the meeting). Now if ii) and iii) are satisfied i) need not yet be satisfied: the person may have been thwarted somehow or did not act on prudential grounds. There is the "milder" personal requirement in ii) and iii) that the person in question must intend by his own actions to contribute to the collective action in question, but it follows from the satisfaction of ii) and iii) that the analogue of i) must be satisfied for those members whose participation guarantees the satisfaction of ii) and iii). How many such persons there are depends conceptually on the presuppositions of goal iii) and factually (contingently) on how many others take part in the satisfaction of iii).

Whether the situation or state whose existence the satisfaction of the goal G conceptually guarantees can somehow be utilized by all persons having had G as their goal is a different matter. If we have as our collective goal to provide i) streetlights or ii) a barrel of whisky for our village we can say that the satisfaction of a goal is supposed to be rewarding per se: if you get what you want (G) that is somehow satisfying. Thus the provision of i) or ii) is satisfying to all who had the goal in question (and for those who did not succeed in their attempts to help to bring the goal about). Whether all those who had the goal can make use—and be beneficiaries—of the state resulting from the provision of the goal is a matter which does not directly relate to my analysis. The question about who can be beneficiaries depends on what the members of the group decide or accept about the situation. This matter is independent of whether the goal is "indivisible" (or, equivalently, "in joint supply") as in case i) or "divisible" (case ii)) in the economists' sense. Thus, as economists typically define public goods in terms of the conjunction of the ontic feature of divisibility and the "accessibility" feature of non-excludability, a collective goal in my sense can be either a public or a non-public one.

It can be noted here that situation dealt with by *ICG*) can be compared with a game-theoretic situation involving a coordination problem and perhaps some conflict. In the present case the game has been solved and G represents an equilibrium. It is to be noted, however, that due to Collectivity Condition and assuming the correctness of belief in b), a collective goal G in the sense of *ICG*) can be regarded as a coordination equilibrium, but obviously not any coordination equilibrium will satisfy *ICG*).

It is a background assumption of our analysis of the notion of a collective intention that such an intention can and will be dropped when there is a true mutual belief among the participants that it has been realized by the participants. It will also be dropped—without being satisfied—when there is a mutual belief among the participants that some other party has brought about the goal-state without the participants' contribution; and the same can be said when there is a mutual belief that the intention is not realizable or that the underlying motivation for it has ceased to exist or that some other generally recognized revocability condition applies (e.g., that some of the participants have been misinformed or coerced, etc.). I will not here defend these conditions (but see the discussion in Cohen and Levesque, 1991).

In view of what has been said the following thesis about shared collective goals is plausible: If agents A and B share a collective intention G each must be disposed to have thoughts that can be expressed (at least by us theoreticians) by "We will act together to satisfy the collective intention and, hence, will also be disposed to contribute to the satisfaction of this collective intention". The disposition to contribute to the satisfaction of the collective intention is grounded in the agents' acceptance of the collective intention (and not *vice versa*). Thus we can say in this kind of situation, first, that an agent has the personal action-intention to contribute on the basis of the collective intention and, secondly, that unless the agents had had the collective goal they would not have had the personal goal (but not *vice versa*).

It actually suffices in this kind of case that A and B each only believe that G is their shared collective intention or goal. If they in addition also have the mutual belief that G is their shared collective goal, we can speak of their intersubjectively shared collective intention. Finally, G will be their objectively and intersubjectively shared intention if the mutual belief is true. Even more, can be had: The mutual belief can be communication-based and amount to mutual knowledge. This is the strongest case of sharing of a collective goal, and it is what agreement-based shared collective goals in standard cases give us. (Cf. Tuomela, 1996, for a discussion.)

On the basis of what has been said, I finally give my analysis of (intended) joint goals:

(*JG*) G is a *joint goal* of some persons A₁,....,Aₙ forming a collective C in a situation S if and only if G is a state or (joint) action such that
a) each member accepts the statement: "G is our goal in S" (or an equivalent of this statement), and this entails that they conatively endorse "We will realize G in S";
b) part of each participant's reason for intending G as their goal, is that there is a—normally communication-based—mutual belief among these participants to the effect that a);
c) necessarily, if G is satisfied for a member Aᵢ of C it is satisfied for every member of C.

This analysis basically says that a G is joint goal if and only if it is jointly intended by the agents. The analysis (*JG*) contains lots of inbuilt assumptions, viz. assumptions concerning the content of joint intentions, including an analogue of the collectivity condition c) of (*ICG*); see Tuomela (1995), Chapter 3. Note that in my analysis of joint intentions (see (*JI*) of note 1) joint intentions are (technically) based on we-intentions, which in are taken to be responsive to the relevant underlying beliefs. According to my analyses (*ICG*) and (*JG*) each joint goal is an intended collective goal, but not conversely.

4. Cooperation

According to the view I defend in my recent work (Tuomela, 1997), cooperating (viz. intentionally cooperating) means acting together intentionally either in the pursuit of an intended collective (or joint) goal or in the pursuit of an intended private goal. Acting together involves sharing in an action. Thus there must be at least this much jointness or togetherness in cooperation. Any acting together—viz. joint action in a broad or a narrow sense—in principle qualifies (cf. (*AT*)). Thus also agreement-based joint action involving conflict (cf. an organized fight) will do on suitable occasions. The joint action with respect to which the agents cooperate may be a goal in itself or it can be a means for the agents to achieve their shared collective goal—when such a goal exists in the situation in question—or their private goals. Whichever of these three possibilities concerning further goals is involved the joint action in question can in any case be regarded as at least a proximate goal—*telos*—that the agents share. Thus it is possible to say that when cooperating they share an intended collective goal—at least the very joint action with regard to which they cooperate. Whichever more distant goals they either collectively or merely personally have is a different matter and the existence of such goals is not required for cooperation to occur. In accordance with what has just been said, cooperation must involve a "jointness-aspect"—viz. something joint, which need not be more than the jointness any joint action involves. I will call this jointness the agents' shared (proximate) collective goal. Let me also note that the thing shared here can be a joint or collective action defined by reference to a state—for instance, saving a house from a fire or cooking a kettleful of peasoup. Let me illustrate what has been said in terms of the peasoup-example. The state of there being a kettleful of peasoup could be some agents' a) collective goal in the sense of (*ICG*), or it could be each agent's b) private goal, or it might be c) nobody's goal of any kind in this situation (the agents might love acting together, independently what the activity results in). In cases b) and c) there must clearly be cooperative collective cooking activity for cooperation to occur. This cooking activity would be the collective action-goal my theory requires. But also in case a) there must be cooperative acting together—cf. clause i) of (*ICG*). (However, if the presupposition of the collective goal so specifies, only one of the participants might perform the actual cooking.) Fully adequate cooperation requires in addition that the participants willingly (as opposed to reluctantly) participate in the collective cooking activity.

To be a little more specific, I argue that all full-blown cooperation must, firstly, involve commitment toward a (cooperative) collective goal or plan. Secondly, if the participants' interests or preferences, *qua* participants of the action, are highly correlated that makes the action situation cooperative in nature (by making helping desired and rational). This contrasts with the case where the interests of the participants are opposed. Thirdly, the cooperative nature of an action is enhanced if the participants act out of a cooperative attitude. (See Tuomela, 1993 and 1997, for a defense.)

Some of the specific central theses that I defend in Tuomela (1997)—but do not have space for in this paper—are the following:

T1) Two or more actors cooperate in the full sense of the notion if and only if they share a collective (or joint goal) and act together in order to achieve that goal.

This thesis is a rough statement of what cooperation in a general but full-blown sense can be taken to involve. However, this thesis must be understood broadly enough so that it is compatible with the claim that not all cooperation need be acting towards a collective end-state. The truth of this claim is based on the possibility that there can be cooperation which only involves shared activity—a collective action-goal—but which shared activity does not purport to causally lead to a collective end —but only to private ends or no ends separate from the action at all. Note, too, that cooperation in the sense of T1) does not require an agreed-upon joint plan but needs only satisfy (*AT*).

T2) Cooperation is more likely to get initiated and carried out successfully and—speaking of rational cooperative situations—to give the expected rewards the more there is commonality of interest in the situation, understanding rewardingness to involve reward from acting together rather not so acting.

That cooperation is successful in the sense of T2) has to do with improvements related to a) the possibilities of helping the other participants to succeed in their part-performances and in other relevant features concerning the achievement of the cooperation-generating collective goal in question (cf. T1)); b) the selection of a collective goal and the means for reaching it, c) the stability of the commitment to the collective goal-directed action, and d) flexibility concerning the change of a means or a goal when it is called for.

In general, cooperation is expected to be rewarding:

T3) All intentionally, knowingly, and reflectively undertaken cooperation by normal and normally acting human agents is expected to be rewarding (considered relative to non-cooperation) to the participants.

By intentionally and knowingly undertaken cooperation here is meant, roughly, a case of cooperative activity, in which the people know "what is going on", viz. that they to an adequate extent possess the concept of cooperation and correctly apply it to the situation at hand. Of such adequate possession we require, for example, that when a person asks somebody else to join him in performing a task the latter understands the request at least in the sense concerned with his performing his part of the joint action. In T3) the reward concerns the reward coming from the collective cooperative activity itself as compared with not acting so. (The reward coming from reaching the collective goal involved in cooperation is still a separate matter.) In view of T3) all conceptually and informationally adequate cooperation can be called rational—rational in the sense of involving a reward expectation. The normality assumption excludes, e.g., small children and mentally ill, and also unreflectively acting normal agents will be excluded.

However, in view of T1) thesis T3) is compatible with the existence of cooperation without reward-expectation: People can cooperate—less than fully intentionally or without adequate knowledge of the nature of the situation—just by adopting a joint (or collective) goal—whose joint achievement need not be actually rewarding for the agents nor expected to be rewarding (even in favorable conditions).

There are weaker kinds of cooperation, I call them quasi-cooperation, such as cooperative activity based on reciprocity, where no collective goal but only personal goals need to be present. What is discussed under the heading 'cooperation' in game-theoretic setting often belongs here.

5. Conclusion

In this paper the notion of an intended collective goal in its full-blown sense was investigated. Roughly speaking, a state or action is an intended collective goal in a group when the members intend to contribute—together with the others—to the satisfaction of that goal, mutually believe or know that the others similarly have that goal and intend to contribute together with the others to its achievement. Furthermore, they must also in part maintain that goal of theirs because of this mutual belief. Part of the collectivity of a collective goal derives from the intuitive idea that it is a collective's goal. This idea is taken into account—in part—in the given analysis by the requirement that, on "quasi-conceptual" grounds, if the goal is satisfied it is satisfied for the whole collective, viz. for all its members. The resulting notion of a collective goal is stronger than what game-theory delivers or is capable of adequately delivering.

Collective goals (especially action-goals) are central for cooperation—or this is the view which this paper advocates. However, although some general theses about cooperation were presented in the paper, the reader was referred elsewhere for a proper discussion of them.

Acknowledgements

I wish to thank Kaarlo Miller, Maj Bonnevier-Tuomela, and Cristina Bicchieri for helpful comments related to this paper.

Notes
[1] This paper relies to some extent on some technical notions analyzed and discussed elsewhere. One of them is the notion of we-intention (cf. Tuomela, 1984, Tuomela, 1995). Basically a we-intention involves the we-intending person's acceptance of a conative intentions expression of the form "We will do X", and his being disposed to perform relevant practical reasonings and act in accordance with them (see especially the schemas W1) and W2) in Tuomela, 1995, Chapter 3). Also the further summary analysis holds true of we-intentions:

(WI) A member A_i of a collective G we-intends to do X if and only if, based on the (explicit or implicit)

agreement to perform X jointly made by the agents $A_1,...,A_i,...,A_m$,
(i) A_i intends to do his (agreement-based) part of X (as his part of X);
(ii) A_i has a belief to the effect that the joint action opportunities for an intentional performance of X will obtain (or at least probably will obtain), especially that a right number of the full-fledged and adequately informed members of G, as required for the performance of X, will (or at least probably will) do their parts of X, which will under normal conditions result in an intentional joint performance of X by the participants;
(iii) A_i believes that there is (or will be) a mutual belief among the participating members of G (or at least among those participants who do their parts of X intentionally as their parts of X there is or will be a mutual belief) to the effect that the joint action opportunities for an intentional performance of X will obtain (or at least probably will obtain);
(iv) (i) in part because of (ii) and (iii), 'because' expressing at least a presupposition reason.
Group-intentions (not to be confused with intentions that groups have) are analyzed in terms of acceptances of "We will do X":
(GI) The conatively used sentence "We will do X" is true of A (relative to A's group G) if and only if, based on the (explicit or implicit) agreement by the members of A's group G to perform X jointly,
1) A we-intends to do X (in the sense of (WI)); or
2) A has formed a standing group-intention to do X, which is a disposition to we-intend to do X (provided X has a part-division).
Group-intentions can now be regarded as either we-intentions or dispositions to we-intend.
My analysis of the notion of joint intention is this:
(JI) Agents $A_1,...,A_i,...,A_m$ have the *joint intention to perform a joint action X* if and only if
a) these agents have the group-intention to perform X; and
b) there is a mutual belief among them to the effect that a).
[2] The following comment on the logical aspects goal ascriptions may be made in this connection. Joint and collective goals (or goal-predicates, to be precise) in their basic sense apply to a number of agents. Thus a collective goal can be expressed by an $(m+1)$-place predicate $ICG(A_1,...,A_m,G)$ standing for "the agents $A_1,...,A_m$ have as their intended collective goal to achieve G". The analogous point can be made of intended joint goals (JI). In a derivative sense we can also speak of a single agent having a collective intention. This is the case when the agent is one to which the predicate ICG applies, entailing also that the agent in question endorses or accepts the collective intention in a commitment-generating sense (to be commented on later). As to my technical notions, the notion of we-intention is a social intention that an individual has: $WI(A_i,X)$ standing for "the agent A_i we-intends to do X". A group-intention is a we-intention or a disposition to acquire a we-intention. Finally, a group G can have an intention to perform something: $I(G,Y)$ standing for "group G intends to perform the group action Y" (Y could be "invading the town" or "painting the house").
[3] The argument just presented can be put precisely as follows (in the case of two agents A and B, the symbols used with rather obvious meanings). The conclusion derived from the example is that at least the following is needed (assuming each one bases his participation on his intention to participate):
i) $I_A(X_A$ because $I_B X_B$ & $B_B I_A X_A)$.
More generally (but simplifying the joint plan idea slightly) we require:
ii) $I_A(X_B$ because $MB_{A,B}(I_A X_A$ & $I_B X_B))$.
Requirement ii) comes from my agreement-view of joint intention, the view that joint intentions in their fullest sense require that the participants explicitly or implicitly agree on a plan for joint action: Agreement-making is essentially intentional. Thus if the agents have made an agreement there is mutual knowledge (or at least mutual belief) that they have made the agreement, and this mutual belief in the agreement and agreement-involving joint intention entails ii).
    The converse does not hold, and the tie provided by ii) is not yet sufficiently strong to account for proper joining of the wills: that requires agreement-making. Let me note here that in ii) the reason-relation 'because' is meant to be an objective or intersubjective one. Thus I intend to do my part for the reason that there is the mutual belief in question.
[4] A broad notion of a collective is meant here. I will not try to characterize it precisely here. Suffice it to say somewhat circularly that a collective in the present sense is a collection of people capable of sharing a collective goal.
[5] See Tuomela, 1984, p. 115, for a discussion of a related principle: Given that there are m participants in the joint action X in question X is contextually identical—amounts to—the type conjunctions $X_1 \& ...X_m$, where X_i is A_i's part-action. Thus it follows from this principle that X is "satisfied" (is duly performed by the m agents in question) only if each X_i is appropriately "satisfied" (performed). The converse entailment also holds when the notion of a part-performance is understood in a sufficiently "thick" sense requiring that the collective committed related to it has been appropriately satisfied. My present account simply applies this idea of "collectivity" to intention contents (goals), which may be states or joint actions.

References

Cohen, P. and Levesque, H. (1991) Teamwork, *Noñs 35*, 487-512.

Tuomela, R. (1984) *A Theory of Social Action*. Synthese Library. Reidel Publishing Company. Dordrecht and Boston.

Tuomela, R. (1991) We Will Do It. An Analysis of Group-Intentions. *Philosophy and Phenomenological Research LI*, 249-277.

Tuomela, R. (1993) What is Cooperation?, *Erkenntnis 38*, 87-101.

Tuomela, R. (1995) *The Importance of Us: A Philosophical Study of Basic Social Notions*, Stanford University Press, Stanford.

Tuomela, R. (1997) *Cooperation: A Philosophical Study*, book ms.

Tuomela, R. and Bonnevier-Tuomela (1997) From Social Imitation to Teamwork, in G. Holmstrom-Hintikka and R. Tuomela (eds.), *Contemporary Action Theory, vol. II: Social Action*, Kluwer, Dordrecht, pp. 1-46.

A LOGICAL APPROACH TO REASONING ABOUT UNCERTAINTY: A TUTORIAL

J. Y. HALPERN
Computer Science Department
Cornell University
Ithaca, NY 14853
USA
halpern@cs.cornell.edu
http://www.cs.cornell.edu/home/halpern

1. Introduction

Uncertainty is a fundamental—and unavoidable—feature of daily life. In order to deal with uncertainty intelligently, we need to be able to represent it and reason about it. These notes describe a systematic approach for doing so. I have made no attempt to be comprehensive here; I have been guided by my biases and my own research.

Reasoning about uncertainty can be subtle. Perhaps the best way to see this is to consider a number of puzzles, some of them very well-known. These puzzles are presented under the assumption that the uncertainty is quantified in terms of probability, but the issues that they bring out arise whatever method we use to represent uncertainty.

The second-ace puzzle [Bar-Hillel and Falk (1982), Freund (1965), Shafer (1985)]:
> Suppose we have a deck with four cards: the ace and deuce of hearts, and the ace and deuce of spades. After a fair shuffle of the deck, two cards are dealt to Alice. It is easy to see that, at this point, there is a probability of 1/6 that Alice has both aces, probability 5/6 that Alice has at least one ace, probability 1/2 that Alice has the ace of spades, and probability 1/2 that Alice has the ace of hearts: Out of the six possible deals of two cards out of four, Alice has both aces in one of them, at least one ace in five of them, the ace of hearts in three of them, and the ace of spades in three of them.
> Alice then says "I have an ace" Conditioning on this information, Bob computes the probability that Alice holds both aces to be 1/5. This seems reasonable: The probability of Alice having two aces goes up if we find out she has an ace. Next, Alice says "I have the ace of spades". Conditioning on this new information, Bob now computes the probability that Alice holds both aces to be 1/3. Of the three deals in which Alice holds the ace of spades, she holds both aces in one of them. As a result of learning not only that Alice holds at least one ace, but that the ace is actually the ace of spades, the conditional probability that Alice holds both aces goes up from 1/5 to 1/3. Similarly, if Alice had said "I have the ace of hearts", the conditional probability that Alice holds both aces would be 1/3.
> But is this reasonable? When Bob learns that Alice has an ace, he knows that she must have either the ace of hearts or the ace of spades. Why should finding out

X. Arrazola et al. (eds.), Discourse, Interaction and Communication, 141–155.

which particular ace it is raise the conditional probability of Alice having two aces?

The Monty Hall Puzzle [vos Savant (1991), Morgan et al. (1991)]: Suppose you're on a game show and given a choice of three doors. Behind one is a car; behind the others are goats. You pick door 1. Before opening door 1, Monty Hall, the host (who knows what is behind each door), opens door 2, which has a goat. He then asks you if you still want to take what's behind door 1, or to take what's behind door 3 instead. Should you switch?

The Two-Coin Problem [Fagin and Halpern (1994)]: Alice has two coins. One of them is fair, and so has equal likelihood of landing heads and tails. The other is biased, and is twice as likely to land heads as to land tails. Alice chooses one of her coins (assume she can tell them apart by their weight and feel) and is about to toss it. Bob knows that one coin is fair and the other is twice as likely to land heads as tails. He does not know which coin Alice has chosen, nor is he given a probability that the fair coin is chosen. What is the probability, according to Bob, that the outcome of the coin toss will be heads? What is the probability according to Alice? (Both of these probabilities are for the situation *before* the coin is tossed.)

The Single-Coin Problem [Fagin and Halpern (1994)]: This time both Bob and Alice know that Alice is using the fair coin. Alice tosses the coin and looks at the outcome. What is the probability of heads according to Bob? (Note I now want the probability *after* the coin toss.) One argument would say that the probability is still 1/2. After all, Bob hasn't learned anything about the outcome of the coin toss, so why should he change his valuation of the probability? On the other hand, runs the counterargument, once the coin has been tossed, can we really talk about the probability of heads? It has either landed heads or tails, so at best, Bob can say that the probability is either 0 or 1, but he doesn't know which.

There is certainly far more to representing uncertainty than dealing with puzzles such as these. Nevertheless, the analysis of these puzzles and paradoxes will give us deeper insight into the process of reasoning under uncertainty and the problems involved with getting a good representation.

So how do we represent and reason about uncertainty? I shall use the *possible-worlds* framework. This is the standard approach for giving semantics to modal logic. The intuition is that besides the true state of affairs, there are a number of other possible states of affairs or "worlds", that an agent considers possible. We can view the set of worlds that an agent considers possible as a qualitative way to measure her uncertainty. The more worlds she considers possible, the more uncertain she has as to the true state of affairs, and the less she knows. We can then quantify this uncertainty by adding a probability distribution to the possible worlds (or using some other means of "grading" the uncertainty). This is not quite enough for dealing with the puzzles above. We need to add time to the picture. That means we need to have possible worlds describing not only the current state of affairs, but the state of affairs at each time point of interest. As we shall see, it is also useful to assume that these states have some internal structure. The resulting framework, incorporating knowledge, time and probability in a concrete setting, is a powerful modeling tool.

The rest of this paper is organized as follows. Section 2 reviews modal logic and the possible-worlds framework. Section 3 discusses a concrete framework for modeling knowledge and time in multi-agent systems. Probability is added in Section 4. The various puzzles are analyzed in the resulting framework in Section 5. Other topics are briefly discussed in Section 6.

2. Basic modal logic: knowledge, belief, and time

Let us start by considering a simple model to capture an agent's knowledge, using ideas that go back to Hintikka (1962).

Suppose we have an agent with some information, and we want to reason about her beliefs. Given her current information, the agent may not be able to tell which of a number of possible worlds describes the actual state of affairs. We say that the agent *believes* or *knows* [1] a fact ϕ if ϕ is true in all the worlds the agent considers possible.

To capture this intuition, we use the language of modal logic. We start with a set Φ of primitive propositions, where a primitive proposition $p \in \Phi$ represents a basic fact of interest like "it is raining in Spain". We then close off under conjunction and negation, as in propositional logic, and modal operators $K_1, ..., K_n$, where $K_i\phi$ is read "agent i knows ϕ". Thus, a statement such as $K_1 K_2 p \wedge \neg K_2 K_1 K_2 p$ says "agent 1 knows agent 2 knows p, but agent 2 does not know that 1 knows that 2 knows p".∙ More colloquially: "I know that you know it, but you don't know that I know that you know it."

Next we need a semantics. Suppose for simplicity we start with just one agent (and write $K\phi$ rather than $K_1\phi$). We define a *simple structure* M to be a triple (W, w_0, π), where W can be thought of as the set of worlds the agent considers possible, w_0 is the actual world, and π associates with each world a truth assignment to the primitive propositions. That is, $\pi(w)(p) \in \{\text{true, false}\}$ for each primitive proposition $p \in \Phi$ and world $w \in W \cup \{w_0\}$. Notice that I am not identifying a world with a truth assignment. There may be two worlds associated with the same truth assignment; that is, we may have $\pi(w) = \pi(w')$ for $w \neq w'$. This amounts to saying that there may be more to a world than what can be described by the primitive propositions in our language. For the simple logic I am about to present, it would actually be safe to identify worlds with truth assignments (and thus "combine" two worlds that were associated with the same truth assignment), but once we move to multiple agents, or even to somewhat more sophisticated logics involving just one agent, this cannot be done.

In propositional logic, a formula is true or false given a valuation. In the possible-worlds approach, of which this is an example, the truth of a formula depends on the world. A primitive proposition such as p may be true in one world and false in another. Thus, we define truth relative to a world in a structure, writing $(M,w) \models \phi$, which is read "ϕ is true in world w of structure M". We define $\models$ by induction on the structure of formulas:

$(M,w) \models p$ (for a primitive proposition $p \in \Phi$) iff $\pi(w)(p) = \text{true}$

$(M,w) \models \phi \wedge \phi'$ iff $(M,w) \models \phi$ and $(M,w) \models \phi'$

$(M,w) \models \neg\phi$ iff $(M,w) \not\models \phi$

$(M,w) \models K\phi$ iff $(M,w') \models \phi$ for all $w' \in W$.

The first three clauses are just what we would expect from propositional logic; the last captures the intuition that the agent knows ϕ if ϕ is true in all the worlds the agent considers possible. We remark that occasionally when M is clear from context, we write $w \models \phi$ instead of $(M,w) \models \phi$.

In simple structures, it is implicitly assumed that the set of worlds the agent considers possible in world w is the same as the set of worlds the agent considers possible in world w', even if $w \neq w'$. In general, this is clearly inappropriate. The set of worlds the agent considers possible when it is raining is clearly different from the set of worlds the agent considers possible when it is sunny. This may seem less objectionable if we think of W as the set of worlds that the agent considers possible given some fixed information (or set of observations and perceptions). Then our implicit assumption amounts to saying that the set of worlds the agent considers possible is determined by her "internal state"—roughly speaking, what she has seen and heard thus far, together with her genetic makeup and so on. The impact of the external world on the set of worlds she considers possible is summarized by her *internal* state. We return to this viewpoint in the next section.

There are times when we want the set of worlds the agent considers possible to depend on the actual world. This can be done in a straightforward way. We define a *Kripke structure* M to be a tuple $(W, \mathcal{K}, \pi)$, where $\mathcal{K}$ is a binary relation on W—that is, a set of pairs $(w, w') \in W \times W$. Intuitively, $(w, w') \in \mathcal{K}$ if the agent considers w' a possible world in world w. In a Kripke structure there is no distinguished "actual world" (although we could add one if desired). If we define $\mathcal{K}(w) = \{w': (w, w') \in \mathcal{K}\}$, then we can think of $\mathcal{K}(w)$ as describing the set of worlds the agent considers possible in world w. We thus define

- $(M, w) \vDash K\phi$ if $(M, w') \vDash \phi$ for all $w' \in \mathcal{K}(w)$.

Of course, this framework allows us to generalize easily to multiple agents. We simply have one possibility relation for each agent. In particular, if we have n agents, we take a Kripke structure for n agents to be a tuple $(W, \mathcal{K}_1, ..., \mathcal{K}_n, \pi)$, where each $\mathcal{K}_i$ is a binary relation on W. Of course, we now define:

- $(M, w) \vDash K_i\phi$ if $(M, w') \vDash \phi$ for all $w' \in \mathcal{K}_i(w)$.

The simple structures above are essentially Kripke structures for one agent where $\mathcal{K}(w) = \mathcal{K}(w')$ for $w, w' \in W$.

We can maintain the intuition that the worlds that the agent considers possible depend only on the agent's internal state without resorting to simple structures, but by taking the $\mathcal{K}_i$ relation to be transitive and *Euclidean*.[2] This guarantees that the set of worlds the agent considers possible is the same in all worlds that he considers possible. An even stronger assumption, that further ensures that what the agent knows is true, is to take the $\mathcal{K}_i$ relation to be an equivalence relation.[3]

Up to now, we have considered knowledge (and belief). In our examples, time also formed a crucial element. Clearly an agent's beliefs change over time. Thus, to capture this, we need to have time in our model. It is easy to construct a simple model of time, along the lines above. We take a temporal structure T to consist of a pair $((w_0, w_1, w_2, ...), \pi)$, where, intuitively, w_k is the world at "time" k, and π associates with each world a truth assignment, as before. Thus, we are implicitly assuming that time is discrete, linear (for each time, there is a unique next time), and infinite. While each of these assumptions can be (and have been!) challenged, let us make them for now. The assumption of discreteness certainly seems reasonable in human affairs (we can allow an arbitrarily fine level of granularity), linearity seems reasonable in our applications (as we shall see, if we want to consider different possible futures, we can combine knowledge with time), and if we want to model a situation where there are only finitely many steps, all we have to do is to repeat the last step infinitely often to get an infinite sequence.

The type of modal operators that are typically considered when dealing with time are $\bigcirc$ and $\square$, where $\bigcirc$ means "at the next time interval" while $\square$ means "now and at all times in the future". Thus, for example,

$$(T,w_k) \models \bigcirc\phi \text{ if } (T,w_{k+1}) \models \phi, \text{ and}$$

$$(T,w_k) \models \bigcirc\phi \text{ if } (T,w_m) \models \phi, \text{ for all } m \geq k.$$

Of course, we can also have structures that combine knowledge and time. A concrete framework for doing so is presented in the next section.

3. A concrete framework for multi-agent systems

The possible-worlds framework of the previous section is somewhat abstract. Possible worlds are represented as elements of a set. But where are these possible worlds coming from? I shall now consider a more concrete framework, that incorporates both knowledge and time, and takes an agent's knowledge to be determined by the agent's internal state. The ideas presented here are mainly taken from Halpern and Fagin (1989), and Fagin et al. (1995).

Suppose we want to analyze a multi-agent system. The phrase "system" is intended to be interpreted rather loosely here. Players in a poker game, agents conducting a bargaining session, robots interacting to clean a house, and processes in a computing system can all be viewed as multi-agent systems. The only assumption I shall make here about a system is that, at all times, each of the agents in the can be viewed as being in some *local* or *internal* state. Intuitively, the local state encapsulates all the relevant information to which the agent has access. For example, if we are modeling a poker game, a player's state might consist of the cards he currently holds, the bets made by the other players, any other cards he has seen, and any information he may have about the strategies of the other players (for example, Bob may know that Alice likes to bluff, while Charlie tends to bet conservatively).

It is also useful to view the system as a whole as being in a state. The first thought might be to make the system's state be a tuple of the form $(s_1,..., s_n)$, where s_i is agent i's state. But, in general, more than just the local states of the agents may be relevant when doing an analysis of the system. If we are analyzing a message-passing system where agents send messages back and forth along communication lines, we might want to know about messages that are in transit or about the status of each communication line (whether it is up or down). If we are considering a system of sensors observing some terrain, we might need to include features of the terrain in a description of the state of the system. Thus, we conceptually divide a system into two components: the agents and the *environment*, where we view the environment as "everything else that is relevant". In many ways the environment can be viewed as just another agent, but one that we often ignore, since we are not usually interested in what the environment knows. We define a *global state* of a system with n agents or agents to be an $(n+1)$-tuple of the form $(s_e,s_1,...,s_n)$, where s_e is the state of the environment and s_i is the local state of agent i.

A system is not a static entity. It is constantly changing over time. A *run* is a complete description of what happens over time in one possible execution of the system. Thus, formally, a run is a function from the natural numbers to global states. Given a run r, $r(0)$ describes the initial global state of the system in r, $r(1)$ describes the next global state, and so on. We refer to a pair (r,m) consisting of a run r and time m as a point. If

$r(m) = (s_e, s_1, ..., s_n)$, we define $r_e(m) = s_e$ and $r_i(m) = s_i$, $i = 1, ..., n$; thus, $r_i(m)$ is agent i's local state at the point (r, m)

How do we incorporate knowledge into this framework? The basic idea is that a statement such as "agent i does not know ϕ" means that, as far as i is concerned, the system could be at a point where ϕ does not hold. The way we capture that "as far as i is concerned, the system could be at a point where ϕ does not hold" is closely related to the notion of possible worlds in Kripke structures. We think of i's knowledge as being determined by its local state, so that i cannot distinguish between two points in the system in which it has the same local state, and it can distinguish points in which its local state differs. In fact, all that prevents us from viewing a distributed system as a Kripke structure is that we have no primitive propositions, and no function π telling us how to assign truth values to the primitive propositions. We now rectify this problem.

Assume that we have a set Φ of primitive propositions, which we can think of as describing basic facts about the system. These might be such facts as "Alice holds the ace of spades", "there is a goat behind door 3", or "process 1's initial input was 17". An *interpreted system* I consists of a pair $(\mathcal{R}, \pi)$, where $\mathcal{R}$ is a system and π associates with each point in $\mathcal{R}$ a truth assignment to the primitive propositions in Φ. We say that the point (r, m) is in the interpreted system $I = (\mathcal{R}, \pi)$ if $r \in \mathcal{R}$.

We can associate with an interpreted system $I = (\mathcal{R}, \pi)$ a Kripke structure $M_I = (S, \mathcal{K}_1, ..., \mathcal{K}_n, \pi)$ in a straightforward way. The set S of states in M_I consists of the points in I. We can define $\mathcal{K}_i$ so that $\mathcal{K}_i((r, m)) = \{(r', m'): r_i(m) = r'_i(m')\}$. Thus, $\mathcal{K}_i((r, m))$ consists of all points indistinguishable from (r, m) by agent i, where we think of two points as being by agent i if agent i has the same local state in both.

We can now define what it means for a formula ϕ in our language of knowledge to be true at a point (r, m) in an interpreted system I by applying the definitions of the previous section to the related Kripke structure M_I. Thus we say that $(I, r, m) \models \phi$ exactly if $(M_I, s) \models \phi$, where $s = (r, m)$. For example, we have

- $(I, r, m) \models p$ (for $p \in \Phi$) if $\pi(r, m)(p) = $ **true**

- $(I, r, m) \models K_i\phi$ iff $(I, r', m') \models \phi$ for all (r', m') such that $r_i(m) = r'_i(m')$.

Interpreted systems also allow us to reason about time, since each run provides a temporal model. Thus, for example, we have

- $(I, r, m) \models \bigcirc\phi$ if $(I, r, m+1) \models \phi$.

We can also combine temporal and epistemic statements; a formula such as $K_1 \bigcirc \neg K_2 \square p$ makes perfect sense.

Where do the runs in the system come from? Typically, they are generated by means of a *protocol*. I do not want to go into the formal definitions here (these can be found in Halpern and Fagin (1989), and Fagin et al. (1995)), but intuitively, a protocol is a description of the actions that an agent takes as a function of her local state. We shall see some examples of protocols later in the paper.

4. Adding probability

Up to now we have considered time and knowledge. The next step is to add probability. The idea now is to assume that besides having a set of worlds that she considers possible, an agent puts probability on these worlds. To reason about the probability, we need to enrich the language. I shall do so by allowing formulas of the form $\mathrm{pr}_i (\phi) \geq \alpha$,

$pr_i(\phi) \leq \alpha$, and $pr_i(\phi) = \alpha$, where ϕ is a formula in the language and α is a real number in the interval $[0,1]$. A formula such as $pr_i(\phi) \geq \alpha$ can be read as "the probability of ϕ, according to agent i, is at least α". It is easy to allow even more complicated formulas such as $pr_i(\phi) + 2pr_i(\psi) \leq \alpha$ (and this, in fact, is done in Fagin et al. (1990)), but all the basic ideas should already be clear with the simple language we are considering.

To give semantics to such formulas, we need to augment the Kripke structures used in Section 2 with a probability distribution. To bring out the main ideas, let's start by assuming there is one agent (so that we can temporarily drop the subscript on pr). We take a *simple probability structure M* to be a tuple of the form (W, Pr, π), where Pr is a *discrete probability distribution* on W. A discrete probability distribution Pr just maps worlds in W to numbers in the interval $[0,1]$, with the constraint that $\Sigma_{w \in W}Pr(w) = 1$. We extend Pr to subsets of W by taking $Pr(A) = \Sigma_{w \in A}Pr(w)$.[4] We can now define satisfaction ($\models$) in simple probability structures; the only interesting case comes in dealing with formulas such as $pr(\phi) \geq \alpha$. Such a formula is true if the set of worlds where ϕ is true has probability at least α:

$$(M,w) \models pr(\phi) \geq \alpha \text{ if } Pr(\{w: (M,w) \models \phi\}) \geq \alpha.$$

Of course, the treatment of $pr(\phi) \leq \alpha$ and $pr(\phi) = \alpha$ is analogous.

Like the simple structures of Section 2, simple probability structures implicitly assume that the agent's probability distribution is independent of the state. We can generalize simple probability structures analogously to the way we extended simple structures, by having the probability distribution Pr depend on the world, and by allowing different agents to have different probability distributions. We thus define a probabilistic Kripke structure M to be a tuple of the form $(W,\mathcal{PR}_1,...,\mathcal{PR}_n,\pi)$, where for each agent i and world w, we take $\mathcal{PR}_i(w)$ to be a discrete probability distribution, denoted $Pr_{i,w}$, over W. (Actually, as we shall see, it is sometimes useful to view $Pr_{i,w}$ as a distribution, not on W, but on some subset of W; that is, its domain is some $W' \subseteq W$ rather than all of W. Of course, we can identify a distribution over $W' \subseteq W$ with a distribution over W by just making all the worlds in $W - W'$ have probability 0.) To evaluate the truth of a formula such as $pr_i(\phi) \geq \alpha$ at the world w we use the distribution $Pr_{i,w}$:

$$(M,w) \models pr_i(\phi) \geq \alpha \text{ if } Pr_{i,w}(\{w: (M,w) \models \phi\}) \geq \alpha.$$

We can easily combine reasoning about knowledge with reasoning about probability. A Kripke structure for knowledge and probability is a combination of a Kripke structure (for knowledge) and a Kripke structure for probability; thus, it is a tuple of the form $(W,\mathcal{K}_1,....,\mathcal{K}_n,\mathcal{PR}_1,...,\mathcal{PR}_n,\pi)$. Such a structure can be used to give semantics to a language that has both knowledge operators and probability operators. A natural assumption in that case is that, in world w, agent i assigns probability only to the worlds that he considers possible, namely $\mathcal{K}_i(w)$. We can model this either by assuming that $Pr_{i,w}$ is defined only on $\mathcal{K}_i(w)$ or by taking $Pr_{i,w}(w')$ to be 0 if $w' \notin \mathcal{K}_i(w)$. There may be times, however, when this is not appropriate.

Example 4.1: Let us reconsider the two-coin problem from the introduction. Recall that Alice has two coins, one of which is fair, the other biased. She chooses one of them. There are four possible worlds, which we can denote (F,H), (F,T), (B,H), (B,T): the fair coin is chosen and will land heads, the fair coin is chosen and will land tails, and so on.[5]

Bob cannot distinguish any of these worlds; in any one of them, he considers all four possible. (His internal state is the same in all four, since he does not know which coin is chosen.) On the other hand, if a world of the form (F,x), Alice considers only worlds of the form (F,y) possible, while in a world of the form (B,x), Alice considers only worlds of the form (B,y) possible. Describing Alice's probability distributions $\mathrm{Pr}_{A,w}$ is straightforward: In a world of the form (F,x), she knows the fair coin is being used, so her probability space consists of the two worlds (F,H) and (F,T), each of which gets probability $1/2$. Similarly, in a world of the form (B,x), she knows the biased coin is being used, so her probability space consists of the two worlds (B,H) and (B,T); the former gets probability $2/3$, while the latter gets probability $1/3$. Suppose we take as primitive propositions f, b, h, and t, representing that Alice chooses the fair coin, Alice chooses the biased coin, the coin will land heads, and the coin will land tails, respectively. Then, for example, $(F,T) \models K_A f \wedge K_A(\mathrm{pr}_A(h) = 1/2)$: in the world where the fair coin is chosen and will in fact land tails, Alice knows that the fair coin is chosen and knows that the probability that it will land heads is $1/2$.

What about Bob? Clearly we have $(F,T) \models \neg K_B f$: Bob does not know which coin has been chosen. But what probability distribution should Bob use? As I said above, if Bob knew the probability of Alice's picking the coin was α (or, for that matter, if Bob's subjective probability that Alice would pick the fair coin were α), then there would be no problem: (F,H) and (F,T) would both get probability $\frac{1}{2}\alpha$, (B,H) would get probability $\frac{2}{3}(1-\alpha)$, and (B,T) would get probability $\frac{1}{3}(1-\alpha)$. Unfortunately, the problem statement does not give us α. A Bayesian would say that Bob should just go ahead and choose some α (and perhaps go on to say that in the absence of any information, $\frac{1}{2}$ would be the best choice for α).

This is not the place to get into a discussion about the merits of the Bayesian approach. Whatever its merits, we certainly want the model to be rich enough to allow us to model the fact that Bob does not know the probability that Alice chooses the fair coin. This is, after all, supposed to be an approach with which we can represent Bob's knowledge (or lack of it). One way to do this is to consider a family of models, one for each choice of α. But doing this negates the point of using the possible-worlds framework: We want to be able to represent Bob's uncertainty within one model, not by considering a family of models. Perhaps the simplest approach to doing this is not to take Bob's probability space to consist of all the four worlds he considers possible, but to split up these four worlds into two separate probability spaces: W_F, consisting of the two worlds (F,H) and (F,T) and W_B, consisting of the two worlds (B,H) and (B,T). W_F consists of the worlds where Alice chose the fair coin and W_B consists of the worlds where Alice chose the biased coin. In each of these worlds, Bob's probability distribution is the obvious one: For example, $\mathrm{Pr}_{B,(B,H)}$ assigns the world (B,H) probability $2/3$ and the world (B,T) probability $1/3$.

It is easy to see that, at each world, Bob's probability distribution is the same as Alice's: $\mathrm{Pr}_{A,w} = \mathrm{Pr}_{B,w}$ for each world $w \in W$. The difference between Bob and Alice is not captured in the probability distributions they use, but in the set of worlds they consider possible. We already observed that in the world (F,H), the formula $K_A(\mathrm{pr}_A(h) = 1/2)$ is true. This is because in both of the worlds that Alice considers possible— namely, (F,H) and (F,T)—the formula $\mathrm{pr}_A(h) = 1/2$ holds. Now since Bob is using the same probability distribution as Alice, it is also the case that at both (F,H) and (F,T), the formula $pr_B(h) = 1/2$ holds. However, the formula $K_B(pr_B(h) = 1/2)$ does *not* hold at the world (F,H) since Bob, unlike Alice, also considers the worlds (B,H) and (B,T) possible: Bob does not know whether Alice chose the fair coin or the biased coin. In the latter two worlds, the formula $pr_B(h) = 2/3$ is true. Thus, we have $(F,H) \vDash K_B(pr_B(h) = 1/2 \vee pr_B(h) = 2/3)$. All Bob can say is that the probability of heads is either 1/2 or 2/3, but he does not know which. I would argue that this indeed is a reasonable representation of Bob's ignorance regarding which coin was chosen. ∎

Example 4.2: Armed with the insights from the previous example, we can now also consider the single-coin problem from the introduction. Despite its apparent simplicity, it involves a number of subtleties. Using the notation from the previous example, since Bob now knows that Alice used the fair coin, the only worlds that he considers possible are (F,H) and (F,T). Alice also knows the outcome of the coin toss, so in world (F,H), the only world she considers possible is (F,H), while in (F,T), the only world she considers possible is (F,T). Obviously she assigns probability 1 to the only world that she considers possible, so, for example, we now have $(F,H) \vDash K_A(h) \wedge K_A(pr_A(h) = 1)$. How about Bob? What probability distribution should he place on the two worlds he considers possible. One obvious choice would be to make them equally likely, as in the previous example. After all, he does not know the outcome of the coin toss. Thus, if we take M_1 to be the structure where Bob's probability functions $Pr_{B,(F,H)}$ and $Pr_{B,(F,T)}$ give each of the two worlds (F,H) and (F,T) probability 1/2, then we have $(M_1,(F,H)) \vDash K_B(pr_B(h) = 1/2)$. This seems like a reasonable answer: Bob still believes that heads has probability 1/2.

On the other hand, as we saw in the previous example, the framework does not force us to assign probability to all of Bob's possible worlds. We can divide them up. In particular, just as in the previous example, we can take Bob's probability distribution to be identical to Alice's: let $Pr_{B,(F,H)}$ assign probability 1 to the world (F,H) (and hence probability 0 to (F,T)) and let $Pr_{B,(F,T)}$ assign probability 1 to the world (F,T) (and hence probability 0 to (F,H)). If M_2 is the structure where $\mathcal{PR}_B$ is defined in this way, then $(M_2,(F,H)) \vDash K_B(pr_B(h) = 1 \vee pr_B(h) = 0)$, since at the world (F,H), $pr_B(h) = 1$ holds, while at the world (F,T), $pr_B(h) = 0$ holds.

I was careful in this example to include the structure. M_1 and M_2 are identical in all respects except for $\mathcal{PR}_B$, which determines Bob's probability distribution at each of the worlds. This is precisely the crucial distinction though. M_1 and M_2 capture formally the two competing intuitions we discussed in the introduction: in M_1, Bob assigns probability 1/2 to heads; in M_2, the probability of heads is either 0 or 1, but Bob does not know which. It is beyond the scope of these notes to delve into which of the two approaches is "right". (This issue is discussed in some detail by Halpern and Tuttle (1993), where the point is made that a useful way of approaching this issue is to think in terms of the nature of the adversary against which Bob is playing.) ∎

5. Combining knowledge, probability, and time

We can now put all the pieces together, and combine knowledge, probability, and time, using the framework of runs and systems. The basic idea is to put a probability on runs, and then condition. But the subtleties that we observed before we considered time carry over here.

Where does the probability come from? Typically, if we are given a protocol that generates the set of runs, then some of the transitions are probabilistic. The probability of the transitions then determines the probability of the runs. For example, suppose we first toss a biased coin (with heads having probability 2/3) and then toss a fair coin. There are four runs, depending on the outcome of the coin tosses. These runs are best thought of as being the paths in the tree in Figure 1, where we go left in the tree if the outcome of coin toss is heads, and go right if the outcome is tails. The branches of the tree are labeled by the probability of the outcome, so, for example, the top left branch is labeled by 2/3, since the probability of getting heads on the first coin toss is 2/3. The probability of a run is then just the product of the probabilities of the path in the tree that determines it, so, for example, the probability of getting two heads is 1/3, just as we would expect.

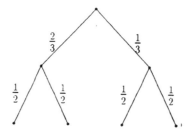

Figure 1: Tossing two coins

The first problem in this approach comes if not all transitions are probabilistic. Some may be nondeterministic, with no probabilities attached. This is precisely what happens if we model the two-coin example using runs. At the first step Alice chooses a coin. She can choose either a fair coin (go left) or a biased coin (go right). This step is nonprobabilistic; the problem does not give us probabilities with which to label this transition. The second step—tossing the coin—is probabilistic, as shown in Figure 2. The solution we take is just the same as that in Example 4.1: we separate the four runs into two probability spaces, one consisting of the runs corresponding to the fair coin (the paths labeled r_1 and r_2 in Figure 2) and one consisting of the runs corresponding to the biased coin (r_3 and r_4 in Figure 2). In the space consisting of $\{r_1, r_2\}$, each run gets probability 1/2. In the space consisting of $\{r_3, r_4\}$, the run r_3 gets probability 2/3 and r_4 gets probability 1/3.

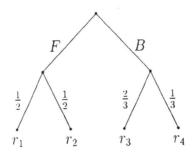

Figure 2: The two-coin example

Putting a probability on the runs (or on various subsets of runs) is not enough. We want to know what probability each agent assigns to various events at each point. In general, the probability that an agent assigns to an event like "the coin landed (or will land) heads" changes over time, depending on what information the agent obtains. To capture this, we need to have, for each agent at each point in the system, a probability. Clearly, we would like that probability to be related to the probability on runs. The obvious way to do this is to condition, but what do we condition on? There is not enough space here to go into all the details (see Halpern and Tuttle (1993) for those) but the general answer is to condition on the agent's knowledge.

To make this clearer, let us consider the two-coin example in a little more detail, by putting in the local states for Alice and Bob. At time 0, we assume that Alice's local state is 0; this essentially captures the fact that she knows the time. At time 1, she is either in state F or B, depending on which coin she has chosen. At time 2, she is in one of the states (F,H), (F,T), (B,H), or (B,T), depending on the outcome of the coin toss. (The fact that Alice's state also contains either B or F encodes the fact that Alice does not forget which coin she has tossed.) Call the four runs where Alice ends up in these states $r_1,...,$ r_4, respectively. Bob never finds out which coin was tossed nor how it landed, but we assume that he does know which step of the protocol is currently being followed. Thus, we take his local state at time m, $m \leq 2$, to be just m.

What are Alice's probability spaces? At time 0, she considers all the points $(r_1,0),...,(r_4,0)$ possible. (She knows the time is 0.) As in Example 4.1, we partition these points into two subspaces, one corresponding to the fair coin being chosen, and one corresponding to the biased coin being chosen. At time 1, Alice knows what coin she chose, so, for example, at the point $(r_1,1)$, she only considers $(r_2,1)$ possible. She puts the obvious probability on these two points, judging them to be equally likely. At time 2, Alice knows the outcome of the coin toss. Her probability spaces are singletons, and she puts probability 1 on the one point in each probability space.

Bob never learns what happens. At each time m, he considers all the points $(r_1,m),...,(r_4,m)$ possible. He can divide these points up into two probability spaces, as we have seen, but he also has the possibility of dividing it up into four probability spaces, just like Alice, at time 2. This will mean that, after the coin toss, he believes that the probability of heads is either 0 or 1, although he does not know which.

We can apply the same methodology to the Second-Ace problem from the introduction. As Shafer (1985) points out, the ambiguities in the problem become clearer when we specify the protocol that Alice and Bob are following. One possible protocol that is consistent with the story is that, at step 1, Alice is dealt two cards. At step 2, Alice tells Bob whether or not she has an ace. Then, at step 3, Alice tells Bob she has the ace of spades if she has it and otherwise she says she hasn't got it. In this case, the analysis described in the introduction is correct. There are six possible pairs of cards that Alice could have been dealt; each one determines a unique run. Since we assume a fair deal, each of these runs has probability 1/6. Bob conditions on his information, as discussed above. When Alice tells Bob that she has an ace in step 2, then at time 2, Bob can eliminate the run where Alice was not dealt an ace, and his conditional probability that Alice has two aces is indeed 1/5, as suggested in the story. At time 3, Bob can eliminate two more runs (the runs where Alice does not have the ace of spades), and he assesses the probability that Alice has both aces as 1/3. Notice, however, the concern as to what happens if Alice had told Bob that she has the ace of hearts does not arise. This cannot happen, according to the protocol.

Now suppose we consider a different protocol (although, again, one consistent with the story). Again, at step 2, Alice tells Bob whether or not she has an ace. However, now, at step 3, Alice tells Bob which ace she has if she has an ace (otherwise we can assume she says nothing). This still does not completely specify the protocol. What does Alice tell Bob at step 3 if she has both aces? One possible response is to say that she says "I have the ace of hearts" and "I have the ace of spades" with equal probability in this case. With this protocol, there are seven runs: each of the six possible pairs of cards that Alice could have been dealt determines a unique run, with the exception of the case where Alice is dealt two aces, for which there are two possible runs (depending on which ace Alice tells Bob she has). Each run has probability 1/6 except for the two runs where Alice was dealt two aces, which each have probability 1/12.

Again, Bob conditions on the information he receives, and again, at time 2, his conditional probability that Alice has two aces is 1/5. What is the situation at time 3, after Alice says she has the ace of spades? In this case Bob considers three points possible, those in the two runs where Alice has the ace of spades and a deuce, and the point in the run where Alice has both aces and tells Bob she has the ace of spades. Notice, however, that after conditioning, the probability of the point on the run where Alice has both aces is 1/5, while the probability of each of the other two points is 2/5! This is because the probability of the run where Alice holds both aces and tells Bob she has the ace of spades is 1/12, half the probability of the runs where Alice holds only one ace. Thus, Bob's probability that Alice holds both aces at time 3 is 1/5, not 1/3, if this is the protocol. The fact that Alice says she has the ace of spades does not change Bob's assessment of the probability that she has two aces. Similarly, if Alice says that she has the ace of hearts at step 3, the probability that she has two aces remains at 1/5.

Suppose we modify Alice's protocol so that, if she has both aces, the probability that she says she has the ace of spades is α. In this case, a similar analysis shows that Bob's probability that Alice holds both aces at time 3 is $\alpha/(\alpha + 2)$. In the special case we started with, we have $\alpha = 1/2$, and $\alpha/(\alpha + 2)$ reduces to 1/5. If $\alpha = 0$, then Alice never says "I have the ace of spades" if she has both aces. In this case, Bob's probability that Alice has both aces is 0, as we would expect. If $\alpha = 1$, which corresponds to Alice saying "I have the ace of spades" either if she has only the ace of spades or if she has both aces, Bob's probability that Alice has both aces is 1/3.

What if Alice does not choose which ace to say probabilistically, but uses some deterministic protocol which Bob does not know? In this case, all Bob can say is that the probability that Alice holds both aces is either 0 or 1/3, depending on which protocol Alice is following.

Finally, let's consider the Monty Hall puzzle. The standard argument says that you ought to switch: you lose by switching if the goat is behind the door you've picked; otherwise you gain. Thus, the probability of gaining is 2/3. Is this argument reasonable? It depends. I'll just sketch the analysis here, since it's so similar to that of the second-ace problem.

What protocol describes the situation? We assume that at the first step Monty places a car behind one door and a goat behind the other two. For simplicity, let's assume that the car is equally likely to be placed behind any door. At step 2, you choose a door. At step 3, Monty opens a door (one with a goat behind it other than the one you chose). Finally, at step 4, you must decide if you'll take what's behind your door or what's behind the other unopened door. Again, to completely specify the protocol, we have to say what Monty does if the door you choose has a car behind it (since then he can open either of the other two doors). Suppose we take the probability of him opening door j if you choose door i to be α_{ij} (where α_{ii} is 0 —Monty never opens the door you've chosen).

Computations similar to those above show that, if you initially take door i and Monty then opens door j, the probability of you gaining by switching is $1/(\alpha_{ij} + 1)$. If $\alpha_{ij} = 1/2$, then we get 2/3, just as in the standard analysis. Intuitively, the standard analysis presumes that learning which door Monty opens does not affect your prior probability that the car is equally likely to be behind each door. If $\alpha_{ij} = 0$, then you are certain that the car can't be behind the door you opened once Monty opens door j. Not surprisingly, you certainly should switch; you are certain to win in this case. On the other hand, if $\alpha_{ij} = 1$, you are just as likely to win by switching as not. Since, with any choice of α_{ij}, you are at least as likely to win by switching as by not switching, it seems that you ought to switch.

However, as pointed out in Morgan et al. (1991), this analysis is carried out under the assumption that, at step 3, Monty must open another door. If we instead modify Monty's protocol so that he is far more likely to open another door if the door that you chose has a car behind it, then this analysis is no longer correct. In particular, if we assume that Monty only opens another door if the door that you chose has the car behind it (in order to tempt you away from the "good" door), then you should clearly stick with your original choice.

6. Conclusion

Uncertainty is pervasive, and it is unlikely that any one approach can handle all of its complexities. Nevertheless, I hope I have made the case that thinking in terms of protocols, runs, and systems can go a long way towards clarifying things. I believe the framework is rich enough to capture much of the reasoning that goes on, natural enough to allow us to model easily many interesting examples, while forcing us to make explicit issues that, when left implicit or unsettled, cause many of the ambiguities and difficulties in reasoning about uncertainty.

As I said in the introduction, I could cover only a small selection of topics here. Let me close with a few words about some related issues that I would have liked to cover, given more space and time:

    • Since the focus here has been on semantics and modeling issues, nothing has been said about axiomatizations. Complete axiomatizations and decision procedures are known for most of the logics presented here. In particular, axiomatizations for modal (multi-agent) logics of knowledge and belief are presented in Halpern and Moses (1992), the case of knowledge and time is considered in Halpern and Vardi (1989), the case of probability is considered in Fagin et al. (1990), and the combination of knowledge and probability is considered in Fagin and Halpern (1994).

    • As Pearl and others have stressed, one of the most important aspects of probabilistic reasoning involves reasoning about dependencies, independencies, and causality. Indeed, Pearl makes a strong case that much human reasoning about uncertainty involves this type of reasoning. *Bayesian networks* have been shown to be a powerful tool for representing (in)dependencies graphically, and many algorithms have been developed for computing with Bayesian networks and learning Bayesian networks. This is an active area of research that holds a great deal of promise; I would encourage the interested reader to consult Pearl (1988) for an overview.

    • The focus here has been on representing uncertainty with probability. There is nothing to stop us from using different, perhaps more qualitative, representations. For example, we might consider a *preferential ordering* on worlds (Kraus et al. (1990)), where, intuitively, one world is preferred to another if it is significantly more likely.

Alternatively, we could use Dempster-Shafer belief functions (Shafer (1976)), possibility measures (Dubois and Prade (1990)), comparative probability (Fine (1973)), or ordinal rankings (Spohn (1987)). Recently, Nir Friedman and I have introduced *plausibility measures* (Friedman and Halpern (1995b)), which generalize all of these approaches. A plausibility measure associates with each set its *plausibility*, which is just some element of a partially ordered set. By taking the set to be [0,1] (with the usual ordering) and imposing some extra requirements on the plausibility, we can get back probability measures. A discussion of how to use preferential orderings rather than probability in the context of systems can be found in Friedman and Halpern (1994); in Friedman and Halpern (1995a), this discussion is redone using plausibility. The changes required are all quite straightforward.

Notes

[1] I will use "belief" and "knowledge" interchangeably here, and ignore the differences between them that the philosophical literature has focused on.

[2] A binary relation $\mathcal{K}$ on W is Euclidean if (u,v), $(u,w) \in \mathcal{K}$ implies $(v,w) \in \mathcal{K}$, for all $u,v,w \in W$.

[3] Readers familiar with modal logic will recognize that if we assume that the $\mathcal{K}_i$'s are Euclidean and transitive, we get the modal logic K45; if we further assume that they are equivalence relations, we get S5 (Halpern and Moses (1992), Hughes and Cresswell (1968)).

[4] An arbitrary—not necessarily discrete—probability distribution is not necessarily defined on all subsets of W, but only on a σ-algebra of subsets of W; that is, a set of subsets that is closed under countable union and complementation. There are added complexities in dealing with arbitrary probability distributions, which I would rather avoid here; see Fagin et al. (1990) for details.

[5] Actually, it would be cleaner to represent this as a two-step process: first the coin is chosen, and then it is tossed. This is done in the next section, using runs and systems

References

Bar-Hillel, M. and R. Falk (1982) Some teasers concerning conditional probabilities. *Cognition* 11:109-122.

Dubois, D. and H. Prade (1990) An introduction to possibilistic and fuzzy logics. In G. Shafer and J. Pearl, editors, *Readings in Uncertain Reasoning*. Morgan Kaufmann, San Francisco, Calif.

Fagin, R. and J. Y. Halpern (1994) Reasoning about knowledge and probability. *Journal of the ACM* 41(2):340-367.

Fagin, R., J. Y. Halpern, and N. Megiddo (1990) A logic for reasoning about probabilities. *Information and Computation*, 87(1/2):78-128.

Fagin, R., J. Y. Halpern, Y. Moses, and M. Y. Vardi (1995) *Reasoning about Knowledge* . MIT Press, Cambridge, Mass.

Fine, T. L. (1973) *Theories of Probability* . Academic Press, New York.

Freund, J. E. (1965) Puzzle or paradox? *American Statistician* , 19(4):29-44.

Friedman, N. and J. Y. Halpern (1994) A knowledge-based framework for belief change. Part I: foundations. In R. Fagin, editor, *Theoretical Aspects of Reasoning about Knowledge: Proc. Fifth Conference*, pages 44-64. Morgan Kaufmann, San Francisco, Calif.

Friedman, N. and J. Y. Halpern (1995a) Modeling belief in dynamic systems. Part I : foundations. Technical Report RJ9965. IBM. Available by anonymous ftp from starry.stanford.edu/pub/nir or via WWW at http://robotics.stanford.edu/users/nir. To appear, *Artificial Intelligence*.

Friedman, N. and J. Y. Halpern (1995b) Plausibility measures: a user's manual. In P. Besnard and S. Hanks, editors, *Proc. Eleventh Conference on Uncertainty in Artificial Intelligence* (UAI '95). Morgan Kaufmann, San Francisco, Calif.

Halpern, J. Y. and M. R. Tuttle (1993) Knowledge, probability, and adversaries. *Journal of the ACM*, 40(4):917-962.

Halpern, J. Y. and M. Y. Vardi (1989) The complexity of reasoning about knowledge and time, I: lower bounds. *Journal of Computer and System Sciences*, 38(1):195-237.

Halpern, J. Y. and R. Fagin (1989) Modelling knowledge and action in distributed systems. *Distributed Computing*, 3(4):159-179. A preliminary version appeared in Proc. 4th ACM *Symposium on Principles of Distributed Computing*, 1985, with the title "A formal model of knowledge, action, and communication in distributed systems: preliminary report".

Halpern, J. Y. and Y. Moses (1992) A guide to completeness and complexity for modal logics of knowledge and belief. *Artificial Intelligence*, 54:319-379.

Hintikka, J. (1962) *Knowledge and Belief*. Cornell University Press, Ithaca, N.Y.

Hughes, G. E. and M. J. Cresswell (1968) *An Introduction to Modal Logic*. Methuen, London.

Kraus, S., D. Lehmann, and M. Magidor (1990) Nonmonotonic reasoning, preferential models and cumulative logics. *Artificial Intelligence*. 44:167-207.

Morgan, J. P., N. R. Chaganty, R. C. Dahiya, and M. J. Doviak (1991) Let's make a deal: the player's dilemma (with commentary). *The American Statistician*, 45(4):284-289.

Pearl, J. (1988) *Probabilistic Reasoning in Intelligent Systems*. Morgan Kaufmann, San Francisco, Calif.

vos Savant, M. (1991) Ask Marilyn. *Parade Magazine*. Sept. 9, 1990; Dec. 2, 1990; Feb. 17, 1991.

Shafer, G. (1976) *A Mathematical Theory of Evidence*. Princeton University Press, Princeton, N.J.

Shafer, G. (1985) Conditional probability. *International Statistical Review*, 53(3):261-277.

Spohn, W. (1987) Ordinal conditional functions: a dynamic theory of epistemic states. In W. Harper and B. Skyrms, editors, *Causation in Decision, Belief Change, and Statistics*, volume 2, pages 105-134. Reidel, Dordrecht, Holland.

HOW COMMITMENT LEADS TO COORDINATION: THE EFFECT OF INDIVIDUAL REASONING STRATEGIES ON MULTI-AGENT INTERACTION

M. E. POLLACK
Department of Computer Science and Intelligent Systems Program
University of Pittsburgh
Pittsburgh, PA 15260 USA
pollack@cs.pitt.edu

1. Introduction

Most agents, human or artificial, are situated in dynamic environments, i.e., environments in which the agent is not itself the only cause of change. Moreover, all agents have computational resource limits: their reasoning processes are not instantaneous, but take time. A dynamic environment may change during the time an agent is reasoning, and, indeed, may change in ways that undermine the very assumptions underlying the ongoing reasoning. Thus an agent that blindly pushes forward with a reasoning task, without regard to the amount of time it is taking or the changes meanwhile going on in the environment, is not likely to make rational decisions. Agents in dynamic environments need a way of deciding what to reason about when, and for how long. Recognition of this fact has led to a number of proposals for mechanisms for controlling reasoning (Russell and Wefald (1991), Dean and Boddy (1988), Horvitz et al. (1989), Zilberstein (1993), Dean et al. (1993).

In our own previous work on this topic (Bratman et al. (1988), Pollack and Ringuette (1990), Pollack (1992), Pollack (1991), Pollack et al. (1994)), my colleagues and I have focused on the development of "meta-level satisficing strategies". These strategies are "meta-level" because they involve (sometimes implicit) reasoning about what to reason about, and "satisficing," because they are not designed to guarantee optimal behavior, but rather to lead to effective enough behavior in the long run (Simon (1957)). That is, meta-level satisficing strategies sometimes trade potential decision quality for decision timeliness: they may lead an agent to make occasional decisions that are suboptimal, in order to achieve a high level of performance overall. An example of a meta-level satisficing strategy that we have explored in detail is *filtering*, in which an agent tends to screen from consideration options for action that are incompatible with its existing intentions. Essentially, an agent that performs filtering is one that has a certain degree of commitment to its own plans, reconsidering them only when a conflicting option is *prima facie* highly promising. Elsewhere, we have argued for the effectiveness of filtering both in principle (Bratman et al. (1988)) and experimentally (Pollack et al. (1994)).

Most of our prior work on meta-level satisficing strategies, like most of the prior work on control of reasoning in general, has focused on the single-agent case. That is, while we

X. Arrazola et al. (eds.), Discourse, Interaction and Communication, 157–163.

studied dynamic environments, we treated exogenous events in those environments as being the result of "black box" processes, not as being caused by agents who themselves are engaged in reasoning tasks. Moreover, we measured the effectiveness of any particular control strategy in terms of its effect on the performance of an individual agent using it. However, agents are frequently in situations in which they can interact with one another, and, hence, in which there is a potential for coordination and cooperation. We have therefore begun exploring the possibility of generalizing the single-agent agent meta-level satisficing strategies, to make them applicable to the multi-agent case. In particular, we have studied a generalization of the filtering strategy, and have conducted preliminary experiments that show how multi-agent filtering, in some circumstances, results in coordination without explicit negotiation (Ephrati et al. (1995)).

In this paper, we briefly survey some meta-level satisficing strategies (Section 2), then discuss the generalization of one of them, filtering, to the multi-agent case (Section 3), and finally describe some related research and note the directions of our ongoing project on this topic (Section 4).

2. Meta-Level Satisficing Strategies

We have been studying the effectiveness of a variety of meta-level satisficing strategies; these include the following:

•**Filtering.** As noted above, filtering involves committing to already adopted goals, and tending to bypass (or "filter out") new options that would conflict with their successful completion. Filtering thus focuses reasoning, by allowing an agent to concentrate on ways of achieving current goals, and to bypass deliberation about the many options that are incompatible with existing goals. Of course, an agent that never considers incompatible options is unlikely to perform rationally; thus, we view filtering as being augmented with an override mechanism that enables the agent to deliberate about options that are *prima facie* important, even when they are incompatible with pre-existing options. In general, even with an override mechanism, agents may sometimes filter options that would have been selected were they subject to consideration; filtering is thus a satisficing strategy (Bratman et al. (1988), Pollack (1992), Pollack et al. (1994)).

•**Overloading.** Using overloading, an agent relies on its existing intentions to suggest solutions to new planning problems. Specifically, if an agent determines that it can achieve some goal G by performing an action A that it already intends for some other purpose, it may, subject to certain conditions, directly adopt the plan containing A without fully weighing it against alternative means to G. (In such a case, we say that A is *overloaded*). Like filtering, overloading may lead to locally suboptimal behavior, for example, when a superior plan that does not involve overloading is missed because of the existence of an overloaded plan. Overloading may nonetheless be justified for resource-limited reasoning because it provides both an added efficiency of action and of reasoning (Pollack (1991)).

•**Case-Based Reasoning.** Case-based reasoning and planning (Kolodner (1988), Hammond (1989)) can be viewed as another meta-level satisficing strategy. Case-based planning involves selecting a plan to achieve some goal by identifying a previous "case" that is sufficiently similar to the current one, and adopting the plan that was used in that case, modifying it as needed for the current situation. This process, like the two mentioned above, may lead to the adoption of a plan that is suboptimal, because full-fledged reasoning from first principles might suggest alternative plans that are superior. However, case-based planning can potentially be much more efficient, and hence useful for a resource-limited agent in a dynamic environment.

•**Abstraction.** A final example of a satisficing strategy is abstraction. This is perhaps best illustrated with an example: Suppose an agent must decide what color to paint a room. The book of paint swatches may be very large, and complete deliberation about all the alternative colors may be infeasible. A reasonable approach is for the agent to deliberate first about the abstract option of painting the room white versus that of painting it another color; once that decision is made, a more detailed deliberation can take place. Note again the satisficing nature of such a strategy. By reasoning about "white" as a single, generic class, the agent may overlook a specific shade of white that is not representative of the class; were the agent to reason about that specific shade, it might have made a different decision than the one it made by grouping all the white shades together. But the added efficiency of reasoning at an abstract level may, in the long run, outweigh the occasional disadvantages of doing so.

3. Multi-Agent Filtering[1]

The first strategy that we mentioned above, filtering, is the one that we have explored the most in previous work. Recently, we have studied a generalization of it to the multi-agent case (Ephrati et al. (1995)). Where single-agent filtering means tending to bypass options that are incompatible with an agent's own goals, multi-agent filtering means tending to bypass options that are incompatible with other agents' known or presumed goals.

It seems clear that if one agent, call it A, avoids interfering with the goals of a second agent, call it B, then B will be better able to achieve its goals. But what about A? Won't its performance be worse, because it is subject to additional constraints on its behavior? If A is the only multi-agent filterer, it seems likely that its performance will suffer, but if A and B are both multi-agent filterers, then the effect is less obvious. What we need to ask is whether the advantage that A derives from B's multi-agent filtering is sufficient to override any penalties A receives from its own multi-agent filtering. And we need to ask the same thing about B. Thus, the central questions we have been exploring are: What happens in multi-agent environments in which all (or most or few or none) of the agents are multi-agent filterers? And do these effects depend, in any interesting and identifiable ways, on properties of the domain?

To answer these questions, we needed, in turn, to address the question of how to interpret interference among agents' goals. The precise interpretation depends on the relationships that hold among the goals of the agents in the environment. For example:

1. The agents may have one common goal, but individual and distinct subgoals. In this case, avoiding conflict means avoiding actions that make it more difficult for another agent to achieve its subgoals. This situation underlies the work on social laws (Moses and Tennenholtz (1990)), where the (implicit) common goal is the maximization of the designer's reward (through the individual activities).

2.   The agents may have one common goal, but potentially overlapping subgoals. Here, "conflict" can mean achieving (or helping in the achievement of) a subgoal for another agent. To some extent, this situation underlies the work on cooperative state-changing rules (Goldman and Rosenschein (1994)), where the common goal is the maximization of the result of the multi-agent activity.

3.   The agents have distinct, possibly conflicting, goals. There may be competition not only for resources to achieve goals, but also for the goals themselves. This case would appear to pose the greatest challenge to a multi-agent filtering strategy. Note that to evaluate multi-agent filtering in this setting, we cannot measure aggregate success of all the agents, but must instead measure the success of each agent.

For each of these cases, we conducted a series of experiments using a multi-agent version of the Tileworld system (Pollack et al. (1994), Pollack and Ringuette (1990)) an abstract testbed, implemented in Lisp, for studying behavior in dynamic environments. We have been studying examples of each type. Like the original Tileworld, MA-Tileworld is an abstract, dynamic, simulated environment, with embedded agents. It is obviously, and intentionally, a highly artificial environment. In keeping the environment divorced from any realistic application, our goal has been to provide a tool that allows researchers concerned with *any* application to focus on what they consider to be key features of that application's environment, without the confounding effects of the actual, complex environment itself. We have, in other words, traded realism—in the short run, at least— for sufficient control to allow for systematic experimentation.

The agents that are embedded in the MA-Tileworld perform filtering both with respect to their own goals and with respect to the goals of other agents in the environment. Various operationalizations of multi-agent filtering have been studied and compared against one another. These include filtering on the basis of:

> *Static geographical boundaries*: The agents' environment is divided into geographical regions, each agent is assigned responsibility for a particular region. It then filters out options to perform tasks in other regions. Because no two agents are assigned the same region, filtering automatically leads to conflict avoidance.
>
> *Dynamic geographical boundaries*: The environment is not partitioned *a priori*. Instead, whenever an agent detects the possibility of completing some task, it determines whether the task location is closer to another agent's current location than to its own, and, if so, filters the option of completing that task. This also leads to conflict avoidance, since every location is nearest to a single agent.
>
> *Intention posting*: The first two cases are clearly "implicit": the agents can follow those filtering strategies without any computations that directly take into consideration the goals of other agents. This third approach is slightly more explicit: here, agents post to a globally accessible data structure each intention they form to carry out a task. Agents then filter from options that have already been declared to be the intentions of other agents.

Our initial experiments, details of which can be found in (Ephrati et al. (1995)), showed that each of these operationalizations of multi-agent filtering improves the average performance of MA-Tileworld agents, even under conditions of extreme *boldness* (i.e., absolute filtering, without any possibility of overriding). Subsequent experiments showed the conditions under which overriding leads to further improvement. Interestingly, the relative performance of the various operationalizations depended on the nature of the environment. In relatively uniform environments—ones in which all tasks have more or less equal value and are more or less equally easy to accomplish—an intention posting strategy outperformed the geographically-based strategies. However, in the more heterogeneous environments in which overloading is important, the reverse is true. Analysis showed that this is due to the fact that the strategies behave differently with respect to maintaining the agents' geographical separation in the different environments.

In the uniform environments of the first set of experiments, all the filtering strategies lead to geographical separation of the agents. With geographical boundaries filtering, the agents focus on tasks in distinct areas, and so tend to stay separated. With intention posting filtering, agents dynamically create separate regions because they tend first to form plans to complete nearby tasks, and thus create territories that are avoided by other agents. Moreover these territories tend to stay fixed, because filtering is absolute (and can be, in these environments). However, once the environments become heterogeneous, and overriding must be introduced, the stability of these local areas decreases. With a relatively low threshold, posted intentions will frequently be overridden by other agents, and there is nothing to prevent the agents from becoming clustered in one area and thus missing many remote opportunities. In contrast, although geographical-boundaries filtering will also be subject to frequent overrides, once any particular out-of-region goal is completed, the agent will return to its original territory.

Although this result in some sense is quite specific to the MA-Tileworld environment, it can be related to a much more general claim about the importance of resource distribution in coordination. What is interesting about this case is that the resources are both goals and objects needed to satisfy those goals.

Another set of experiments was aimed at analyzing the potential usefulness of multi-agent filtering in situations of type 3, as defined above—that is, the type of situation in which agents have distinct, and possibly conflicting, goals. Note that in such situations, an improvement in average performance does not guarantee that agents will adopt a filtering strategy.[2] This is because in type 3 setting, what agents (are built to) care about is maximization of their individual utility—not necessarily maximization of overall average utility.

Game theory has addressed many type 3 interactions, analyzing them to determine what an agent's chosen strategies would be, given the rules of the interaction. In particular, game theorists are concerned with the notion of *dominant strategies*:

> The strategy S is a *dominant strategy* if it is an agent's strictly best response to any strategies that the other agents might pick, in the sense that whatever strategies they pick, his payoff is highest with S.

A *dominant strategy equilibrium* is a strategy combination of each agent's dominant strategy.

A key question then, is whether each agent performing multi-agent filtering is a dominant strategy equilibrium, relative to a fixed alternative of not performing filtering. To explore this question, we conducted an experiment using MA-Tilewords populated by fifteen agents, only some of whom were cooperative. We varied the number of cooperative agents across trials, and measured the performance of the cooperative agents, the performance of the non-cooperative agents, and the global performance. Details of the experiment can, again, be found in (Ephrati et al. (1995)), in which we show that the higher the percentage of filtering agents, the better the global performance is. In addition, at any given ratio of filtering to non-filtering agents, the filtering agents are doing better. That fact implies that regardless of the other agents' behavior, each agent, if rational, should choose to cooperate (engage in multi-agent filtering) and thus guarantee itself a higher utility: within the bounds of this experiment, multi-agent filtering is in dominant strategy equilibrium.

Multi-agent filtering is a natural extension to single-agent filtering, and has several highly desirable characteristics, such as simplicity and efficiency. Moreover, our experiments to provide preliminary evidence that multi-agent filtering is a good candidate for achieving coordination. Clearly the experiments conducted so far raise at least as many questions as they answer, and further research is needed to refine these initial hypotheses about the usefulness of multi-agent filtering, as well as to develop additional such strategies.

4. Related and Ongoing Research

Resource-limited reasoning has mostly been studied in the single-agent context. At the same time, other branches of AI, notably Distributed AI, have focused on issues of coordination and cooperation. Broadly speaking, two main approaches have been proposed in this literature. The first involves explicit coordination and cooperation: agents are designed to reason about their potential interactions, and negotiate with one another as needed. Examples of this approach include (Durfee et al. (1987), Sycara (1988), Rosenschein and Zlotkin (1994)). A difficulty with explicit coordination and negotiation is that it can be extremely time-consuming, and in dynamic environments, agents may not be able to afford the time required. The second approach involves implicit coordination: agents are designed to follow "local" rules of behavior that lead to their acting in apparently coordinated ways; see, for example, Moses and Tennenholtz (1990), Goldman and Rosenschein (1994)). This approach is motivated in part by a belief that one can design simple rules that are easy for an agent to follow, yet result in coordination. Our own approach of generalizing the single-agent meta-level satisficing strategies falls within this second class.

We conducted several other investigations of implicit coordination. Part of our effort involves refining our analysis of multi-agent filtering, and also looking at potential generalizations of other single-agent meta-level satisficing strategies, such as those noted above. In addition, we have begun to study the ways in which the tools of noncooperative game theory can be used to achieve cooperation in intelligent agent settings. In particular, where most of the DAI literature that has employed game theory has relied on the techniques of *cooperative* game theory, we are attempting to apply the tools of *noncooperative* game theory to the problem of agent design (Bicchieri et al. (1997)).

Acknowledgments

This work has been supported by the Air Force Office of Scientific Research (Contract F49620-92-J-0422), by the Rome Laboratory (RL) of the Air Force Material Command and the Advanced Research Projects Agency (Contract F30602-93-C-0038), and by an NSF Young Investigator's Award (IRI-9258392). I would like to thank Eithan Ephrati and Sigalit Ur, who have been heavily involved in the work on multi-agent filtering described in this abstract.

Notes

[1] Much of the material in the section is taken from Ephrati et al (1995).
[2] Actually, we may either be concerned with what strategy agent *designers* adopt, if the agents have fixed strategies, or with what strategy the agents themselves adopt, if they are adaptive. For ease of presentation, we will talk as if agents adopt their own strategies, although nothing here hinges on this assumption.

References

Bicchieri, C., Pollack, M.E., Rovelli, C., and Tsamardinos, I. (1997): The Potential for the Evolution of Cooperation among Web Agents. *International Journal of Computer-Human Systems*. To appear.
Bratman, M.E., Israel, D.J., and Pollack, M.E. (1988): Plans and resource-bounded practical reasoning. *Computational Intelligence* 4 (1988), 349-355.
Dean, T., and Boddy, M. (1988): An analysis of time-dependent planning, in *Proceedings of the Seventh National Conference on Artificial Intelligence*, St. Paul, MI, 49-54.
Durfee, E.H., Lesser, V.R., and Corkill., D.D. (1987): Cooperation through communication in a distributed problem solving network. in M.N. Huhns (ed). *Distributed Artificial Intelligence*, Kaufmann Publishers, Morgan, 29-58.
Ephrati, E., Pollack, M.E., and Ur. S. (1995): Deriving multi-agent coordination through filtering strategies, in *Proceedings of the 14th Joint International Conference on Artificial Intelligence (IJCAI)*, 679-685.
Goldman, C., and Rosenschein, J.S. (1994): Emergent coordination through the use of cooperative state-changing rules, in *Proceedings of the Twelfth National Conference on Artificial Intelligence (AAAI-94)*, 408-413.
Hammond, K. (1989): Opportunistic memory, in *Proceedings of the 11th International Joint Conference on Artificial Intelligence*, Detroit, MI.
Horvitz, E.J., Cooper, G.F., and Heckerman, D.E. (1989): Reflection and action under scarce resources: Theoretical principles and empirical study, in *Proceedings of the Eleventh International Joint Conference on Artificial Intelligence*, Detroit, MI, 1121-1127.
Kolodner, J. (ed.) (1988): *Proceedings of the DARPA Case-Based Reasoning Workshop*, Morgan Kaufmann.
Moses, Y., and Tennenholtz, M. (1990): Artificial social systems, part I: Basic principles. Technical Report CS90-12, Weizmann Institute, Rehovot, Israel.
Moses, Y., and Tennenholtz, M. (1992): On computational aspects of artificial social systems, in *Proceedings of the 11th International Workshop on Distributed Artificial Intelligence*, Glen Arbor, Michigan, 267-283.
Pollack, M.E. (1991): Overloading intentions for efficient practical reasoning, *Nous* 25(4) (1991), 513-536.
Pollack, M.E. (1992): The uses of plans, *Artificial Intelligence* 57 (1992), 43-68.
Pollack, M.E., Joslin, D., Nunes, A., Ur, S., and Ephrati, E. (1994): Experimental investigation of an agent-commitment strategy, Technical Report 94-31, Univ. of Pittsburgh Dept. of Computer Science, Pittsburgh, PA.
Pollack, M.E., and Ringuette, M. (1990): Introducing the Tileworld: Experimentally evaluating agent architectures, in *Proceedings of the Eighth National Conference on Artificial Intelligence*, Boston, MA, 183-189.
Rosenschein, J.S., and Zlotkin, G. (1994): *Rules of Encounter*, MIT Press, Cambridge, MA.
Russell, S.J, and Wefald, E.H. (1991): *Do the Right Thing*, MIT Press, Cambridge, MA.
Simon, H.A. (1957): *Models of Man*, Macmillan Press, New York.
Sycara, K.P. (1988): Resolving goal conflicts via negotiation, in *Proceedings of the Seventh National Conference on Artificial Intelligence (AAAI-88)*, 245-250.
Zilberstein, S. (1993): Operational rationality through compilation of anytime algorithms. Technical report, Computer Science Division, University of Berkeley. Ph.D. Dissertation.

BUILDING A COLLABORATIVE INTERFACE AGENT

C. L. SIDNER
Lotus Development Corp.
One Rogers St.
Cambridge, MA 02142 USA

1. Introduction

At a time when intelligent software agents are the buzz word of every media article, agents that collaborate with people have received very little attention, even in research. Perhaps this lack of attention results from researchers' fear of the formidable task of creating an agent that understands natural language. To understand agents that can collaborate with users, rather than being their slaves, we are creating a software agent that communicates and collaborates with a user by adhering to established principles of multi-person human collaboration and communication but without using natural language.

Among the questions we address in this research are:

• How can a principled collaborative and communicating software agent be designed?
• What theories would inform the design?
• Would such an agent be useful to a user?

In this paper, we will discuss the viewpoint we take on software agents, as well as discuss the design of an agent that we are building that adheres to principles of collaboration and communication. We will review the principles and theories that are informing the work and evaluate how well these principles apply to the software agent, specially in comparison to human collaborators on a similar task.

To begin, we illustrate in Figure 1 the basic view of the relationship between a software agent and users we have in mind.

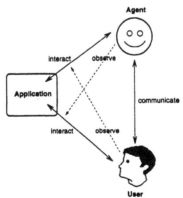

Figure 1. The Collaborative Interface Agent Paradigm

X. Arrazola et al. (eds.), Discourse, Interaction and Communication, 165–177.

In this view, an user and a software agent each interact with an application. In addition, the user and agent can communicate with one another, and each can observe the interactions that the other has with the application. To give deeper meaning to this picture, we must answer the question "how do we characterize the software agent in this picture?"

We take the software agent to be an **autonomous** software process that interacts with humans as well as with elements of the software environment; the agent does some sort of "intelligent" task, and is presented anthropomorphically. Unlike Schneiderman's (1995) list of features, this agent does not work when and where the user is not, although this lack is not an inherent limitation in the design.

Our software agent is a **communicating** agent because it behaves according to the principles of human discourse structure, in particular, the computational models in Grosz and Sidner [1986, 1990], Grosz and Kraus [1994], Lochbaum [1994, 1995] and Sidner [1994a]. While we will return to this matter in more detail later in this paper, these principles include:

- modeling the segments of a conversation and relating the segments' purposes to the user and agent's shared goals,
- tracking and communicating changes in purposes,
- establishing mutual beliefs relevant to the collaboration,
- negotiating beliefs held mutually by the user and agent, and
- recognizing and producing utterances in an artificial language related to purposes and beliefs.

We take our software agent to be a **collaborating** agent because it understands its shared goals with a user well enough to contribute to the goals' accomplishment. It does so in two ways:
- by having and achieving the beliefs, intentions, and actions that are relevant for the goal, and
- by understanding its human partner's participation as a collaborator rather than a mere master to be followed.

To limit the effort in the project, our design is constrained in several ways. First, communication between user and agent does not use full natural language, but rather an artificial language (c.f. Sidner [1994]); we did not want to undertake all the complexities of natural language understanding engines as part of this project. However, because communication is critical to collaboration, some linguistic-like graphical communication is necessary. Second, we limited the domain of interaction in two ways: the agent and the user collaborate by sharing a direction manipulation graphical user interface (GUI). Because GUIs are a very common and successful interface technology, we decided that rather than supplant it, our agent would work with the user in this typical format. We chose a "vertical" domain, that is, one that performs tasks related to one overall function. By contrast, a horizontal domain would be one where several different functions occur, such as those in a suite of software products for personal computers. The vertical domain for our experimental system is choosing air travel itineraries.

While some research to date has explored applications of the discourse model in Grosz and Sidner [1986], that work has considered either human-to-human discourse (e.g. Grosz and Hirschberg [1992]) or human-to-computer discourse with full natural language capabilities (e.g. Lambert and Carberry [1991]). Cohen [1994] has explored interface agents in which a user can specify rules for a collection of agents to use in performing tasks, but his agents do not attempt to model conversational interaction (though see Cohen [1992] for extensions to direct manipulation languages that incorporate anaphoric reference and make previous context directly available). Yanklovich [1994] reported on a speaking agent for answering questions about calendars, todos and email. Stein and Thiel [1993] reported on a multi-modal non-agent interface which models both linguistic and non-linguistic dialogue acts and allows the user to use the interface to gain access to the dialogue model as well as the interface task (retrieval from a database). This work makes no explicit attempt to model collaboration.

Among the questions we are addressing with this research is the value of a collaborating agent for GUI users. As part of our research, we plan a series of tests with users performing tasks with and without the agent, to determine such factors as the ease with which they accomplish the tasks, the speed of accomplishment and their overall satisfaction with the agent.

2. The domain of TT, the collaborating software agent

TT is a software agent that is being designed to collaborate and communicate in the world of air travel itineraries. While TT has significant knowledge about this domain, it is the goal of the research to build TT as a set of software tools that could be used in another domain by replacing its domain specific knowledge about airlines, flights, scheduling and the associated actions with a different domain and interface (see Rich [1994, 1995] for further discussion of this aspect of TT).

The graphical user interface built for an air travel itinerary is shown in Figure 2. The user can click on various cities of a USA map to indicate the desired route for an itinerary, as in Figure 2a. The cities on that route are also displayed in small boxes that can be positioned in the slider window below the map to represent times that the user wishes to be in the particular city. The boxes in effect provide constraints on arrivals and departures of flights. Whenever the user sets a city constraint, as in Figure 2b, the number of possible itineraries is updated in a small window marked "itineraries." By touching the "Display?" button in that window, the user can see all the possible itineraries in the large scrollable window at the bottom of the screen. In general, users find that displaying more than five to ten flights is too much information, and so they add constraints or look only at the first few flights displayed. Users can also add constraints by checking off boxes to the left of the USA map; these boxes represent airlines on which the user prefers to fly. When none are checked, all airlines are allowed for search; when some are checked, only flights on those airlines considered.

Figure 3 shows the interface with TT, the software agent, and a user, each with a "home window" superimposed on the application GUI. TT can wave its hand to get the user's attention, use its hand as a cursor to press buttons, drag boxes, and the like on the shared GUI. The user communicates with TT by pressing buttons or selecting from dynamically produced menus of utterances in her home window.

168 C. L. SIDNER

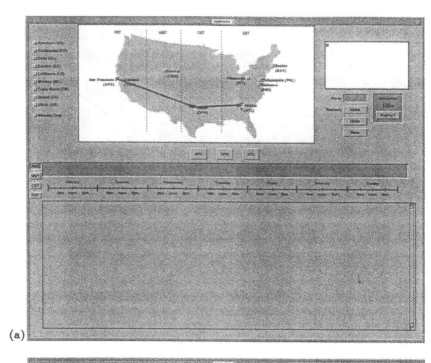

(a)

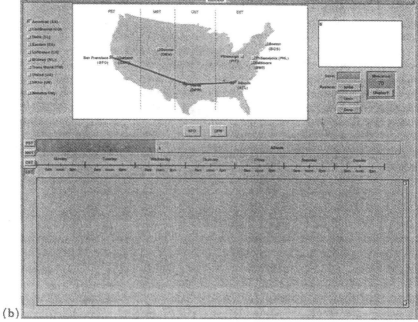

(b)

Figure 2: The Graphical User Interface for the Air Travel Application

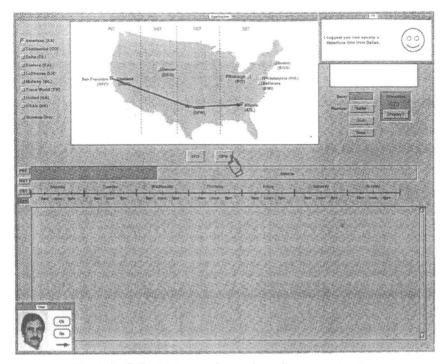

Figure 3: GUI with home window for software agent and user

TT is being designed to collaborate with a user on problems in planning air travel itineraries. For comparison, Figure 4 below is a transcript of an actual conversation between a customer and an American Express agent as they plan an itinerary [Kowtko and Price, 1989]. In this discourse the customer is uncertain about when he might leave because he is aware that constraints on the arrival at his final destination (Green Bay) affect his departure time, so he proposes working backwards from the destination constraints.

TA: and the date you need to leave?
BC: well um I have to work a little bit backwards here
TA: ok
BC: I want to leave on the first flight out of ORD uh Monday morning
TA: M- Monday (the first BC: the eighth) the eighth
TA: ok
BC: and I want to take whatever red eye or any other flight that I have to take to get there in time to make that transfer
TA: where are you going from Chicago to where?
BC: Greenbay. so the first I need to catch the first flight from ORD out to Greenbay, Wisconsin uh Monday morning
TA: it looks like the first one is a seven forty on American uh Eagle that arrives Greenbay at eight fifty one

Figure 4: A Human-to-Human conversation about airline itineraries

Our design goals aim for TT to participate in interactions with users in a way that is similar in discourse content though not in natural language form to this conversation. A sample portion of a TT and user interaction, which is not yet operational, is shown is Figure 5. The artificial language form of the interaction is shown with an English gloss; we are exploring various approaches to producing palatable English glosses without using full natural language. In this sample, the user wishes to travel from San Francisco via Dallas to Atlanta for a Wednesday 9 am meeting. The user first specifies the route for his trip using the map interface shown in Figure 2a. The conversation in figure 5 includes these actions as (0).

---

(0) User: <User manipulates GUI to display route from SF to Dallas to Atlanta>
(1)   TT: (Propose (Collaborate (user, TT) (user-trip (source San Francisco) (destination Atlanta))))
        Shall we collaborate on your trip from San Francisco to Atlanta?
(2) User: OK.
(3) User: <User manipulates GUI to specify for the constraints on the arrival time in Atlanta.>
(4) TT: (Propose (Recipe (user) (Work-backwards SF Atlanta)))
        You are working backwards from your arrival in Atlanta.
(5) User: Ok.
(6) TT: (Propose (Should-do (user) (specify (departure (latest) Atlanta)))) (TT points to the DFW box to be placed on the slider window.)
        Specify your latest departure from Dallas.
(7) User: Ok. <User gestures to put in departure time.>
(8) TT: <points to count box in the Display? window>
(9) User: Ok.
(10) TT: (Propose (collaborate (user, TT) (workbackwards SF Dallas))).
            Now let's work backwards to the San Francisco departure.
        (Propose (Should-do (user) (specify (departure (latest) San Francisco))))
        Specify a departure time from San Francisco to Dallas.
        (Propose (Should-do (user) (specify (preferred airline))))
        Specify airline constraints also.
(11) User: Ok.
        <User specifies for a departure time before noon on Monday with flights on American airlines.>
(12) TT: <TT points to the count box in the Display? window>
(13) User: Ok.
        <User clicks for display of the itineraries.>

Figure 5. A Hypothetical Conversation between TT and a User

In this conversation, TT guides the user through the establishment of constraints for the desired trip. These constraints specify the arrival time in Atlanta, the departure time from Dallas and the departure time from San Francisco, as well as the requirement to fly on American Airlines.

The constraints are relatively straightforward in this example, and the user might have easily planned this trip without TT. However, in general specifying constraints without producing either too many or too few candidate itineraries can be difficult for users. TT's knowledge of the different recipes that users bring to bear in specifying constraints can be critical when the number of legs in a trip is bigger than just two and the number of constraints produces no itineraries without significant trial and error on the part of the user.

3. The Application of Discourse Structure and Theory of Collaboration

TT's domain-independent knowledge of human communication is based on a two interrelated theories of language and collaborative behavior, due to Grosz and Sidner [Grosz and Sidner, 1986, 1990] and extensions due to Grosz and Kraus [1994] and Lochbaum [1994]. The discourse structure theory of Grosz and Sidner proposed a model of discourse structure with three interacting components:
1) The linguistic structure contains the segmentation of the utterances of the discourse into units, called segments, as well as the user of anaphoric and tense elements of human language.
2) The attentional state of the discourse represents the shift of the focus of attention of the discourse participants and is modeled as a stack of focus spaces.
3) The intentional structure captures the intentions and beliefs (called the discourse segment purposes) of the participants that were conveyed in the discourse. The structure also represents relations among purposes.

The collaborative plan theory of Grosz and Sidner [1990], revised and extended by Grosz and Kraus [1994], proposed that human collaboration necessitated a model (called the SharedPlan) of the mental states of the collaborators. This model predicted that, for successful collaboration, the participants needed to have mutual beliefs about the actions of the collaboration, about the capabilities of the participants performing the actions, about the intentions of the participants, and about their commitment to the overall success of the collaboration.

In the air travel domain, these beliefs can be illustrated with the following example. When two collaborators plan a trip where collaborator A knows the constraints on travel and collaborator B knows how to find itineraries, then each collaborator must have mutual beliefs that:

1) A and B share a common goal G (to choose flights that meet the specified constraints);
2) Each knows the sequence of actions (the recipe) to accomplish G (e.g. a route is chosen, followed by specifying constraints on the component flights, followed by searching for itineraries that satisfy the constraints);
3) Each can do his or her particular actions (e.g. A will tell B the constraints and B will search the database);
4) Each intends to do the actions;
5) Each is committed to the overall group success (and not just the successful accomplishment of his or her own part).

All these beliefs must be mutually held by both A and B because otherwise they could not be certain that their goal would succeed. For example, if only A knew that A could do certain actions of the recipe, then B would have no means of being sure that all the actions of the recipe were accounted for. B might decide to go ahead anyway, but the success in that case would be left to chance. Mutual belief is also critical for agreement on what actions and participants will be associated with the goal.

Several important features of collaboration should be noted here. First, participants do not begin a collaboration with all of these beliefs and intentions "in place." They start instead with only partial knowledge of themselves and others. Using communication with each other as well as private information gathering, they determine the recipe and the other types of beliefs given above. Second, their knowledge about their context and ability to act is distributed and incomplete as well. As a result, they must share information about acting, intending to act and the current context. The acting which they undertake can be distributed as well, although some of it may also be joint action. Finally, the planning (coming to hold the beliefs and intentions for the collaboration) as well as the acting (upon the intentions) are generally interleaved.

Most of the beliefs and intentions of individual collaborators relevant to a common goal are established through communication. Lochbaum [1994] proposed a model of collaboration and communication that links the discourse structure theory and the SharedPlan model and demonstrated how a group comes to collaborate on a common goal through natural language utterances. In her model, each segment of discourse contributes intentions and beliefs that extend a partial SharedPlan. Every utterance in a segment is explained in terms of its contribution to the unfolding SharedPlan. Lochbaum developed an algorithm that determines whether the propositional content of an utterance contributes to the beliefs and intentions of the current SharedPlan, completes the current SharedPlan, or initiates a SharedPlan that is subsidiary to the current SharedPlan.

Dialogues in TT's travel world are also modeled using an artificial language of proposals and counterproposals [Sidner, 1994]. The purpose of the artificial language is to provide a semantics for relating the content of utterances to proposals for believing that content. The semantics of the language specifies the state of belief just after utterances are first presented to a conversational partner as well as the state of mutual belief of the conversational partners after one partner accepts or rejects the belief conveyed by an utterance from the other partner. Lochbaum's SharedPlan algorithm provides reasons for why one of the partners might accept or reject the propositional content of a belief given the current context of SharedPlans.

The artificial language is defined in terms of meta-operators, whose arguments are propositions that range over a domain language. The operators' semantics specifies the beliefs and mutual beliefs are associated with each operator. In TT's world, the domain language is one in which there are names for objects such as flights, times, and places, and verbs for actions such as specifying a route, specifying constraints on departure times or using a particular recipe. For example, an utterance such as (4) in Figure 5 is a proposal (to believe) a proposition that the user is working backwards from the arrival time in Dallas. After the user receives utterance (4) and confirms it, the user and TT can assume that there is mutual belief that the user is working backwards.

To illustrate Lochbaum's model, let us return to the dialogue between TT and the user of Figure 5.

The user's gestures (0) preceding utterance (1) provide the initial information that the user wants to fly to Atlanta from San Francisco via Dallas. TT takes GUI manipulations to be non-linguistic utterances akin to linguistic ones. It also understands these gestures as communication of the user's intention that TT and the user undertake a SharedPlan to find itineraries. TT confirms its understanding with the user before proceeding. The user (who has the option of declaring that no collaboration was intended) in this example accepts TT's confirmation, and hence TT and the user now know that they are collaborating. Their SharedPlan is the task of choosing flights from San Francisco to Atlanta via Dallas. Using Lochbaum's algorithms, TT is prepared to view the rest of the dialogue as contributing to accomplishing this SharedPlan.

The user manipulates the GUI to constrain the arrival time of the second leg of the overall trip (utterance 3). TT recognizes this action as a portion of a private recipe of the user that contributes to the SharedPlan. TT requests confirmation of its understanding in utterance 4 by checking with the user to see if the recipe it recognized is the one the user believes she has undertaken.

The gestures in (3), TT's utterance in (4), and the user's response in (5) are modeled by TT as a discourse segment, the purpose of which is to contribute to the SharedPlan via the user's private recipe and the mutual sharing of information about that recipe. While the user did not tell TT directly which recipe she was using, she acts according to that recipe and can assume TT has enough intelligence to recognize her actions as intentional and about the recipe of working backwards.

TT uses its own knowledge of recipes to guide the user in ordering the constraints on the second leg of the trip (utterances 6-7). There are at least two recipes in play at this point: the user's private recipe for working on the second leg, and the overall recipe for finding a flight by constraining the second leg of the trip and then constraining the first ("working backwards"). TT could simply watch to see if the user specified a departure time for the Atlanta leg, and if not, point out what the user should do. However, in this dialogue, TT takes a more active role and utters (6).

When the constraints do not limit the number of itineraries sufficiently (end of utterance (8)), TT proposes that the collaboration focus on an additional SharedPlan, one to establish the first leg of the itinerary (utterances 10-11). TT is able to propose a collaboration because it knows the relevant recipes and has enough model of its own capacities and the user's to decide that a collaboration is feasible in this case. This additional SharedPlan produces sufficient constraints to reduce the itineraries to a number that can be easily viewed on screen. As in the earlier portion of the discourse, TT recognizes the user's gestures as part of enacting a recipe for constraining the flights. It also models its own utterances in (10) as a segment that contributes to the second SharedPlan by bringing about TT's intentions to do actions that are part of the recipe.

4. Principles that govern TT's behavior

TT's behavior is both collaborative and discourse-wise for several reasons. First, TT pays careful attention to the establishment of the mutual beliefs that are necessary for collaboration. It must distinguish between beliefs that are already shared and ones that are not, so that it can communicate the non-shared ones that further the collaboration. Beliefs that result from TT's indirect inference are communicated, but beliefs that are directly represented in the GUI are not. For example, because the displayed map directly represents information about the route, TT does not need to confirm beliefs that derive from this source--it just assumes that directly represented information is shared by TT and the user without further checking. This choice helps keep TT's part of the conversation from becoming overly verbose.

In contrast, TT has special concern for its beliefs that result from recipe recognition or deductive rules. TT always checks out its beliefs with the user when it concludes that the user is performing GUI actions that indicate a possible collaboration. We designed

TT to treat this circumstance with an extra layer of checking because collaboration is a powerful interactive behavior and because users of GUIs are not accustomed to having agents perform as collaborators. These choices determine TT's utterance (1) in figure 5.

TT also proposes and awaits confirmation of any beliefs it wants to become shared with the user. The pattern of proposing and gaining confirmation we call a "proposal round." An example positive proposal round in Figure 5 is the set in utterances (4) and (5). TT proposes a belief to the user, which the user chooses to believe (in fact already believes and is establishing as mutually believed with her response). A negative proposal round is found in each of the dialogues in Figure 7 discussed below. More complex proposal rounds can consist of one or more negative rounds followed by a positive one or proposals from one participant followed by counterproposals by the other participant, as in Figure 6 below.

```
TT:    Shall we collaborate on a flight from Chicago to San Francisco?
User: ok.
TT:    Specify the departure time from Chicago.
User: I want to specify the arrival time in San Francisco.  That's the most important
part of the trip for me.
```

Figure 6. A Sample Proposal and Counterproposal

In this example, TT proposes that the user constrain the first part of a trip, while the user counter-proposes that the second part be planned first. The user's second utterance offers a belief that is meant to be understand as support for the counterproposal. The user's utterances are not rejections of TT's proposal, but can be seen as alternatives. Counterproposals have the valuable function of exploring alternate paths of a search space through conversation. One proposal need not be rejected until it is clear which is wiser.

Because TT does not rely on any of the rich means by which human conversational partners signal indirectly that the content of an informing has been accepted, TT awaits (and will request) explicit confirmation of its proposals (c.f. Sidner [1994a]). Seeking explicit confirmation is a somewhat laborious and potentially unnatural activity in dialogue, and we hope to explore in the future ways to permit TT to use some subset of the confirming signals that people use.

TT performs recipe recognition following the algorithms of Lochbaum [1994]. It uses its observations of the user's GUI actions to find a recipe that explains those actions. Furthermore, TT assumes that the user intends for it to recognize her recipes; thus like utterances that can convey intention recognition, GUI manipulations are understood as "utterances" that are intended to be recognized as part of a recipe for action (see Pollack [1990] for further discussion). Because the inference that TT does is rather complex, it checks with the user about the recipes it recognizes, as indicated in utterance (4) of Figure 5.

TT must also communicate about its own capabilities and actions because it does not believe that this information is shared with the user. In each of its communications with the user, TT keeps track of the portion of the SharedPlan to which they contribute.

Following Lochbaum [1994, 1995], each of TT's interactions with the user is modeled as a segment, the purpose of which is seen in terms of its contribution to the SharedPlan for finding an acceptable itinerary. TT not only understands that there is an overall collaboration between itself and the user, but also recognizes that portions of an interaction constitute sub-collaborations on parts of the trip planning. For example, the trip leg from San Francisco to Dallas represents a sub-collaboration which contributes to accomplishing the overall collaboration on planning a trip from San Francisco to Atlanta. TT represents each sub-collaboration as a SharedPlan in service of the main SharedPlan. It uses these additional SharedPlans to explain the user's utterances and to generate utterances to express its own beliefs about actions and intentions relevant to the sub-collaborations.

When a sub-collaboration is concluded, TT returns its focus to the more general collaboration for the whole trip. The overall collaboration provides the framework for the interaction and for recognizing sub-collaborations as they occur (c.f. Lochbaum [1994, 1995]). For example, TT knows that the "working backwards" recipe includes choosing an acceptable flight for the San Francisco to Dallas leg. It can undertake actions to accomplish that sub-goal, or recognize another portion of the conversation as establishing a sub-collaboration to accomplish that sub-goal.

When TT seeks confirmation for the performance of one of its actions, the user can react and offer a different recipe for the collaboration. TT can follow such a response by means of the SharedPlan constructs and knowledge that beliefs come to be shared sometimes only after negotiating the beliefs during additional sub-conversation. In this way, negotiation of belief, while not directly "encoded" in a SharedPlan, can be recognized as conversational activity in service of collaboration. In the simple sample negotiations below, the user either rejects TT's role as a collaborator (Dialogue 1) or rejects a collaboration in which both TT and the user act for a collaboration where only TT performs any actions (Dialogue 2).

TT: I can choose a flight that meets all the displayed constraints.
User: No, no collaboration.

Dialogue 1

TT: Shall we collaborate on finding a flight from Dallas to Atlanta?
User: Ok.
TT: Fill in the constraints on departure and arrival times.
User: No. Just choose any flight on Monday and Friday.

Dialogue 2

Figure 7. Sample Simple Negotiations

5. Comparing TT and a Human Travel Agent

TT's interaction with a user is guided by communication and collaborative principles. TT organizes its graphical and linguistic utterances into segments and relates them to the collaboration undertaken by it and the user. It makes use of recipes for accomplishing activities in the air travel domain, and it uses these recipes to guide its behavior and to understand proposed and actual actions of a user. Finally, TT focuses a part of its processing on the beliefs that become shared between user and itself and on the negotiation of beliefs that may be necessary during the collaboration.

To inform the development of TT, especially the recipe library, we studied a set of transcripts provided by the Speech Group at SRI of staff and American Express travel agents planning trips (c.f. Kowtko and Price [1989]). As discussed in Sidner [1994b], human agents negotiate about their beliefs, a feature we carry forward into TT. They also are not always explicit about accepting the beliefs of others, a feature we did not build into TT because we do not expect TT to be as robust as a human communicator.

In many ways the example of TT and the user presented here parallels the sample human-human discourse in Figure 4. That discourse indicates that people do work backward in travel planning and tell their partners when they do so. However, TT makes explicit its knowledge of recipes for finding itineraries, while in human-to-human travel dialogues, the recipes are just assumed as part of the travel agent's repertoire without further comment. Both human participants in the dialogue in Figure 4 have clear expectations of what the travel agent can and cannot do: they do not discuss their roles; they simply act from them. While the user in the TT domain does likewise, TT is more explicit about what it is doing with the user. TT's explicitness results from its less than human knowledge of language and context. Finally, in general TT has much less fluid language ability than a human collaborator, and while it tries to take control and guide the user, its control is more choppy than that shown in the human discourse in Figure 4.

Acknowledgments

Many of the ideas reported here were developed in collaboration with Charles Rich, Mitsubishi Electric Research Labs, Cambridge, MA 02139, rich@merl.com. Thanks also to Steve Whittaker for editorial review.

References

Cohen, P. (1994) An Open Agent Architecture, in Working Notes of the AAAI Spring Symposium Series, AAAI Press.

Cohen, P. (1992) The role of natural language in a multimodal interface, in Proceedings of the Fifth Annual Symposium on User Interface Software and Technology, ACM Press, New York, pp. 143-149.

Grosz, B.J. (1977) The representation and use of focus in dialogue understanding, Technical Report 151, Artificial Intelligence Center, SRI International, Menlo Park, California.

Grosz, B.J., and Hirschberg, J.(1992) Some intonational characteristics of discourse structure, in Proceedings of the International Conference on Spoken Language Processing, Banff, Alberta, Canada, pp 429-432.

Grosz, B.J., and Kraus, S. (1993) Collaborative plans for group activities, in Proceedings of IJCAI-13, Chambery, France, September, pp. 367-373.

Grosz, B.J., and Sidner, C.L. (1986) Attention, intentions, and the structure of discourse, Computational Linguistics 12(3),175--204.

Grosz, B.J., and Sidner, C.L. (1990) Plans for discourse, in P.R. Cohen, J.L. Morgan, and M.E. Pollack (eds.), Intentions in Communication, MIT Press.

Kowtko, J.C., and Price, P. (1989) Data Collection and analysis in the Air Travel Planning Domain, in DAPRA Workshop Proceedings, Cape Cod, MA.

Lambert, L., and Carberry, S. (1991) A tripartite plan-based model of dialogue, in Proceedings of the 29th Annual Meeting of the ACL, Berkeley, CA.

Lochbaum, K.E. (1994) Using Collaborative plans to Model the Intentional Structure of Discourse, Technical Report TR-25-94, Aiken Computational Laboratory, Harvard University, Cambridge, MA.

Lochbaum, K.E. (1995) The use of knowledge preconditions in language processing, in Proceedings of the IJCAI-95, Montreal, Canada.

Pollack, M. (1990) Plans as Complex Mental Attitudes, in P.R. Cohen, J.L. Morgan, and M.E. Pollack (eds.), Intentions in Communication, MIT Press.

Rich, C. (1994) Negotiation in collaborative activity: an implementation experiment, Knowledge-Based Systems 7(4),268-270.

Rich, C. (1995) Window Sharing with Collaborative Interface Agents, Mitsubishi Electric Research Labs TR-95-12, Cambridge, MA.

Schneiderman, B. (1995) Perspectives: Looking for the Bright Side of User Interface Agents, in Interactions: New Visions of Human-Computer Interaction.

Sidner, C.L. (1994a) An artificial discourse language for collaborative negotiation, in Proceedings of AAAI-94, AAAI Press/MIT Press, Cambridge.

Sidner, C.L. (1994b) Negotiation in collaborative activity: a discourse analysis, *Knowledge-Based Systems* 7(4), 265-267.

Stein, A., and Thiel, U. (1993) A Conversational Model of Multimodal Interaction, in Proceedings of the 11th National Conference on AI, AAAI Press/MIT Press, Cambridge, pp 283-288.

Yanklovich, N. (1994) Talking vs. Taking: Speech Access to Remote Computers, in Proceedings of the ACM CHI Conference, ACM, New York, pp 275-276.

NAME INDEX

PHILOSOPHICAL STUDIES SERIES

PHILOSOPHICAL STUDIES SERIES

28. Terence Penelhum: *God and Skepticism*. A Study in Skepticism and Fideism. 1983
ISBN 90-277-1550-5
29. James Bogen and James E. McGuire (eds.): *How Things Are*. Studies in Predication and the History of Philosophy of Science. 1985 ISBN 90-277-1583-1
30. Clement Dore: *Theism*. 1984 ISBN 90-277-1683-8
31. Thomas L. Carson: *The Status of Morality*. 1984 ISBN 90-277-1619-9
32. Michael J. White: *Agency and Integrality*. Philosophical Themes in the Ancient Discussions of Determinism and Responsibility. 1985 ISBN 90-277-1968-3
33. Donald F. Gustafson: *Intention and Agency*. 1986 ISBN 90-277-2009-6
34. Paul K. Moser: *Empirical Justification*. 1985 ISBN 90-277-2041-X
35. Fred Feldman: *Doing the Best We Can*. An Essay in Informal Deontic Logic. 1986
ISBN 90-277-2164-5
36. G. W. Fitch: *Naming and Believing*. 1987 ISBN 90-277-2349-4
37. Terry Penner: *The Ascent from Nominalism*. Some Existence Arguments in Plato's Middle Dialogues. 1987 ISBN 90-277-2427-X
38. Robert G. Meyers: *The Likelihood of Knowledge*. 1988 ISBN 90-277-2671-X
39. David F. Austin (ed.): *Philosophical Analysis*. A Defense by Example. 1988
ISBN 90-277-2674-4
40. Stuart Silvers (ed.): *Rerepresentation*. Essays in the Philosophy of Mental Representation. 1988 ISBN 0-7923-0045-9
41. Michael P. Levine: *Hume and the Problem of Miracles*. A Solution. 1989
ISBN 0-7923-0043-2
42. Melvin Dalgarno and Eric Matthews (eds.): *The Philosophy of Thomas Reid*. 1989
ISBN 0-7923-0190-0
43. Kenneth R. Westphal: *Hegel's Epistemological Realism*. A Study of the Aim and Method of Hegel's *Phenomenology of Spirit*. 1989 ISBN 0-7923-0193-5
44. John W. Bender (ed.): *The Current State of the Coherence Theory*. Critical Essays on the Epistemic Theories of Keith Lehrer and Laurence BonJour, with Replies. 1989
ISBN 0-7923-0220-6
45. Roger D. Gallie: *Thomas Reid and 'The Way of Ideas'*. 1989 ISBN 0-7923-0390-3
46. J-C. Smith (ed.): *Historical Foundations of Cognitive Science*. 1990
ISBN 0-7923-0451-9
47. John Heil (ed.): *Cause, Mind, and Reality*. Essays Honoring C. B. Martin. 1989
ISBN 0-7923-0462-4
48. Michael D. Roth and Glenn Ross (eds.): *Doubting*. Contemporary Perspectives on Skepticism. 1990 ISBN 0-7923-0576-0
49. Rod Bertolet: *What is Said*. A Theory of Indirect Speech Reports. 1990
ISBN 0-7923-0792-5
50. Bruce Russell (ed.): *Freedom, Rights and Pornography*. A Collection of Papers by Fred R. Berger. 1991 ISBN 0-7923-1034-9
51. Kevin Mulligan (ed.): *Language, Truth and Ontology*. 1992 ISBN 0-7923-1509-X
52. Jesús Ezquerro and Jesús M. Larrazabal (eds.): *Cognition, Semantics and Philosophy*. Proceedings of the First International Colloquium on Cognitive Science. 1992
ISBN 0-7923-1538-3
53. O.H. Green: *The Emotions*. A Philosophical Theory. 1992 ISBN 0-7923-1549-9
54. Jeffrie G. Murphy: *Retribution Reconsidered*. More Essays in the Philosophy of Law. 1992 ISBN 0-7923-1815-3

PHILOSOPHICAL STUDIES SERIES

55. Phillip Montague: *In the Interests of Others*. An Essay in Moral Philosophy. 1992
ISBN 0-7923-1856-0
56. Jacques-Paul Dubucs (ed.): *Philosophy of Probability*. 1993   ISBN 0-7923-2385-8
57. Gary S. Rosenkrantz: *Haecceity*. An Ontological Essay. 1993   ISBN 0-7923-2438-2
58. Charles Landesman: *The Eye and the Mind*. Reflections on Perception and the Problem of Knowledge. 1994   ISBN 0-7923-2586-9
59. Paul Weingartner (ed.): *Scientific and Religious Belief*. 1994   ISBN 0-7923-2595-8
60. Michaelis Michael and John O'Leary-Hawthorne (eds.): *Philosophy in Mind*. The Place of Philosophy in the Study of Mind. 1994   ISBN 0-7923-3143-5
61. William H. Shaw: *Moore on Right and Wrong*. The Normative Ethics of G.E. Moore. 1995   ISBN 0-7923-3223-7
62. T.A. Blackson: *Inquiry, Forms, and Substances*. A Study in Plato's Metaphysics and Epistemology. 1995   ISBN 0-7923-3275-X
63. Debra Nails: *Agora, Academy, and the Conduct of Philosophy*. 1995
ISBN 0-7923-3543-0
64. Warren Shibles: *Emotion in Aesthetics*. 1995   ISBN 0-7923-3618-6
65. John Biro and Petr Kotatko (eds.): *Frege: Sense and Reference One Hundred Years Later*. 1995   ISBN 0-7923-3795-6
66. Mary Gore Forrester: *Persons, Animals, and Fetuses*. An Essay in Practical Ethics. 1996   ISBN 0-7923-3918-5
67. K. Lehrer, B.J. Lum, B.A. Slichta and N.D. Smith (eds.): *Knowledge, Teaching and Wisdom*. 1996   ISBN 0-7923-3980-0
68. Herbert Granger: *Aristotle's Idea of the Soul*. 1996   ISBN 0-7923-4033-7
69. Andy Clark, Jesús Ezquerro and Jesús M. Larrazabal (eds.): *Philosophy and Cognitive Science: Categories, Consciousness, and Reasoning*. Proceedings of the Second International Colloquium on Cogitive Science. 1996   ISBN 0-7923-4068-X
70. J. Mendola: *Human Thought*. 1997   ISBN 0-7923-4401-4
71. J. Wright: *Realism and Explanatory Priority*. 1997   ISBN 0-7923-4484-7
72. X. Arrazola, K. Korta and F.J. Pelletier (eds.): *Discourse, Interaction and Communication*. Proceedings of the Fourth International Colloquium on Cognitive Science. 1998
ISBN 0-7923-4952-0
73. E. Morscher, O. Neumaier and P. Simons (eds.): *Applied Ethics in a Troubled World*. 1998   ISBN 0-7923-4965-2

KLUWER ACADEMIC PUBLISHERS – DORDRECHT / BOSTON / LONDON

CPSIA information can be obtained
at www.ICGtesting.com
Printed in the USA
LVHW051040030520
654914LV00002B/416

9 780792 349525